Pitkin County Library

PITKIN COUNTY LIBRARY
1 13 0001704017

120 North Mill Street
Aspen, Colorado 81611

REF 917.8804 W185   11.95
Walker, T. J., 1956-
Colorado : a newcomer's
manual : everything you need
to know about living in
Colorado

L

SCHOOLS, BUSINESSES, ORGANIZATIONS
This book is available at quantity discounts with bulk purchase for educational, business or sales promotional use. Special booklets, excerpts or expanded sections can be created to fit your specific needs. Mail, FAX, or E-Mail:

MILLENNIUM PUBLICATIONS
P.O. Box 9941
Denver, CO 80209
FAX: (303) 733-9821 E-Mail: Mpubs @ aol.com

"O.K. Mom, let's head for Colorado!"

COLORADO:
A NEWCOMER'S MANUAL
Everything You Need to Know About
Living in Colorado

By T.J. Walker

First Edition

Millennium Publications
Denver, Colorado

COLORADO: A NEWCOMER'S MANUAL
Everything You Need to Know About Living in Colorado

By T.J. Walker

Published by Millennium Publications, Denver, CO, U.S.A.

Copyright © 1996 by T.J. Walker

All rights reserved. No part of this book may be reproduced or transmitted in any form or by any means, electronic or mechanical, including photocopying, recording or by any information storage and retrieval system without written permission from the author, except for the inclusion of brief quotations in a review.

Cover Design by Vango Graphics, Denver, Colorado
Edited by Jane Kopp, Ph.D.

First Edition
ISBN 0-9628192-1-2
Library of Congress Catalog Card Number: 95-79220

Printed and bound in the United States by Gilliland Printing
10 9 8 7 6 5 4 3 2 1   98 97 96 95

Publisher's Cataloging in Publication
(Prepared by Quality Books Inc.)

Walker, T.J., 1956-
  Colorado : a newcomer's manual : everything you need to know about living in Colorado / by T.J. Walker. -- 1st ed.
  p. cm.
  Includes bibliographical references and index.
  ISBN 0-9628192-1-2

  1. Colorado--Guidebooks. 2. Colorado--Miscellanea. I. Title.

F774.3.W35 1995   978.8'033
                        QBI95-20491

ACKNOWLEDGMENTS

To my wife. For her patience, support, and encouragement.

The information in this book was compiled from over 100 separate government, business and private resources. In every case, someone had to respond to my request for data. To list them all would require more space than is available. My thanks go to everyone who contributed and cooperated with this endeavor.

ABOUT THE ADDITIONAL BOOKS RECOMMENDED HEREIN

Colorado is home to more than 125 small to mid-size, independent publishers. These people are entrepreneurs in the true sense of the word. Having information to share or a story to tell, most became frustrated with the rejections of the big publishing houses and decided to strike out on their own. A few have grown and now have hundreds of titles in print, while the majority remain "mom and pop" operations with but one or two titles. I would sincerely like to thank the dozen or so who so readily agreed to provide information and assistance in the preparation of this book.

All the additional books recommended in this manual have been personally reviewed by me and are considered to be excellent resources to compliment and enhance the data contained in these pages. If applicable, each chapter begins with acknowledgment of the additional titles which were used for reference. A complete list of the publishers, all their related titles, and ordering information is contained in Appendix A.

Cover Design by Vango Graphics
Edited by Jane Kopp, Ph.D.

Warning—Disclaimer

This book is designed to provide information about the subject matter covered. It is sold with the understanding that the publisher and author are not engaged in rendering legal, accounting or other professional services. If legal or other expert assistance is required, the services of a competent professional should be sought.

It is not the purpose of this book to reprint all the information that is otherwise available. For additional information, see the many references throughout each chapter and in Appendix A.

Every effort has been made to make this book as complete and accurate as possible. **However, there may be mistakes both typographical and in content.** This text should be used only as a general guide and not as the ultimate source of information on the subject matter covered.

The author(s) and publisher assume no responsibility for errors, inaccuracies, omissions or any other inconsistency herein. Neither shall the author(s) or publisher assume any liability to any person or entity with respect to any loss or damage caused, or alleged to be caused, directly or indirectly by the information contained in this book.

If you do not wish to be bound by the above, you may return this book to the publisher for a full refund.

Printed on Recycled Paper

"Because We Care"

UPDATES AND FUTURE EDITIONS
We Need Your Help

During the process of outlining the information to be contained in this book, many newcomers to Colorado were consulted in regards to what type of information and data would be most useful to them as recent arrivals to the state. The results of that survey are the twelve chapters contained herein. However, by no means do we consider this book to be a definitive work.

Regardless if you have lived here for a week or 20 years, we would like to hear from you if you have suggestions about additional material which should appear in future editions of this book. Keep in mind this book is not intended to be a "tour book" or "restaurant guide" type of publication. What we are looking for is specific information which you may have had a difficult time obtaining while trying to adjust to daily life in Colorado. In addition, this book contains a tremendous amount of information in the form of points of contact, addresses, and phone numbers. We strived to insure such data was up-to-date. Even our best efforts can not guarantee this. If you have updates or suggestions that would be helpful in the next edition of this book please forward them to us via FAX, mail or E-Mail. If you are the first one to submit a specific update which is used in the next edition, we will send you a free copy of that edition. Use the same addresses if you would like to be placed on our mailing list for future editions or would like to send us your comments if you found this book particularly useful or helpful in some way (yes, we *are* fishing for compliments).

Thanking You In Advance,

Millennium Publications
P.O. Box 9941
Denver, CO 80209
FAX (303) 733-9821   E-Mail: Mpubs @ aol.com

TABLE OF CONTENTS

CHAPTER ONE
ONCE UPON A TIME IN THE WEST (Dire Straits, 1979)
THE STATE OF COLORADO	**15**
COLORADO FACTS AT A GLANCE	16
PRE-HISTORY OF COLORADO	21
MODERN HISTORY	22
COLORADO'S GEOGRAPHY/TOPOGRAPHY	24
COLORADO'S WEATHER	25

CHAPTER TWO
THE POWERS THAT BE (Roger Waters, 1987)
COLORADO'S GOVERNMENT	**27**
COLORADO'S POLITICAL PROCESS	**28**
THE VOTING PROCESS	28
INITIATIVES AND REFERENDUMS	29
THE BRANCHES OF GOVERNMENT	**31**
THE EXECUTIVE BRANCH	31
THE JUDICIAL BRANCH	33
BECOMING A JUDGE	34
JURIES	35
THE LEGISLATIVE BRANCH	**35**
THE LEGISLATORS	35
THE LEGISLATIVE COUNCIL	35
THE LEGISLATIVE COMMITTEES	36
STATE GOVERNMENT DEPARTMENTS/AGENCIES	**37**
COLORADO STATE GOVERNMENT	37
GOVERNOR'S OFFICE	37
DEPARTMENT OF ADMINISTRATION	37
DEPARTMENT OF AGRICULTURE	37
DEPARTMENT OF CORRECTIONS	38
DEPARTMENT OF EDUCATION	38
DEPARTMENT OF HEALTH CARE	38
DEPARTMENT OF HIGHER EDUCATION	39
DEPARTMENT OF HUMAN SERVICES	39
DEPARTMENT OF LABOR AND EMPLOYMENT	40
DEPARTMENT OF LOCAL AFFAIRS	40

DEPARTMENT OF MILITARY AFFAIRS	40
DEPARTMENT OF NATURAL RESOURCES	41
DEPARTMENT OF PERSONNEL	41
DEPARTMENT OF PUBLIC HEALTH AND ENVIRONMENT	41
DEPARTMENT OF PUBLIC SAFETY	42
DEPARTMENT OF REGULATORY AGENCIES (DORA)	42
DEPARTMENT OF REVENUE	43
DEPARTMENT OF TRANSPORTATION	43
DORA	**45**
OFFICE OF THE EXECUTIVE DIRECTOR	45
OFFICE OF CONSUMER COUNSEL	45
OFFICE OF POLICY AND RESEARCH	46
OFFICE OF REGULATORY REFORM	46
DIVISION OF ADMINISTRATIVE SERVICES	47
DIVISION OF BANKING	48
DIVISION OF CIVIL RIGHTS	48
DIVISION OF FINANCIAL SERVICES	49
DIVISION OF INSURANCE	50
PUBLIC UTILITIES COMMISSION	50
DIVISION OF REAL ESTATE	51
DIVISION OF REGISTRATIONS	51
DIVISION OF SECURITIES	56

CHAPTER THREE

SCHOOL'S OUT FOREVER (Alice Cooper, 1972)

STATE SCHOOL SYSTEMS	**57**
AN OVERVIEW OF PUBLIC SCHOOLS	**57**
SCHOOL CHOICES IN COLORADO	**59**
SELECTING THE RIGHT SCHOOL	**60**
PARENT INVENTORY OF EDUCATIONAL PREFERENCES	60
INDEX OF CITIES AND SCHOOL DISTRICTS	**62**
PRIVATE SCHOOLS	**67**
HIGHER EDUCATION	**68**
THE COLORADO COMMISION ON HIGHER EDUCATION	68
FACTS ABOUT PUBLIC HIGHER EDUCATION	68
STUDENT FINANCIAL ASSISTANCE PROGRAMS	69
DEFINITION OF DEGREES	70
COLORADO INSTITUTIONS OF HIGHER EDUCATION	70
LIBRARIES	**72**
THE NEW DENVER CENTRAL LIBRARY	73
CORPORATE, SPECIAL AND PRIVATE LIBRARIES	73

CHAPTER FOUR
THIS MUST BE THE PLACE (Talking Heads, 1983)
STATE-WIDE STATISTICS	**77**
GENERAL STATISTICS	78
POPULATION GROWTH	78
80 SAFEST COMMUNITIES	80
EMPLOYMENT	82
COLORADO LARGEST EMPLOYERS	84
HEALTH CARE	85
FACTS AT A GLANCE	85
HEALTH CARE FACILITIES	85
TAXES	86
STATE INCOME TAX	86
STATE/COUNTY/CITY SALES TAX	86
HIDDEN TAXES	86

CHAPTER FIVE
BEHIND THE WHEEL (Depeche Mode, 1987)
VEHICLES	**87**
REGISTRATIONS/TITLES	88
TRANSFERRING STATES	89
BUYING FROM A DEALER	89
BUYING FROM A PRIVATE OWNER	89
PHONE LIST FOR COUNTY CLERKS	90
LICENSE PLATES (TAGS)	91
VEHICLE INSURANCE	92
EMISSIONS TESTING	92
ENHANCED PROGRAM AREA	93
BASIC PROGRAM AREA	94
DRIVER'S LICENSE	94
NEW RESIDENTS WITH A VALID LICENSE	95
POINTS ASSESSED	96
EXPRESSED CONSENT LAW (ALCOHOL & DRUGS)	98
IDENTIFICATION CARDS	98
THE DRIVER EXAMINATION	98
OFFICE LOCATIONS	98

CHAPTER SIX
SEND LAWYERS, GUNS AND MONEY (Warren Zevon, 1978)
LAWS, RULES AND REGULATIONS   101

DUI/DWAI	102
LIQUOR LAWS	102
BAD CHECKS	102
EVICTIONS	103
MARRIAGE	103
DIVORCE	104
REAL ESTATE	105
LOTTO	106

CHAPTER SEVEN
CHANGES IN LATITUDES, CHANGES IN ATTITUDES
(Jimmy Buffett, 1977)
THE TEN FASTEST GROWING COUNTIES   107

GUIDING PRINCIPLES FROM THE COLORADO LEADERSHIP SUMMIT ON SMART GROWTH AND DEVELOPMENT	108
ADAMS COUNTY	112
ARAPAHOE COUNTY	114
BOULDER COUNTY	116
CITY AND COUNTY OF DENVER	119
DOUGLAS COUNTY	120
EL PASO COUNTY	123
JEFFERSON COUNTY	125
LARIMER COUNTY	128
SUMMIT COUNTY	130
WELD COUNTY	132

CHAPTER EIGHT
MONEY FOR NOTHING (Dire Straits, 1985)
SMALL AND HOME-BASED BUSINESS START-UP   135

SO YOU WANT TO BE AN ENTREPRENEUR?	136
CHECK-LIST FOR NEW BUSINESS START-UP	137
NEW, ESTABLISHED, OR FRANCHISE	138
AVOIDING COMMERCIAL FRAUD	138

LEGAL STRUCTURE AND REGISTRATION	140
WHERE TO REGISTER YOUR NEW BUSINESS	142
COLORADO SALES TAX LICENSES	143
COLLECTING SALES TAXES	143
EMPLOYER RESPONSIBILITIES	144
PAYROLL TAX FILING REQUIREMENTS AND FORMS	146
BUSINESS INSURANCE	147
INCOME AND PROPERTY TAX	149

CHAPTER NINE

THINGS TO DO IN DENVER WHEN YOU'RE DEAD
(Warren Zevon, 1991)

STATE-WIDE RECREATION AND ENTERTAINMENT	157
COMMUNING WITH NATURE	158
WINTER SPORTS	161
WATER SPORTS	163
BICYCLING	164
SKY-HIGH ADVENTURE	165
WEEKEND GETAWAYS	166
TOURS	167
PROFESSIONAL SPORTS	168
DOWNTOWN DENVER	168
LEISURE, FUN & THE UNUSUAL	169
THE ARTS & CULTURE	170

CHAPTER TEN

EIGHT MILES HIGH (The Byrds, 1966)

HIGH-ALTITUDE LIVING	175
HEALTH PRECAUTIONS	176
HIGH-ALTITUDE COOKING	178
HIGH-ALTITUDE GARDENING	182

CHAPTER ELEVEN
SO FAR AWAY (Dire Straits, 1985)
GETTING FROM THERE TO HERE   **185**
- MOVING TIPS   186
- MOVING WITH CHILDREN   187
- TEMPORARY HOUSING/RELOCATION SERVICES   188

CHAPTER TWELVE
NEW KID IN TOWN (Eagles, 1976)
RESOURCES / PHONE LISTS   **189**
- INDEX OF PHONE LISTS ELSEWHERE IN THIS BOOK   189
- PREFIXES IN THE NEW 970 AREA CODE   190
- CONVENTION & VISITORS BUREAUS   191
- REFFERAL SERVICES   191
- CIVIC CLUBS AND ORGANIZATIONS   192
- DAILY / WEEKLY NEWSPAPERS   197
- RADIO / T.V. STATIONS   200
- CREDIT UNIONS   202
- PUBLIC UTILITY COMPANIES   206
- VOLUNTEER CENTERS   207

APPENDIX A *RECOMMENDED READING*   **208**
APPENDIX B *MAPS & PHOTOS*   **211**
- THE NEW DENVER CENTRAL LIBRARY   211
- COLORADO COUNTIES   212
- SUB-STATE REGIONS   213
- COLORADO NATIONAL FOREST   214
- COLORADO STATE PARKS   215

BIBLIOGRAPHY   **216**
INDEX   **219**

CHAPTER ONE
ONCE UPON A TIME IN THE WEST

THE STATE OF COLORADO
Facts At A Glance
History
Geography/Topography
Weather

The information in this chapter was compiled from various sources including, but not limited to, government reports and publications (Federal, State, and Local); materials provided by business and civic organizations; and books produced by independent Colorado publishers including:

A Colorado History, Seventh Edition, Pruett Publishing Company
Ancient Walls, Fulcrum Publishing
Colorado, A History of the Centennial State, University Press of Colorado
Denver, Mining Camps to Metropolis, University Press of Colorado
Leadville's Ice Palace, Ice Castle Productions
The Archaeology of Colorado, Johnson Books
The Four Corners Anasazi, Johnson Books

For a complete description of the above books and related titles, please see the Publisher's listing in Appendix A.

 COLORADO: A Newcomer's Manual

I moved to Colorado almost a decade ago. I fell in love with the breathtaking beauty of the mountains and the easy-going manner of the people I would meet while visiting my sister who had moved here exactly one year before me. To this day, I am still amazed by the new sights, sounds, smells, and discoveries the state freely offers on a seemingly unlimited basis. Also, to this day, I still have to ask my wife or sister where this town or that city is located, how to dress for mountain ventures, or about the history of a pile of sawdust which used to be a mining town.

I never bothered to learn much about this state. Trying to put a limit on the number of facts, figures, data, maps, and stories I seem to constantly cram into my head, I would acquire new knowledge about Colorado only on a need-to-know basis. Being a self-employed entrepreneur, I quickly learned almost everything about conducting business here. Yet, before researching the material for this book, I couldn't tell you much about Colorado's history (weren't there cowboys and Indians here?), geography (the mountains are West of Denver), weather (it can rain in December and snow in July), unique laws (you can be fined 3 times the amount of a bad check), or high-altitude living (things just don't cook the same this high up).

In fact, while gathering information for this chapter from other Colorado publishers, one asked me if I planned to include a section on the state's pre-history. My first thought was "If something is *pre*-history, how do we know anything about it?" Allowing for the non-literal meaning of the word, I soon discovered this state has a very rich and interesting *pre*-history. Moving forward from there, I found the modern, high school type of history (which previously bored me to tears) to be full of wonderment. AND, after I completed writing this chapter, I can proudly say "I know about the cliff dwellings in Mesa Verde, I know the location of Montrose, I know Colorado gets an average of 300 days of sunshine a year, and I can even tell you Colorado has 35 registered motorcycles per 1,000 residents!"

However, all that being said, I still have this thing for learning a new subject in two stages. First, I want to see the bare-bones facts. Statistics that give me an outline understanding. Then, at my leisure, I will go back and fill in the blanks with dialog, prose and explanations. In keeping with this tradition, the first section of this chapter contains more bare-bone facts about Colorado than you ever wanted to know, followed by some fascinating lessons on the pre-history, modern history, geography, topography, and weather of the most beautiful state in the country.

COLORADO FACTS AT A GLANCE

(Please Note: All demographic information about population is the most current available. However, Colorado's incredible growth since the 1990 census should be considered when evaluating this data)

PEOPLE OF COLORADO

POPULATION, 1990: 3,294,394; 1994: 3,655,647
PROJECTED POPULATION, YEAR 2000: 4,018,309
POPULATION DENSITY, 1990: 31.76 persons per sq mile
POPULATION, 1980-1990: +14.0% change
POPULATION OVER 18 YEARS, 1990: 2,433,128
POPULATION UNDER 18 YEARS, 1990: 861,266

16

CHAPTER ONE: ONCE UPON A TIME IN THE WEST

POPULATION 65 YEARS OLD AND OVER: 9%
ASIAN/PACIFIC ISLANDER POPULATION, 1990: 59,862
ASIAN/PACIFIC ISLANDER POPULATION RATE: 1.82%
BLACK POPULATION, 1990: 133,146
BLACK POPULATION RATE, 1990: 4.04%
HISPANIC POPULATION, 1990: 424,302
HISPANIC POPULATION RATE, 1990: 12.88%
NATIVE AMERICAN POPULATION, 1990: 27,776
NATIVE AMERICAN POPULATION RATE, 1990: 0.84%
WHITE POPULATION, 1990: 2,905,474
WHITE POPULATION RATE, 1990: 88.19%
METROPOLITAN AREA POPULATION: 81.7%
METROPOLITAN AREA POPULATION, 1980-1990: 15.5% change
HOUSING UNITS, 1990: 1,477,349
HOUSEHOLDS, 1990: 1,282,000
HOUSEHOLDS, 1980-1990: 20.8% change
BIRTH RATE: 16.30 per 1,000 population
BIRTHS TO TEENAGE MOTHERS: 10.20% of total
BIRTHS TO UNMARRIED WOMEN: 18.9% of total
LIFE EXPECTANCY, BOTH SEXES: 75.30 years
LIFE EXPECTANCY, FEMALE: 78.80 years
LIFE EXPECTANCY, MALE: 71.78 years
DEATH RATE: 6.4 deaths per 1,000 population
MARRIAGE RATE: 9.6 marriages per 1,000 population
DIVORCE RATE: 5.7 divorces per 1,000 population
VIETNAM VETERANS: 155,000

Lark Bunting

Bighorn Sheep

GEOGRAPHY IN COLORADO

TOTAL AREA: 104,091 square miles
LAND AREA: 103,595 square miles
WATER AREA: 496 square miles
AVERAGE ELEVATION: 6,600 feet
HIGHEST POINT: Mt. Elbert, 14,433 feet
LOWEST POINT: Arkansas River, 3,350 feet
HIGHEST TEMPERATURE: 118 degrees Fahrenheit
LOWEST TEMPERATURE: -61 degrees Fahrenheit
NATURAL RESOURCES: Petroleum, natural gas, coal
LAND IN NATIONAL PARKS: 588,200 acres
AREA IN STATE PARKS: 5,455,000 acres
VISITORS TO STATE PARKS: 7,670,000
FEDERAL LANDS: 36.2% owned by federal government
FRESH WATER CONSUMPTION: 4,850,000,000 gallons per day
ANNUAL SOIL EROSION: 121,600,000 tons
HAZARDOUS WASTE SITES: 16 sites on national priority list

Cutthroat Trout

Stegosaurus

 COLORADO: A Newcomer's Manual

EDUCATION IN COLORADO

EXPENDITURES FOR PUBLIC SCHOOLS: $787 per resident
PUBLIC SCHOOL EXPENDITURES: $4,633 per pupil
PUPIL/TEACHER RATIO: 19.08 pupils per teacher
TEACHER SALARIES, ELEMENTARY: $28,800 average
TEACHER SALARIES, SECONDARY: $30,300 average
SPENDING, PUBLIC HIGHER EDUCATION: $2,780 per student
TUITION REVENUES, HIGHER EDUCATION: $1,883 per student
COLLEGE ENROLLMENT, TOTAL: 184,000 students
COLLEGE ENROLLMENT, FEMALE: 97,000 students
COLLEGE ENROLLMENT, FRESHMEN: 30,000 students
COLLEGE ENROLLMENT, PART-TIME: 74,000 students

GOVERNMENT OF COLORADO

OFFICIAL NAME: State of Colorado
CAPITAL: Denver
ADMITTED TO UNION: Aug. 1, 1876
ORDER OF STATEHOOD: 38
ELECTORAL VOTES: 8
EXECUTIVE TERM: 4 years
GOVERNOR: Roy Romer (D) 1994
SENATORS: Hank Brown (R) 1996, Ben Nighthorse Campbell (R) 1998
NUMBER OF U.S. REPRESENTATIVES: 6
FLAG: Three alternating horizontal stripes of blue, white and blue with a large red C containing a gold disk in the center.
MOTTO: Nil Sine Numine (Nothing without providence)
SYMBOLS:
Animal: Rocky Mountain bighorn sheep
Bird: Lark bunting
Fish: Cutthroat Trout
Fossil: Stegosaurus
Flower: White and lavender columbine
Gem: Aquamarine
Song: Where The Columbines Grow
Tree: Blue spruce
AGE OF BUYING ALCOHOL: 21
AGE OF LEAVING SCHOOL: after age 16
AGE OF MAJORITY (FULL CIVIL RIGHTS): 18
AGE OF MARRIAGE WITH CONSENT: 16
AGE OF MARRIAGE WITHOUT CONSENT: 18
VOTERS, 1988 PRESIDENTIAL ELECTION: 55.1% casting votes
DISTRIBUTION OF FEDERAL FUNDS: $3,943 per capita
FEDERAL EMPLOYEES, CIVILIAN: 52,000
FEDERAL INCOME TAXES PAID: $1,483 per capita
FEDERAL SPENDING, DEFENSE PROGRAMS: $4,616,000,000
STATE GOVERNMENT EXPENDITURES: $1,430 per capita

State Flag

State Seal

CHAPTER ONE: ONCE UPON A TIME IN THE WEST

STATE FUNDING FOR ART: $0.40 per capita
SOCIAL SECURITY RECIPIENTS: 12.0% of population
PUBLIC AID RECIPIENTS: 3.9% of population
FOOD STAMP RECIPIENTS: 6.1% of population

CRIME IN COLORADO (See Chapter Four)

ECONOMY OF COLORADO

INCOME PER CAPITA: $16,463
DISPOSABLE PERSONAL INCOME: $14,110.00 per capita

Columbine

GROSS STATE PRODUCT, TOTAL: $ 59,177,000,000
GROSS STATE PRODUCT, AGRICULTURAL: $1,517,000,000
GROSS STATE PRODUCT, CONSTRUCTION: $3,510,000,000
GROSS STATE PRODUCT, FINANCE: $9,688,000,000
GROSS STATE PRODUCT, GOVERNMENT: $ 8,275,000,000
GROSS STATE PRODUCT, MANUFACTURING: $7,631,000,000
GROSS STATE PRODUCT, MINING: $1,704,000,000
GROSS STATE PRODUCT, RETAIL TRADE: $6,285,000,000
GROSS STATE PRODUCT, SERVICES: $10,218,000,000
GROSS STATE PRODUCT, TRANSPORTATION: $6,564,000,000
GROSS STATE PRODUCT, WHOLESALE TRADE: $3,784,000,000
SERVICE BUSINESS ESTABLISHMENTS: 125,767
SERVICE BUSINESS ESTABLISHMENT EMPLOYEES: 256,147
SERVICE BUSINESS RECEIPTS: $13,235,666
WHOLESALE BUSINESS ESTABLISHMENTS: 7,100
WHOLESALE BUSINESS EMPLOYEES: 76,393
WHOLESALE BUSINESS RECEIPTS: $29,971,953
RETAIL BUSINESS ESTABLISHMENTS: 36,131
RETAIL BUSINESS ESTABLISHMENT EMPLOYEES: 267,899
RETAIL SALES: $21,287,132
RETAIL SALES PER HOUSEHOLD: $17,205
RETAIL SALES PER HOUSEHOLD, 1982-1987: 18.7% change
MANUFACTURING WORKERS, 1982-1987: -6. 4% change
UNION MEMBERSHIP, MANUFACTURING: 10.0% unionized
VALUE ADDED BY MANUFACTURING: $11,876,000,000
LABOR FORCE: 1,597,000
FEMALE LABOR FORCE: 61.1% of total
EMPLOYED/POPULATION: 65.3% of total population
UNEMPLOYMENT RATE: 6. 4%
PATENTS GRANTED: 675
DEPARTMENT OF DEFENSE CONTRACTS: $2,891,000,000
EXPORTS: $1,783,000,000
EXPORT RELATED FACTORY EMPLOYMENT: 14.0% of total employment
NEW BUSINESS FAILURES: 248 per 10,000 concerns
NEW HOUSING STARTS: 11,900 units
MORTGAGE LOANS FORECLOSED: 7.7%

 *COLORADO: A Newcomer's Manual*

NONRESIDENTIAL CONSTRUCTION: $544,000,000
MINERALS PRODUCED (NON-FUELS): $373,000,000
MINERAL FUELS PRODUCED: $1,118,000,000
CRUDE PETROLEUM PRODUCTION: 29,000,000 barrels
NATURAL GAS PRODUCTION: 163,000,000,000 cubic feet marketed
ELECTRICITY, GENERATION: 30,900,000,000 kWh
ELECTRICITY, INSTALLED CAPACITY: 7,300,000 kW
NUCLEAR POWER PLANTS: 1

AGRICULTURE IN COLORADO

NUMBER OF FARMS: 27,284
SIZE OF FARMS: 1,241 acres per farm
LAND IN FARMS: 34,048,433 acres
FARMLAND, 1982-1987: 1.5% change
VALUE OF FARM LAND AND BUILDINGS: $364 per acre, average
NET FARM INCOME: $751,000,000
NET FARM INCOME/DEBT RATIO: 23.4%
FARM NET CASH RETURN: $15,476
AGRICULTURAL SALES: $3,143,131,000
PRINCIPAL FARM COMMODITIES: In order of marketing receipts cattle, wheat, corn, dairy products (79%)
PRINCIPAL CROPS: In order of value: hay, corn, wheat, potatoes
CROPLAND HARVESTED: 5,677,000 acres
BARLEY PRODUCTION: 12,160,000 bushels
BARLEY YIELD: 76 bushels per acre
CORN PRODUCTION: 134,850,000 bushels
CORN YIELD: 145 bushels per acre
HAY PRODUCTION: 3,450,000 tons
HAY YIELD: 2 tons per acre
OATS PRODUCTION: 3,025,000 bushels
OATS YIELD: 55 bushels per acre
POTATO PRODUCTION: 22,587,000 CWT
POTATO YIELD: 333 CWT per acre
SUGARBEET PRODUCTION: 912,000 tons
WHEAT PRODUCTION: 62,100,000 bushels
WHEAT YIELD: 27 bushels per acre
CATTLE: 2,900,000 head on farms
HOGS AND PIGS: 230,000 head on farms
SHEEP AND LAMBS: 840,000 head on farms

COMMUNICATIONS IN COLORADO

COMMERCIAL TELEVISION STATIONS: 13
EDUCATIONAL TELEVISION STATIONS: 3
COMMERCIAL AM RADIO STATIONS: 77
COMMERCIAL FM RADIO STATIONS: 68
EDUCATIONAL FM RADIO STATIONS: 20
DAILY NEWSPAPERS: 26

Blue Spruce

CHAPTER ONE: ONCE UPON A TIME IN THE WEST

TRAVEL IN COLORADO

INTERSTATE HIGHWAYS: 942 miles
REGISTERED AUTOMOBILES: 675 per 1,000 population
REGISTERED MOTORCYCLES: 35 per 1,000 population
LICENSED DRIVERS: 2,244,000
MOTOR VEHICLE TRAVEL: 352 miles traveled per road mile
MOTOR VEHICLE ACCIDENT DEATHS: 18 per 100,000 population
STATE GASOLINE TAX RATES, 1991: 22.00 cents per gallon

PRE-HISTORY OF COLORADO

In the beginning was the Word, or maybe the Big-Bang, or perhaps both (maybe the sound of the Big-Bang was the Word). Regardless, we can jump ahead a few billion years to only 300 million years ago. This was a time of the Ancestral Rockies. A vast mountain range which was eventually washed away and became part of a great ocean. Evidence of this can be found in the sandstone deposits around the town of Lyons which was used for most of the sidewalks as Denver grew into a city. Many of the state's highways and buildings were produced from concrete made from the shells of billions of sea creatures turned into Colorado limestone.

Between the Ancestral Rockies and the beginnings of the modern Rockies (about 70 million years ago), what would become Colorado was home to such dinosaurs as the bony-backed stegosaurus, the three-horned triceratops, and the 85-foot long diplodocus. In fact, Colorado has produced some of the richest fossil finds in the country. Also, during this time period, much of this region was swamp-land, leaving behind debris that would eventually become vast deposits of coal and natural gas. Volcanoes were not uncommon and their lava flows created many geological features of Colorado including the Table mountains near Golden.

Skipping ahead to more recent pre-history, we can look at the nomadic tribes of the first Americans who lived here for more than 10,000 years before the first frontier city was built.

At one site, 40 miles north of Denver, artifacts have been carbon-dated to at least 11,250 years ago. Artifacts dating back over 10,000 years have also been found in another site 25 miles southeast of Denver. The origin of the first humans in the southwest is still debated; however, it is generally agreed that some 15-20 thousand years ago, nomadic hunters followed herds of prey across a temporary land bridge which is now the Bering striate between Alaska and Siberia. Dependent on traveling with their food source, these Asian visitors eventually migrated south. As these tribes evolved from nomadic hunters into agricultural farmers, they laid down roots in places such as Mesa Verde, Colorado, some 2,000 years ago.

Mesa Verde is located in Four Corners, the place where Arizona, Colorado, New Mexico, and Utah meet. This entire area was home to early tribes collectively known as the Anasazi. During the thirteenth century the Anasazi numbered more than 50,000. Yet a half-century later there were none. They didn't die out, their descendants still live in New Mexico and Arizona. For some unknown reason, they simply abandoned

 COLORADO: A Newcomer's Manual

the area. And we are not talking about leaving some tents or caves here. By the thirteenth century, Mesa Verde was filled with over 500 cliff dwellings, from one-room houses to large communal structures three or four stories high containing more than 200 rooms.

Between the 14th and 19th centuries, Colorado was inhabited by other more familiar tribes including the Ute, Comanche, Navajo, Apache, Kiowa and Shoshoni. Numerous wars and slaughters took place between various tribes, the Spanish, French and finally "American" pioneers, and this is really becoming reminiscent of high school history class so I believe it's time to move on. For those closet archaeologists, great delight will be found in several of the books mentioned at the beginning of this chapter. A couple are coffee table books, full of fantastic full-color photos of ancient ruins and, while the others may not be able to compete with a rainbow, they are loaded with B/W photos and unlimited details about every major archaeological site in Colorado. See Appendix A for details.

MODERN HISTORY

Colorado is among the handful of states with a very colorful and interesting history. Risking a deluge of nasty letters, what's so interesting about the history of say North Dakota or Nebraska? That being said, let's jump ahead to the mid-eighteen hundreds, to a time before Colorado actually became the 38th state in 1876.

After the end of the Mexican/American War in 1848, large portions of Colorado were settled by farmers from New Mexico. This slow migration and settlement increased dramatically with the discovery of gold. Virtually all the older towns and cities of Colorado have their origins in mining and prospecting. In 1858, the Green-Russel party found gold along Little Dry Creek near the junction of the South Platte River and Cherry Creek. Exaggerated accounts of the discovery spread eastward, causing the Pikes Peak Gold Rush of 1859. Thousands of fortune hunters hurried across the plains, on foot, on horseback, and in wagons. Most of these failed to find any gold and trudged wearily back home. But they had founded several little clusters of huts, known as Montana City, St. Charles, Auraria, and Denver City (named after General James W. Denver, territorial governor of Kansas); and these gradually grew into the capital city of Colorado.

On May 6, 1859, John H. Gregory discovered the Gregory Lode, a vein of gold-bearing quartz, near present-day Central City. Mines were quickly developed on the branches of Clear Creek, in South Park, and across the Continental Divide on the branches of the Blue River.

In 1859 the land that later became Colorado was within the territories of Kansas, Nebraska, Utah, and New Mexico. But the pioneers felt they should have a government of their own, so they created the Jefferson Territory, containing all of present-day Colorado and liberal strips of what is now Utah and Wyoming. Many of the miners ignored the authority of this territorial government and established local laws of their own, electing officials to enforce them.

On February 28, 1861, a law was signed creating the Colorado Territory. William Gilpin, appointed by President Lincoln, was the first governor. The territory was named for the river that rises in Grand Lake and flows through rugged chasms and

CHAPTER ONE: ONCE UPON A TIME IN THE WEST

fertile valleys to the great depths of the Grand Canyon and finally to the Pacific Ocean. (Other rivers rising in Colorado are the Rio Grande, Gunnison, Yampa, White, San Juan, Dolores, Arkansas, Republican, South Platte, and North Platte).

During the first decade following the Pikes Peak Gold Rush, Colorado's development was slow. Refractory ore—ore difficult to extract, process, and transport—was encountered in the mines. The Civil War claimed citizens for soldiers, and Indian resistance threatened the existence of the territory.

But after surviving the ordeals of early years, Colorado made rapid progress in her second decade as a territory. Railways were completed to Colorado in 1870, narrow-gauge rail lines in the mountains tapped the mining regions, colony towns were founded, agriculture was extended, new mines were opened in the San Juan region and immigration escalated.

In 1864, Congress passed an Enabling Act to permit Colorado to become a state. However, the people voted against it because they did not want to pay the taxes needed to support a state government. Finally, more than ten years later, Colorado entered the Union on August 1, 1876, and was called the "Centennial State" in honor of the 100th anniversary of the Declaration of Independence.

During the 1880s progress continued on a grand scale. Mineral wealth poured forth from Aspen and other mining centers such as Leadville. Many other towns flourished, colleges and opera houses were built, and brownstone mansions rather than log cabins became representative of the times. Agriculture expanded with the construction of irrigation systems and the introduction of dry farming. The range livestock industry prospered. Wood production soared. Smelters were erected for the reduction of ores. Although the Panic of 1893 (which followed a devaluation of silver) was a severe blow to the mining industry, Colorado rallied. The great gold camp at Cripple Creek aided revival. Farming continued to expand, and new crops such as sugar beets created new wealth. By 1890, Colorado claimed a population exceeding 413,000.

The city of Leadville, mentioned above, was also home to one of the most unique human-made structures. Built in 1895, Leadville's Ice Palace was constructed by approximately 300 craftsmen in under 60 days. The main building materials were 8,000 tons of ice and 307,000 board feet of lumber. When completed, this crystal castle housed a skating rink, ballroom, banquet room, riding gallery, lounges, a kitchen and more. It covered over 5 acres, was electrically lighted and heated by coal burning stoves. If you are fond of quirky little pieces of history, get a copy of *Leadville's Ice Palace* by Ice Castle Productions. Weighing in at 391 pages, this fascinating book is the definitive work on the bizarre project one city used in an attempt to boost its economy (maybe another book is due about Denver International Airport?). See Appendix A for more information on *Leadville's Ice Palace* and also a book entitled *Tales, Trails and Tommyknockers* by Johnson Books. The latter is a great Colorado history book for children.

This brings us up to the beginning of the 20th century. Since the turn of the century, historically significant events have been multiplying in geometric proportions. The great depression, World Wars I & II, the Korean War, the civil rights movement, more wars, on and on. To describe Colorado's involvement in all these events would take much more space than can be alloted. If you are interested in more recent history,

 COLORADO: A Newcomer's Manual

please check the Additional Resources section of this chapter or the books listed in Appendix A.

COLORADO'S GEOGRAPHY/TOPOGRAPHY

Colorado is the eighth largest state in the nation, with an area of 104,247 square miles and with over 35% of this area owned by the federal government. The State is rectangular, extending 387 miles east to west and 276 miles north to south.

The main feature of the state's geography is the Continental Divide, extending Northeast to Southwest and roughly bisecting Colorado into the Eastern and Western Slopes. Waters west of the Divide flow into the Pacific, east of the Divide into the Atlantic. The major rivers are the Arkansas, Platte, Rio Grande and Colorado. The state's largest natural lake is Grand Lake which human enterprise has outdone with projects like the John Martin Reservoir on the Arkansas River and Blue Mesa Reservoir on the Gunnison River.

Colorado contains 75 percent of all the area in the United States over 10,000 feet high. It contains 53 peaks of more than 14,000 feet with the highest being Mt. Elbert at 14,433 feet, and over one thousand peaks two miles high. In fact, the mountainous area of Colorado is six times that of Switzerland. Three of the nation's highest highways are in Colorado. The roads to the summits of both Pikes Peak and Mt. Evans are over 14,000 feet above sea-level and Trail Ridge Road, which crosses through Rocky Mountain National Park and over the Continental Divided at 12,183 feet, is the nation's highest continuous paved highway. The principal mountain ranges are the eastern Front Range, the central Sawatch Range, the Park range in the north, the southern Sangre de Cristo Mountains and the San Juan Mountains in the southwest.

Plateaus, mesas, and canyons make up the western 25% of the state while high plains bordering Wyoming, Nebraska, Kansas, Oklahoma and New Mexico being 40% of the state to the east. Sloping upward from Kansas, Colorado's central plains gently rise approximately 2,000 feet from 3,386 to 5,200 feet above sea-level.

Colorado has two national parks, six national monuments, 12 national forests, 43 state parks, three national recreation areas, and 16 hazardous waste sites on the national priority list.

Colorado's 63 counties are divided into five informal substate regions (see maps on pages 212 & 213):

Front Range	Adams, Arapahoe, Boulder, Denver, Douglas, El Paso, Jefferson, Larimer, Pueblo, Weld
Western Slope	Archuleta, Delta, Dolores, Eagle, Garfield, Grand, Gunnison, Hinsdale, Jackson, La Plata, Mesa, Moffat, Montezuma, Montrose, Ouray, Pitkin, Rio Blanco, Routt, San Juan, San Miguel, Summit
Eastern Plains	Baca, Bent, Cheyenne, Crowley, Elbert, Kiowa, Kit Carson, Lincoln, Logan, Morgan, Otero, Phillips, Prowers, Sedgwick, Washington, Yuma
San Luis Valley	Alamosa, Conejos, Costilla, Mineral, Rio Grande, Saguache
Eastern Mountains	Chaffee, Clear Creek, Custer, Fremont, Gilpin, Huerfano, Lake, Las Animas, Park, Teller

CHAPTER ONE: ONCE UPON A TIME IN THE WEST

COLORADO'S WEATHER

Unpredictable, unbelievable, unanticipated, calm, chaotic, implausible, improbable, beautiful, nasty, wonderful, violent, serene, ominous, threatening, and blissful are a few of the ways I can describe Colorado's weather.

Having grown-up in Florida, I have experienced my share of violent thunderstorms and hurricanes. However, not until I moved to Colorado did I experience a real-life use of the Emergency Broadcast System. I was driving around Denver, listening to one of my favorite songs, when that nasty, high-pitched tone did its job and startled me back into reality. The clouds had been looking ominous but as of yet, I had not seen any rain, lightening or thunder. The tone was followed by reports of three tornadoes over the area with one touching down and ripping a path along one of Denver's parkways less than a mile from my location. Being a closet thrill-seeker, I stopped my van and climbed on top to watch the show until I realized one mile is not exactly a safe distance from a fast moving, totally unpredictable tornado.

On another occasion, during a morning hike outside of Brekenridge, I experienced bright sunshine, sleet, rain, snow, and more sunshine followed by a heavy misty fog, all before lunch! Fortunately, I had been in Colorado long enough to know to pack the right clothes.

The reason I share these stories is that although I will cover the "for the tourist" descriptions of our weather, such descriptions don't relay the whole story. They consist of basic highs, lows, and averages but don't convey the extreme changes. Every year there are news stories of inexperienced hikers being rescued from snow storms dressed in shorts and T-shirts. After all, it was 90 degrees in the city when they left for the mountains.

If you look in a guide or tour book or break open an encyclopedia, this is basically what you will find about Colorado's weather.

Colorado enjoys an average of nearly 300 days of sunshine per year, with an average humidity of 33 percent. Precipitation varies with respect to elevation and location of a given area. This can range from 60 inches per year on the Western Slope to 16 inches or less on the Great Plains and the Colorado Plateau. Rainfall is concentrated in the spring and summer and the plains are subject to heavy winter snowfalls. The annual average temperature (all Farienheight) ranges from about 51 degrees on the plains to less than 36 degrees in the mountains. The state's recorded high was 118 degrees in 1888 while in 1985 the lowest recorded temperature was -61 degrees. During cold months, Colorado's front range occasionally experiences Chinooks—fast moving (up to 100 mph), warm winds—which can cause local temperatures to rise as much as 50 degrees in a matter of hours. First snows may occur as early as September with the last as late as July or August. At lower elevations, winters are fairly mild and snow seldom stays on the ground more than a few days under the warm, bright sun.

To provide a more rounded, complete picture of Colorado's weather, see the section on high-altitude gardening in Chapter Ten. What follows is a month-by-month account of interesting weather facts provided by Mike Nelson of KUSA 9News and Nolan J. Doesken of the Department of Atmospheric Science, Colordo State University.

 **COLORADO: A Newcomer's Manual**

January: Colorado's coldest New Year's day occured in 1979. A morning temperature of -60 degrees F was reported at Maybell.

February: A remarkable "Fog Storm," February 5-15, 1978 covered much of eastern Colorado. Rime ice several inches thick broke miles of powerlines acroos the region.

March: A massive blizzard over northeast Colorado, March 10-11, 1977. Snow piled into 25 foot high drifts, killed thousands of cattle and resulted in the deaths of nine people.

April: A remarkably strong cold front crossed Colorado on Easter Sunday, April 19, 1987. Afternoon temperatures along the Front Range were in the 80's. By evening it was snowing with Denver receiving 3 inches.

May: A late spring snowstorm dumped 27.8" of snow in Fort Collins within a two day period. Comparable amounts fell in Boulder with larger totals in the foothills.

June: June is Colorado's severe weather month with an average of 15 tornados and 46 damaging hailstorms. On June 6, 1990, a tornado ripped through the town of Limon. Good warnings prevented loss of life although the town itself was almost wiped out.

July: A brutal hailstorm ravaged an area from Estes Park to Colorado Springs on July 11, 1990. In 3 hours, the storm caused more than $600 million in damages to cars and homes.

August: Denver's all time record high reached 105 degrees F on August 8, 1878. Denver's high temperature on August 10, 1968 only reached 58 degrees.

September: An early Front Range snowstorm, September 16-18, 1971 dropped 1-2 feet of snow from Fort Collins to Pueblo. Millions of dollars of damage occurred from broken tree branches. In repeat performance, another early snowstorm hit the front range on September 20, 1995. Over 80% of all the trees in Denver were damaged.

October: Following a very mild autumn, a severe cold wave killed thousands of trees over eastern Colorado. Denver's high temperature on October 30, 1991 was only 21 degrees F.

November: A snowstorm that deposited 20-50" of snow over most of eastern Colorado from November 2-6, 1946, was resposible for at 13 deaths.

December: The worst and most widespread heavy snow to hit the Colorado Front Range occured between December 1-5, 1913. 46" of snow fell in Denver and 86" at Georgetown. Many roofs collasped and locomotives were stranded.

WEATHER/POLLUTION INFORMATION NUMBERS

Clean Air Hotline   758-4848
Wood Burning Hotline   692-3280
Smoking Vehicle Hotline 777-0517
Public Transit   299-6000
Air Quality Information 782-0211
Carpools   458-POOL

CHAPTER TWO
THE POWERS THAT BE

COLORADO'S GOVERNMENT
Colorado's Political Process
State Government Departments and Agencies

> The information in this chapter was compiled from various sources including, but not limited to, government reports and publications (Federal, State, and Local); materials provided by business and civic organizations; and books produced by independent Colorado publishers including:
> *Colorado: The State We're In,* Revised Edition 1995,
>   League of Women Voters of Colorado
> *The Colorado General Assembly,* University Press of Colorado
> For a complete description of the above books and related titles, please see the Publisher's listing in Appendix A.

As a citizen of Colorado you are guaranteed the right of access to your government. The State's constitution states "All elections shall be free and open; and no power, civil or military, shall at any time interfere to prevent the right of suffrage." Of course, this is tempered by the old saying "You can't fight city hall." Either way, you have pre-defined rights and responsibilities as a citizen. This chapter is designed to give you a better understanding of how the state government functions and, more important, who is responsible for what and how to contact them.

COLORADO: A Newcomer's Manual

COLORADO'S POLITICAL PROCESS
THE VOTING PROCESS
VOTER REGISTRATION

The qualifications to become a registered voter in Colorado are:

- 18 years of age by Election day
- United States citizenship
- Address of residence within a given precinct for 30 days by Election day. A citizen who will reach 18 or become a U.S. Citizen during the 30 days prior to the election must register before the 30 days in order to vote.

A yearly function, voter registration is the responsibility of the election commission or county clerk. Both operate during normal business hours and can designate additional sites for registration (shopping malls, grocery stores, etc.) during the weeks preceding an election. If qualified, you can register up to, and including 30 days before an election. If you have moved or changed your legal address since the last election, you must register the change at any location where voter registrations are completed.

In 1984, Colorado voters passed an initiative known as the Motor Voter which allows you to register at all offices where driver's licenses are issued. In addition, in 1992, a law was passed which allows a registrar at each high school to register qualified high school students. You may also register at any social service agency throughout the state.

EARLY VOTING

If you prefer, you may vote in person at a place designated by the county clerk up to 24 days before any election and no later than the Friday prior to the election. Every county must provide a polling place for Early Voting.

MAIL-IN VOTING

Starting January 1 of any election year, you may obtain an application for a mail-in ballot. This option is available the entire year up to the Friday immediately preceding the election. You do not have to provide a reason for exercising this option. All mail-in ballots must reach the county clerk, election commission, or an early voting polling place no later than 7:00 p.m. on Election Day.

ELECTION DAY

This section explains what elections are held in what years. Don't worry if it seems terribly confusing—television, radio, and printed ads provide more than enough information about the issues prior to any election.

General Elections are held on the Tuesday succeeding the first Monday of November in even-numbered years. National and state offices are decided by this election and there may also be ballot issues. Since 1993, initiatives or referenda concerning fiscal matters may be on the ballots of the Statewide Election held in November in odd-numbered years.

CHAPTER TWO: THE POWERS THAT BE

The November General Election is held every fourth year and coincides with the Presidential Election. Colorado's Presidential Election is held on the first Tuesday of March during Presidential Primary Election years. Voters choose their candidates for president and vice-president in the party in which they are affiliated. They also select a slate of delegates for their party's national convention who are committed to support the candidates who won the Presidential Primary Election.

The regular State Primary Election is on the second Tuesday of August in even-numbered years. Contested races within the party are decided by those who have party affiliation. This is the final nomination of the candidate who will represent the party. Only those who have declared a choice of party may vote in the Primary Election. However, any unaffiliated voter may declare a party affiliation at the polling place.

THE VOTING PROCESS ON ELECTION DAY

Each precinct has its own polling place, usually located in public places such as schools, fire stations, churches, or other buildings open to the public. To insure each voter has complete information or to offer assistance, each polling place is staffed by election judges. Provision is made at each polling place for every citizen to cast a secret vote.

The polls are open from 7 a.m. to 7 p.m. The polls are not declared closed until all who were in line at 7 p.m. have voted. Precinct results are reported to the county clerk or the election commission and the final report is sent to the secretary of state.

The League of Women Voters provides nonpartisan information for the public to encourage all who have registered to be informed voters. In addition, a 1994 law requires the nonpartisan research staff of the General Assembly to prepare a ballot information booklet on any initiated or referred constitutional amendment or legislation. This booklet includes the text and title of each measure and a fair and impartial analysis of each measure which includes a summary and the major pros and cons of each issue. The booklet is distributed at no charge to registered voters statewide at least 30 days before the election.

INITIATIVES AND REFERENDUMS

In 1910, Colorado adopted the process of direct legislation by Initiative and Referendum. Initiative proposals seek to amend either the state constitution or the Colorado Revised Statutes. Only the voters can change the constitution, but the General Assembly can amend statutes by passing legislation. These types of ballot proposals have two different forms.

Initiative is the process by which a proposal by citizens who have circulated petitions and gathered the required number of signatures (five percent of the number of votes cast for the secretary of state in the previous election) is placed on the General Election ballot.

Referendum is a proposal passed by a two-thirds of the General Assembly which is then subject to the approval of citizens who voted in the General Election. A referendum may be initiated by citizens to repeal a law passed by General Assembly.

COLORADO: *A Newcomer's Manual*

INITIATIVES

There are seven steps which must be complete before an initiative can be placed on the ballot.

- The proponents must prepare a proposal or statement of the issue.
- The Legislative Council and the Office of Legislative Legal Services must review the proposal. A public meeting must follow and the proposal can be resubmitted after any changes.
- Representatives of the secretary of state, attorney general and the Office of Legislative Legal Services must conduct a Title Setting Hearing. This hearing is open to the public with testimony by both proponents and opponents allowed. Challenges must be made within seven days.
- The complete text of the proposal must be made available to the media and the public.
- The proponents are provided an approved petition format which they use to have petitions printed and circulated for signatures.
- The circulators of such petitions must be registered voters who may be paid for their work. The number of valid signatures required is covered above and has been approximately 50,000 for the past several years. A 6-month window is granted for the circulation and all petitions must be returned to the secretary of state at least three months before the election.
- The secretary of state has a verification and challenge period of 30 days after the deadline to verify if a sufficient number of the signatures are valid. A fifteen days cure period is granted the proponents if the number of signatures is ruled insufficient. However, The entire process must be complete no later than three months before the election.

If approved by the secretary of state, the proposal is given a ballot issue number and appears on the ballot for the November election. The ballot issue must receive a majority of votes in order to be approved.

As a voter, you face two dangers with respect to initiatives and referendums. First, because such proposals can be very lengthy and full of legal terminology they can be difficult to understand and both sides of an issue have been known to use very persuasive—if not entirely accurate—advertisements to sway citizens into voting on an issue they really don't understand. Second, most General Elections end up with so many offices and issues to vote on, a great number of voters simply ignore initiatives and referendums assuming they are of no consequence. Nothing could be further from the truth.

In 1992, Colorado voters approved two controversial issues which continue to have wide-ranging effects on every citizen. Amendment Two, backed by the religious right, appeared to legalize discrimination on the basis of homosexual lifestyles. The passage of this amendment resulted in national attention and major boycotts of the state. At this time, Amendment Two is still being evaluated by the higher courts. Also passed was TABOR—Taxpayer's Bill of Rights. This bill limited taxation to that approved

CHAPTER TWO: THE POWERS THAT BE

by vote of the people and limits annual growth in most government spending to the rate of inflation plus the percentage of change in the state's population. While this sounds like a good thing, the restrictions of this new law have severely hampered all levels of Colorado Government (State, County, and Local) in efforts to provide adequate services for the explosive increase in population. In essence, all services funded by taxes (school systems, law enforcement, etc.) can only be improved through a reactive instead of pro-active approach. Cities and Counties can't adequately prepare for the future because their budgets are restricted to an equation which can't be calculated until well after the need has been established.

Be informed. If you are confused by the legal terminology and political rhetoric of any given proposal, contact The League of Women Voters of Colorado at (303) 863-0437. They can provide an un-biased, easy to understand, plain-English explanation of both sides of upcoming ballot issues.

THE BRANCHES OF GOVERNMENT

The U.S. Constitution established three branches of federal government with a balance of power. Colorado went a step further when they provided for a vote of the people on issues referred by the General Assembly. Although described only briefly herein, a complete understanding of the General Assembly's functions and history can be found in the book *The Colorado General Assembly* mentioned at the beginning of this chapter. Below is a brief description and breakdown of the three branches of Colorado's State Government.

THE EXECUTIVE BRANCH

The Executive Branch encompasses the offices of state elected officials and administrative departments which conduct state business. In 1970, the state constitution was amended to limit the number of executive departments to 20.

THE GOVERNOR OF COLORADO

(Roy Romer, Dem, re-elected in 1994)

The governor is the head of the Executive Branch. The voters elect the governor, lieutenant governor, secretary of state, treasurer, and attorney general for terms of four years each. Appointments for the heads of executive departments are made by the governor (except for the commissioners of Educations and Higher Education). Article IV, Section 2 of the state constitution gives the governor supreme executive power to take care that the laws be faithfully executed.

One of the major powers of this office is the right to appoint approximately 400 judges, heads of departments, board members and commissioners. The governor also has the power to veto bills passed by the General Assembly and has line-item veto of items in the state budget. Also under the control of the governor's office are the Office of State Planning and Budgeting, the Office of Energy Conservation, the Office of Business Development, the International Trade Office and the Colorado Office of Space Advocacy.

The Governor's Cabinet consists of the four other elected officials mentioned above and the heads of the state departments. Included by invitation at cabinet meetings are the commissioners of Education and Higher Education.

31

THE LIEUTENANT GOVERNOR

(Gail Schoettle, Dem, elected 1994)

Also elected to a four-year term, the lieutenant governor is always elected as a package deal with the governor. As with the U.S. vice-president, the lieutenant governor would automatically become governor should the office be vacated.

The Commission on Indian Affairs falls under the control of this office and provides services and coordinates relations between the tribal governments and the state.

THE SECRETARY OF STATE—THE DEPARTMENT OF STATE

(Vikki Buckley, Rep, elected 1994)

The head of the Department of State is the secretary of state. The secretary administers and enforces the laws and codes concerning elections, registration of licenses and incorporation, and also reports political campaign funding.

Additional offices under the Department of State include the Corporations Division, Licensing Division, Administrative Division, and the Elections Division. As explained previously, the secretary of state is also responsible for virtually every aspect of state elections. All initiatives and referendums must be verified and approved through this office.

THE STATE TREASURER—THE DEPARTMENT OF THE TREASURY

(Bill Owen, Rep, elected 1994)

This one should be self-explanatory. This office has three main divisions. The Accounting Division reviews all state bank accounts. The Investment Division is responsible for the safe and profitable investment of state moneys. The Unclaimed Property Program attempts to locate owners of dormant funds. If the owners cannot be found, the moneys go into the state general fund.

THE ATTORNEY GENERAL—THE DEPARTMENT OF LAW

(Gail Norton, Rep, elected 1994)

Charged with protecting the people by enforcing laws concerned with consumer fraud, anti-trust, and consumer credit, the Attorney General acts as the state's lawyer. The Department of Law is the administrative arm of the Attorney General who acts as its executive director. State agencies and the General Assembly receive legal services from assistant attorneys general. They also represent the state in liability cases, review state contracts, and prepare legal opinions. The Attorney General represents the state's interest in state and federal courts.

Consumer protection laws, representing the public interest, are enforced by this department. Cases of fraud and other criminal acts are prosecuted by the department of law. Hazardous waste lawsuits are prosecuted by the Comprehensive Environmental Response Compensation and Liability Act Litigation Unit which is under the direction of the Attorney General.

CHAPTER TWO: THE POWERS THAT BE

THE JUDICIAL BRANCH

The Judicial Branch was created to ensure the balance between individual rights and the powers of the state government. Its major function is to protect the rights of individuals as it interprets and applies the laws. This branch consist of the courts, judges, juries, and the laws.

THE FUNCTION OF THE COURTS

Colorado courts are empowered to resolve conflicts in both criminal and civil matters. Civil cases can include disputes over wills, contracts, personal injuries or family law matters. Procedures in a criminal case are governed by the Colorado Criminal Code and the Colorado Rules of Procedure. Criminal charges are filed by a district attorney. A grand jury can hand down an indictment based on probable cause, but this procedure is seldom used in a criminal case.

SMALL CLAIMS COURT

The Small Claims Court is a division of the County Court. Civil matters involving no more than $3,500 can be argued in this court. Both day and evening sessions are available. Neither side can be represented by an attorney, there are no juries, and sometimes a referee, rather than a judge, may decide the case.

MUNICIPAL COURTS

Violations of city laws committed within city limits are handled by Municipal Courts. This includes offenses of traffic laws, shoplifting (under $300), disturbing the peace, and other petty violations. Any decision of a Municipal court can be appealed to a state court. A defendant has the right to a jury trial in this court.

COUNTY COURTS

Each county has a County Court to handle traffic violations, minor criminal offenses and civil actions involving no more than $10,000. Here again, the defendant has the right to a trial by jury and all decisions can be appealed to the District Courts.

Denver is somewhat different because it is both a city and a county (one of a kind in Colorado). The County Court functions as a municipal as well as a County Court and is funded entirely by Denver taxes and fines paid by offenders. Denver also has the only separate Juvenile Court and a separate Probate Court. These types of cases are handled by the district courts in the rest of the state.

DISTRICT COURTS

District courts are organized into 22 judicial districts. There may be more than one district judge who may serve more than one county in their district. A district court decision may be appealed to the Colorado Court of Appeals or the Colorado Supreme Court.

WATER COURT

The Water Court is a division of the District Court. A district judge from within the water district is appointed by the state Supreme Court to preside over cases concerning water rights or the uses of water resources. There are no juries in this court but decisions can be appealed to the Colorado Supreme Court.

COLORADO: A Newcomer's Manual

THE COURT OF APPEALS
The Court of Appeals serves to hear appeals to decisions in civil and criminal cases. There are 16 judges and their decisions are final unless the Colorado Supreme Court agrees to review a case.

THE COLORADO SUPREME COURT
A decision by this court is final and case reviews are not guaranteed. This court is headed by the Chief Justice who is selected by the seven judges of the court from its own membership. The Chief Justice also serves as the executive head of the Judicial Branch of the state government.
Duties of the Chief Justice include the supervision of all other state courts and the attorneys who practice law in Colorado. The Chief Justice also appoints a Chief Justice in each of the judicial districts. There are four committees which handle the administrative duties of the Colorado Supreme Court.
The State Board of Law Examiners reviews the educational, professional, ethical, and moral qualifications of people who apply for licenses to practice law in Colorado.
The Grievance Committee, composed of 15 attorneys and 4 civilians, investigates all complaints about attorneys. The committee has the power to recommend an attorney be censured or suspended, or that his or her license be revoked.
The Public Defender Commission appoints the state Public Defender, who then appoints assistants in regional offices to serve all the state courts. In mental health cases, a Public Defender may be appointed as *guardian ad litem* to represent the person in a single lawsuit.
The State Court Administrator is responsible for managing court personnel, finances, data processing, research and other responsibilities under the supervision of the Chief Justice.

BECOMING A JUDGE

In 1966, the voters of Colorado approved an initiative which allows state judges to be appointed rather than elected. When a vacancy in any state court occurs, a judicial nominating commission interviews applicants and recommends several to the governor for consideration. The governor appoints the judge for a provisional term of two years. During the general election following that term, the name of the judge is place on the ballot and electors vote to retain or reject that individual.

A judge retained by the voters serves the remaining years of the term to which he or she has been appointed. Upon completion of their terms, they may submit their names for retention in the General Election. In this manner, voters have the opportunity to decide whether or not the performance of a judge merits continuation on the bench. Terms of judges are different for each jurisdiction. A county judge serves for four years, a district judge for six years, an appeals court judge for eight years, and a supreme court justice for ten years. The only exception to this is Denver. Again, being the only city-county, a vacancy is filled by appointment of the mayor from a list of three candidates recommended by the Denver County Court Nominating Commission. The mayor of Denver also has the authority to dismiss a judge when there is sufficient cause.

CHAPTER TWO: THE POWERS THAT BE

JURIES

Every citizen of Colorado is subject to be summoned for jury duty if they meet the following qualifications:

- Citizen of the United States
- At least 18 years of age
- Resident of the county
- Able to read, speak and understand the English Language
- Not currently imprisoned for a felony conviction

Jury summons are issued at random from a data base of the names of registered voters and those who hold a Colorado driver's license. Some people who have lived here most of their lives have never been called for jury duty and others who have only lived here a few years have received multiple summonses. Jurors in Colorado now serve for only one day or one trial in any 12 month period. Employers must pay employed jurors their regular wages for the first three days of a trial and then the state pays $50 per day thereafter. Being summoned to jury duty does not necessarily mean you will serve. However, in the city and county of Denver you can plan on spending the entire day waiting around to find out if you're needed or not.

THE LEGISLATIVE BRANCH

The General Assembly, with its Senate and House of Representatives, is the heart of the Legislative Branch. The organizational structure, functions, responsibilities, and level of funding for the Executive Branch are determined by the General Assembly. In conjunction with the Executive Branch, the Joint Budget Committee develops the state budget which, after modifications, is approved by the General Assembly. Laws passed by the General Assembly also define the responsibilities of the judicial system.

THE LEGISLATORS

The General Assembly has 100 legislators, 35 in the Senate and 65 in the House. Voters in each legislative district elect their representatives to the General Assembly in the General Election. Representatives serve two-year terms, with senators serving four-year terms with half up for re-election at each General Election. Members of the General Assembly are given immunity from arrest except for treason or a felony. They cannot be sued for acts that are part of the legislative procedure.

THE LEGISLATIVE COUNCIL

The council is responsible for computerized legislative research and establishes a data bank on state resources, programs, and expenditures. The council is headed by the majority leader of the Senate and the Speaker of the House who serve *ex officio*, with eight senators and eight representatives serving as the council. The council staffs reference, interim, and statutory committees which include economists who forecast state revenue and costs and prepare fiscal notes estimating the cost of legislation.

COLORADO: A Newcomer's Manual

THE LEGISLATIVE COMMITTEES

COMMITTEE ON LEGAL SERVICES

This committee includes the chairs of House and Senate Committees on Judiciary, four members of the House, two from each major political party, and four members from the Senate, two from each party. This committee supervises the operation of the Office of Legislative Legal Services which consists of lawyers, technical experts, and clerical personnel who are responsible for drafting all bills, resolutions, and memorials introduced in the General Assembly. By law, no bill can be drafted except by the request of a legislator or the governor.

LEGISLATIVE AUDIT COMMITTEE

Members of the General Assembly vote on the selection of a State Auditor who must be a certified public accountant. While formerly elected, this official is now appointed for a five year term. The eight member committee oversees the review of audits of financial transactions and accounts, performance audits, and management studies of all state agencies. The committee consists of two senators from each party and two representatives from each party.

CAPITAL DEVELOPMENT COMMITTEE

This committee was created in 1985 to deal with long-range planning to meet the capital requirements of the state government. It studies capital construction needs and the maintenance requests of state agencies. It also holds public hearings, determines priorities for proposals and makes recommendations to the General Assembly.

SUNRISE AND SUNSET REVIEW COMMITTEE

The House and Senate Majority leadership appoints six or more legislators to serve on the Sunrise and Sunset Review Committee which conducts studies of state boards and commissions and may recommend their termination.

The Sunset Law provides that agencies which no longer serve a purpose shall be terminated. When an occupational group requests state regulation, such as licensing, the committee may recommend it be provided—a sunrise. The final decision is made by the General Assembly.

THE JOINT BUDGET COMMITTEE

This committee reviews the fiscal needs and management of all state agencies and institutions, holds hearings on budget requests, estimates tax revenues, reviews the state's fiscal structure, and prepares the annual budget. It works all year and has a full-time staff.

COMMITTEES OF REFERENCE

These committees have been formed to review proposed legislation and make recommendations to the entire legislative body. Each committee is staffed by a Legislative Council member who prepares a report of the discussions and decisions. These reports are available to the public. The Senate and House have 10 separate committees of reference.

As bills are introduced, they are given a number. Bills introduced to the Senate begin each session with the number SB1. In the House they begin with HB 1001. A prefix is added to identify the year of introduction, such as HB 95-1001. These committees also handle concurrent resolutions, joint resolutions, memorials and tributes.

STATE GOVERNMENT DEPARTMENTS AND AGENCIES

This section provides information about the responsibilities and points of contact for every department and agency of the state government. Believing every citizen should be able to contact a department directly and talk with someone who can help with issues, Governor Roy Romer created the Governor's Advocate Corps. Nearly every state department now has a 1-800 toll-free number for use outside the Denver area and a local number for those within the metro area. A state employee (the advocate) has been assigned in each department to personally assist you or direct you to someone who can.

COLORADO STATE GOVERNMENT
GENERAL INFORMATION
TOLL FREE: 1-800-332-1716
METRO DENVER: (303) 866-5000

GOVERNOR'S OFFICE

136 State Capitol, Denver, CO 80203
ADVOCATE CONTACT: (303) 866-2885
TOLL FREE: 1-800-283-7215
MAIN OFFICE: (303) 866-2471
*TDD NUMBER: (303) 866-5790

DEPARTMENT OF ADMINISTRATION

State Services Building
1525 Sherman St., Second Floor, Denver, CO 80203
ADVOCATE CONTACT/MAIN OFFICE: (303) 866-3221
TOLL FREE: 1-800-886-7682
RESPONSIBILITIES:
- State debt collections
- State vehicle fleet management
- State purchasing
- Administrative hearings
- State liability claims
- State Archives and Public Records

DEPARTMENT OF AGRICULTURE

700 Kipling St., No. 4000, Lakewood. CO 80215-5894
ADVOCATE CONTACT: (303) 239-4110
TOLL FREE: 1-800-886-7683
MAIN OFFICE: (303) 239-4100
RESPONSIBILITIES:
- Pesticide use (agricultural and residential)

- Livestock brand inspection
- Agricultural products bought, sold or stored in Colorado
- Weights and measures certification
- Animal welfare (neglect and cruelty)
- Rodent and predator control

DEPARTMENT OF CORRECTIONS
2862 S. Circle Drive, No. 400, Colorado Springs, CO 80906
ADVOCATE CONTACT: (719) 540-4719
TOLL FREE: 1-800-886-7688
MAIN OFFICE: (719) 579-9580
RESPONSIBILITIES:
- Prisons
- Transitional community correction
- Parole supervision
- Victim Notification Program

OTHER NUMBERS:
Parole Board: (719) 546-0141

DEPARTMENT OF EDUCATION
201 E. Colfax Avenue, Denver, CO 80203
ADVOCATE: CONTACT/MAIN OFFICE: (303) 866-6600
TOLL FREE: 1-800-886-7687
RESPONSIBILITIES:
- Kindergarten through grade 12 standards and assessments
- State Board of Education
- Teacher and administrator licensing
- School for the Deaf and the Blind
- State library services
- Charter schools

OTHER NUMBERS:
Educator licensing: (303) 866-6628
Special education services: (303) 866-6694
*TDD number for special education:
(303) 860-7060
Library for the blind and physically handicapped:
(303)727-9277
Colorado State Library: (303) 866-6900

DEPARTMENT OF HEALTH CARE
POLICY AND FINANCING
State Social Services Building, 1575 Sherman St., Denver, CO 80203
ADVOCATE CONTACT: (303) 866-5825
MAIN OFFICE: (303) 866-2993
*TDD NUMBER: (303) 866-4065
RESPONSIBILITIES:
- Health care reform

- Medicaid
- Medically indigent
- Health Data Commission

OTHER NUMBERS
Colorado indigent care program: (303) 866-2580
Medicaid general information: (303) 866-5901
Medicaid primary care physician program: (303)866-3513 / 1-800-221-3943

DEPARTMENT OF HIGHER EDUCATION

First contact the individual college or university.
If the problem is not resolved, contact the Department of Higher Education.
Colorado History Museum Building
1300 Broadway, Second Floor, Denver, CO 80203
ADVOCATE CONTACT/MAIN OFFICE: (303) 866-4039
OTHER NUMBERS
Student loan hotline: (303) 294-5070
or TOLL FREE: 1-800-727-9834

DEPARTMENT OF HUMAN SERVICES

(formerly Departments of Social Services and Institutions)
State Social Services Building, 1575 Sherman St., Denver, CO 80203
ADVOCATE CONTACT: (303) 866-5825
TOLL FREE: 1-800-536-5298
MAIN OFFICE: (303) 866-5700
*TDD NUMBER: (303) 866-4065
RESPONSIBILITIES:

- Public assistance (AFDC, Food Stamps, AND, OAP, LEAP)
- Medicaid eligibility
- Services for the elderly
- Protection of dependent adults
- Vocational rehabilitation services
- Child protection, social services to families and foster care
- Child care assistance
- Child support enforcement
- State mental institutions/mental health
- Developmentally disabled services
- Juvenile delinquency
- Alcohol and drug abuse services

OTHER NUMBERS:
Low-Income Energy Assistance (LEAP): (303) 866-5970
Community housing services: (303) 762-4441
Governor's Coordinating Council on Housing and
the Homeless: (303) 762-4457
Family centers: (303) 866-5111
Division of youth services: (303) 762-4695
Child support enforcement: (303) 866-5994
Child care assistance and licensing (complaints):

(303) 866-5958 or TOLL FREE: 1-800-799-5871
Mental health: (303) 762-4088
Developmental disabilities: (303) 762-4550
Juvenile Parole Board: (303) 762-4448
Alcohol and drug abuse: (303) 692-2930

DEPARTMENT OF LABOR AND EMPLOYMENT

1515 Arapahoe Street, Denver, CO 80202
ADVOCATE CONTACT/MAIN OFFICE: (303) 620-4718
*TDD NUMBER: (303) 866-6069
RESPONSIBILITIES:
- Labor standards
- Unemployment insurance
- Workers' compensation
- Job services

OTHER NUMBERS:
Unemployment claim filing: (303) 861-5515 / 1-800-388-5515
Unemployment claims inquiries: (303) 837-9933 / 1-800-999-9933
Labor Standards Unit: (303) 572-2241
Workers' compensation: (303) 575-8700
Employer unemployment insurance tax: (303) 620-4791

DEPARTMENT OF LOCAL AFFAIRS

Centennial Building, 1313 Sherman St., No. 518, Denver, CO 80203
ADVOCATE CONTACT: (303) 866-5326
TOLL FREE: 1-800-536-5349
MAIN OFFICE: (303) 866-2771
*TDD NUMBER: (303) 866-5300
RESPONSIBILITIES:
- Property tax administration/appeals
- Financial and technical assistance to local governments
- Rural job training
- Disaster response
- State housing development programs
- Enterprise zones

OTHER NUMBERS:
Economic Development Commission: (303)892-3840
Motion Picture & Television Commission: (303) 620-4500

DEPARTMENT OF MILITARY AFFAIRS

6848 S. Revere Parkway, Englewood, CO 80112
ADVOCATE CONTACT/MAIN OFFICE: (303) 397-3023
RESPONSIBILITIES:
- Army and Air National Guard
- Civil Air Patrol

OTHER NUMBERS
Air space issues: TOLL FREE: 1-800-582-8507

DEPARTMENT OF NATURAL RESOURCES

Centennial Building, 1313 Sherman St., No. 718, Denver, CO 80203
ADVOCATE CONTACT: (303) 866-4628
TOLL FREE: 1-800-536-5308
MAIN OFFICE: (303) 866-3311
*TDD NUMBER (Natural Resources): (303) 866-3543
*TDD NUMBER (Wildlife): (303) 291-7417
RESPONSIBILITIES:
- Mining, energy development and geology
- Parks and recreation
- Water supply, storage and management
- Wildlife management
- Soil and water conservation
- State land management

OTHER NUMBERS:
Division of Wildlife: (303) 297-1192
Big game hunting information: (303) 291-7529
Fishing information: (303) 291-7533
Hunter safety classes: (303) 291-7530
Campground reservations: (303) 470-1144
or TOLL FREE: 1-800-678-2267

DEPARTMENT OF PERSONNEL

Centennial Building, 1313 Sherman St.. No. 122, Denver, CO 80203
ADVOCATE CONTACT: (303) 866-4642
TOLL FREE: 1-800-536-5335
MAIN OFFICE: (303) 866-2321
*TDD NUMBER: (303) 866-2321
RESPONSIBILITIES:
- State employment, testing and recruitment
- Classification and pay, including Fair Labor
- Standards Act for state employment
- Equal Employment Opportunity/Affirmative
- Action for state employment
- State employee benefits

DEPARTMENT OF PUBLIC HEALTH AND ENVIRONMENT

(formerly Department of Health)
4300 Cherry Creek Drive S., Building A, First floor, Denver, CO 80222-1530
ADVOCATE CONTACT: (303) 692-2035
TOLL FREE: 1-800-886-7689 (for complaints only)
MAIN OFFICE: (303) 692-2000
*TDD NUMBER: (303) 691-7700
RESPONSIBILITIES:
- Environmental permits and regulations
- Water supply safety
- Air quality monitoring

- Landfill monitoring
- Food sanitation
- Product safety
- Disease monitoring
- Women, infant and children (WIC) nutrition program
- Family planning
- Immunizations
- Home health care
- Prenatal care
- Programs for children with special needs
- Child health
- Emergency medical services/trauma

OTHER NUMBERS:
Birth and death records: (303) 756-4464
Auto emission program: (303) 692-3143
Smoking vehicle hotline: (303) 777-0517
High pollution day info (Metro Denver): (303)758-4848
Family healthline: 1-800-688-7777
Governor's AIDS Council: (303) 692-2719

DEPARTMENT OF PUBLIC SAFETY

700 Kipling St., No. 3000, Lakewood. CO 80215
ADVOCATE CONTACT: (303) 239-4425
TOLL FREE: 1-800-536-5339
MAIN OFFICE: (303) 239-4398
*TDD NUMBER: (303) 239-4499
RESPONSIBILITIES:
- State Patrol
- Colorado Bureau of Investigation
- Fire safety issues
- Criminal justice issues

DEPARTMENT OF REGULATORY AGENCIES (DORA)

Civic Center Plaza, 1560 Broadway, No. 1550, Denver, CO 80202
ADVOCATE CONTACT: (303) 894-7441
TOLL FREE: 1-800-886-7675
MAIN OFFICE: (303) 894-7855
*TDD NUMBER: (303) 894-7880
RESPONSIBILITIES:
- Licensed occupations (doctors, dentists, plumbers, etc.)
- Insurance issues
- Real estate and investment issues
- Discrimination issues

For a complete breakdown of this department and all Regulatory Agencies and resposibilities, see the DORA section which follows.
OTHER NUMBERS:
Division of Insurance: (303) 894-7499

CHAPTER TWO: THE POWERS THAT BE

Small Business Hotline: (303) 592-5920 / 1-800-333-7798
Public Utilities Commission: (303) 894-2000
   or TOLL FREE: 1-800-456-0858 (for complaints only)
Civil Rights Division: (303) 894-2997
   or TOLL FREE, Bilingual (Spanish/English): 1-800-262-4845

DEPARTMENT OF REVENUE

State Capitol Annex, 1375 Sherman St., No. 404, Denver, CO 80261
ADVOCATE CONTACT: (303) 866-4622
TOLL FREE: 1-800-536-5321
MAIN OFFICE: (303) 866-3091
*TDD NUMBER: (303) 866-4353
RESPONSIBILITIES:
- State sales tax and income tax
- Driver's licensing
- Colorado Lottery
- Limited stakes gaming and regulation
- Horse and dog racing regulation
- Liquor license enforcement

OTHER NUMBERS:
Taxpayer information: (303) 534-1208
Tax forms: (303) 534-1408
Tax practitioners hotline: (303) 534-2916
Tax audit and compliance: (303) 866-3711
Trade name registration: (303) 534-1810
Income tax refund: (303) 534-1417
PTC/Rent rebate: (303) 534-1209

DEPARTMENT OF TRANSPORTATION

4201 E. Arkansas Ave., No. 277, Denver, CO 80222
ADVOCATE CONTACT: (303) 757-9485
TOLL FREE: 1-800-999-4997
MAIN OFFICE: (303) 757-9011
*TDD NUMBER: (303) 757-9087
RESPONSIBILITIES:
- Construction and maintenance of state highways
- Long and short range planning for state transportation
- Coordination and implementation of transportation safety programs, including combating drunken driving
- Support aviation interests, safety, and maintenance needs of airports
- Assisting with alternate modes of transportation, such as public transit in rural areas, bicycle and pedestrian safety programs

OTHER NUMBERS:
Statewide highway conditions: (303) 639-1234
Metro highway conditions (within 2 driving hours of Denver): (303) 639-1111
Metro Denver road and highway construction information: (303) 573-7623
OTHER NUMBERS:

COLORADO: A Newcomer's Manual

Governor's Adjunct Offices:
Office of Business Development: (303) 892-3840
International Trade Office: (303) 892-3850
Governor's Job Training Office: (303) 758-5020
Office of State Planning and Budgeting: (303) 866-3317
Office of Energy Conservation: (303) 620-4292 / 1-800-632-6662
Governor's Initiatives:
Community Partnership Office:
140 E. 19th Ave., No. 100, Denver, CO 80203
MAIN OFFICE: (303) 894-2750 / TOLL FREE: 1-800-376-2728
RESPONSIBILITIES:
- Colorado 2000 (Education)
- Communities for a Drug-Free Colorado
- Youth Violence Prevention and Intervention

Families and Children/First Impressions:
136 State Capitol, Denver, CO 80203, (303) 866-2155/2145
Education Initiative:
136 State Capitol, Denver, CO 80203, (303) 866-2155/2145
Colorado's School-to-Work Initiative:
136 State Capitol, Denver, CO 80203, (303) 866-2155
Workforce Coordinating Council:
1625 Broadway, No. 1710, Denver, CO 80202, (303) 892-3786
Other Helpful Government Numbers:
Lieutenant Governor: (303) 866-2087
Colorado Commission on Indian Affairs: (303) 866-3027
Colorado State House of Representatives: (303)866-2904
Colorado State Senate: (303) 866-4865/4866
Attorney General: (303) 866-4500
    Consumer protection: (303) 866-5189 / 1-800-332-2071
    Anti-Trust: (303) 866-3613 / 1-800-332-2071
- Collection agency board: (303) 866-5304
- Medicaid fraud: (303) 866-5431

Secretary of State: (303) 894-2100
- Corporation filing and reports: (303) 894-2251
- Elections: (303) 894-2680

State Treasurer: (303) 866-2441
- Unclaimed Property: (303) 894-2443

Colorado Judicial Department: (303) 861-1111
- Supreme Court Disciplinary Council:
  (303) 893-8123 (complaints against attorneys)
- Commission on Judicial Discipline:
  (303) 837-3601 (complaints against judges)
- Office of the Circuit Executive: (303) 844-2070
  (complaints against federal judges)

Colorado Uninsurable Health Insurance: 1-800-672-8447 (option 1)
Colorado Counties, Inc.: (303) 861-4076
Colorado Municipal League: (303) 831-6411
Special District Association of Colorado: (303) 863-1733

Colorado Compensation Insurance Authority: (303) 782-4000
Colorado Housing and Finance Authority: (303)297-2432
Public Defender: (303) 620-4888
Colorado Historical Society: (303) 866-3682
Cooperative Extension (main office): (303) 640-5270
Federal Government Information Center: 1-800-359-3997

DORA

The Colorado Department of Regulatory Agencies (DORA) consists of nine differents divisions and several support offices. The major purpose of DORA is to regulate businessess and individuals when the state legislature believes such regulation is necessary for the protection of Colorado citizens. Below is a brief description of the four support offices and the nine divisions including all the boards which regulate professions and occupations which require licensing.

OFFICE OF THE EXECUTIVE DIRECTOR

Executive Director: Joseph A. Garcia
1560 Broadway, Suite 1550, Denver, CO 80202, (303) 894-7850
The Executive Director is responsible for the overall management of the Department and its divisions. Appointed by the Governor, the Executive Director in turn appoints Division directors (with the exception of Insurance and Public Utilities Commissioners who are appointed by the Governor). The Governor makes all appointments to boards and commissions in the Department, and the Executive Director plays a significant role in recommending the names of people for those appointments. The Executive Director presents the Department budget to the Joint Budget Committee, and initiates and recommends legislation affecting the Department.

Complaints relating to persons licensed by any board or agency in the Division of Registrations may be referred to the Executive Director, who in turn may assign the complaint to the Division director or to the appropriate board or agency. The Executive Director may also assign complaints for investigation, or take whatever action he deems appropriate under the circumstances of the complaint.

The Executive Director gives advice to the general assembly and the general public on questions relating to the role of the state in regulating professions and occupations.

OFFICE OF CONSUMER COUNSEL

Director Ronald J. Binz
1580 Logan Street, Suite 610, Denver, CO 80203, (303) 894-2121
The Office of Consumer Counsel (OCC) represents the interests of residential, small business and agricultural consumers before the Public Utilities Commission, certain federal agencies (such as the Federal Communications Commission), and in the courts on appeal. The OCC is Colorado's consumer advocate in electric, gas and telecommunications utility-rate and rule-making matters. The office represents consumers by participating in complex utility cases. The OCC examines the technical evidence filed by the utility, provides expert testimony on consumers' behalf, cross-examines other witnesses, makes legal arguments, and represents consumers in settlement negotiations. Approximately 40 other states have utility consumer advocate offices similar to the OCC.

The OCC has a staff of seven technical and administrative personnel as well as legal representation through the Department of Law. In addition, a statutorily authorized board appointed by the governor gives policy guidance to the OCC. The eleven-member board is appointed to represent the public interest and, specifically, the interests of residential, small business, and agricultural utility consumers. Board members come from all geographic areas of the state.

The office is funded by an assessment on the state's regulated utilities. Since utility companies pass this cost on to their customers, ratepayers fund the office. Each Colorado consumer pays about five cents per month in combined utility bills to fund the OCC. The Office of Consumer Counsel helps consumers by lowering or eliminating utility rate increases and by ensuring that utility rates, regulations and policies are more equitable for residential, small business and agricultural consumers. The OCC is charged with representing the small consumer before the PUC, but is prohibited by statute from representing individuals in complaints with utilities. Instead, the PUC is staffed to resolve individual complaints. The OCC is interested in individual complaints when they show a pattern of rate or service problems the office believes should be addressed.

For more information about the OCC, what it does, what cases it is involved in, and how it benefits consumers, please call (303) 894-2121.

OFFICE OF POLICY AND RESEARCH

Acting Director: Susan L. Warren
1560 Broadway, Suite 1550, Denver, CO 80202, (303) 894-7848
This Office (P&R) is the research arm of the Executive Director. It prepares "sunrise" and "sunset" reports. The Department is required to evaluate both the need for regulation of different occupational groups seeking state regulation and the need for and effectiveness of existing regulatory agencies and functions which are scheduled for termination. The Director of this Office coordinates the research and evaluation effort and the Executive Director submits the Department's findings and recommendations to the Legislature. Final reports are on file in the Executive Director's office and are available to the public. Interested members of the public who wish to provide input on agencies subject to sunset or sunrise evaluations should contact the Director.

OFFICE OF REGULATORY REFORM

Director: Frances V. LeDuke
1560 Broadway, Suite 1530, Denver, CO 80202, (303) 894-7839
The Office of Regulatory Reform (ORR), established by the legislature in 1981, is the only state office in Colorado offering one-stop information on all federal, state and local permit, license and regulatory requirements for starting a new business or expanding an existing business. ORR holds public hearings throughout the state to receive comments, first hand, from business owners about regulations and to help identify areas of duplicative, burdensome and unnecessary requirements. ORR administers the Regulatory Flexibility Act and reviews proposed state agency rules to be certain they do not adversely affect small business.

ORR operates the Small Business Assistance Center (SBAC) at 1560 Broadway, Suite 1530 in downtown Denver. The SBAC is a cooperative effort between ORR, the

Governor's Office of Business Development, Department of Revenue, Taxpayer Services and the Department of Local Affairs. Individuals who wish to start a new business may call one of our business professionals at (303) 592-5920 or 1-800-333-7798. The center also provides walk-in service for trade name registration, state sales tax licenses and wage withholding accounts.

In 1992, ORR was designated to serve as the Ombudsman for small businesses as part of the Colorado Clean Air Act. ORR is responsible for representing small business interests in the formulation of rules and regulations, investigating and facilitating resolution of complaints and disputes concerning the permit process and encouraging the participation of small businesses in the regulatory process.

An advisory council advises ORR on small business issues. The council members are recommended by small business organizations and chambers of commerce and are appointed by the Director of ORR.

Free publications available from ORR include:
Colorado Business Start-Up Kit, containing application forms for state sales tax license, trade name registration, workers' compensation, and state and federal withholding accounts along with information about how to start a business.
Small Business Information Guide, explaining the functions of ORR.
How to Do Business with the State of Colorado, explaining the state's purchasing process.
Small Business News, a quarterly publication explaining state programs regulating or assisting small businesses.
Minority and Women Business Enterprise Certification, a pamphlet explaining the certification process and answering basic questions.

Disadvantaged Business Certification (DBE): ORR also offers the Disadvantaged Business Enterprise (DBE) certification program. The office of Certification conducts certifications for the Colorado Department of Transportation, Regional Transportation District and the Denver Board of Water Commissions. A business must be owned and controlled by women and minorities to be certified. Once certified, a business may participate as a DBE with any of these projects. For more information, call (303) 894-2355.

DIVISION OF ADMINISTRATIVE SERVICES

Director: Susan L. Warren
1560 Broadway, Suite 1550, Denver, CO 80202, (303) 894-7855
The Division of Administrative Services provides services to the department in the areas of planning, budget and fiscal management, payroll and data processing and personnel. The Division provides centralized support in the above areas to all divisions in the Department and also coordinates records management and space planning for the Department. Division staff develop systems for agencies in the Department. The Division also completes special projects as assigned by the Executive Director, and is responsible for implementation of the Americans with Disabilities Act.

The personnel section serves as a liaison between employees in the Department and the State Department of Personnel. Section staff perform desk audits for employees, and coordinate the hiring and examination process for new Department employees.

The staff addresses employee questions and concerns about personnel policies and procedures, and advises employees about job advancement and job enhancement opportunities in state government. Anyone interested in job opportunities with DORA should contact the Personnel Administrator, Fran Armstrong, at 894-7880.

The Division serves as the liaison between the Department and the State Controller, State Archives, State Treasurer, State Department of Personnel, the Office of State Planning and Budgeting, and the Joint Budget Committee staff.

DIVISION OF BANKING

Commissioner: Barbara M. A. Walker
1560 Broadway, Suite 1175, Denver, CO 80202, (303) 894-7575
The Division of Banking is responsible for the regulation of state chartered commercial banks, trust companies, and industrial banks, and of money order companies and debt management companies. The Division holds charter and license application hearings and issues rules and regulations affecting regulated institutions. Division staff conduct examinations of state chartered institutions and licenses. The Division works closely with the Federal Reserve Bank and the Federal Deposit Insurance Corporation in the regulation of commercial banks and industrial banks and certain federal insured trust companies.

Activities include chartering and licensing financial institutions, performing examinations, supervising operations, and closing state chartered banks, industrial banks, and trust companies when necessary. Also, the Division is responsible for the enforcement of the Public Deposit Protection Act, to protect public entity deposits held by state and national banks.

There is an eight-member banking board that is the policy and rule making authority for the Division. The board consists of four members who are executive officers of state banks, a chief executive officer of an industrial bank, a chief executive officer of a trust company, and two public members. The board conducts monthly meetings which are public, and the public is encouraged to attend these meetings. Board members are appointed for four-year terms.

DIVISION OF CIVIL RIGHTS

Director: Jack Langy Marquez
1560 Broadway, Suite 1050, Denver, CO 80202, (303) 894-2997
The Civil Rights Division is a state agency established in 1957 to administer and enforce Colorado civil rights laws in employment, housing and public accommodations. The Division works with federal agencies, such as the Equal Employment Opportunity Commission (EEOC) and the Department of Housing and Urban Development (HUD), and with local human rights agencies. Colorado civil rights laws prohibit discrimination in employment, housing and public accommodations on the basis of race, sex, national origin. ancestry. physical or mental handicap. creed, color and marital status (housing and public accommodations only). Discrimination based on age and marriage to a coworker in employment is also prohibited.

The Colorado Civil Rights Commission is a seven member bipartisan panel appointed by the Governor. The Commission members are selected from across the State to serve four-year terms. Two members represent the business community (one a representative of small business), two represent state or local government entities, and three are from the community at large. At least four commissioners must be from groups who have been or might be discriminated against because of handicap, race, creed, color, sex, national origin or ancestry, marital status, religion or age. The Commission meets monthly to formulate policy and to hear appeals in discrimination cases. The public may attend such meetings.

The Commission and Division implement the civil rights statutes through preventive enforcement (compliance) and outreach (research and education).

DIVISION OF FINANCIAL SERVICES

Commissioner: David L. Paul
1560 Broadway, Suite 1520, Denver, CO 80202, (303) 894-2336
The Division of Financial Services regulates state-chartered savings and loan associations, credit unions, life care institutions, and small business development credit corporations. It also administers the public deposit protection program that covers all uninsured governmental unit deposits in state and federal savings and loan associations.

The Division operates under the policy-making and rule-making authority of the Financial Services Board, which consists of five members appointed by the Governor. The Financial Services Board issues rules and regulations governing the industries regulated by the Division, may delegate many of its authorities to the Commissioner, and hears appeals of actions taken by the Commissioner under delegated authority.

The Division is empowered to approve applications to incorporate new state-chartered savings and loan associations, approve branch office applications for existing associations, approve mergers between associations, and approve changes of ownership. The Division staff examines each state savings and loan association on a regular basis to assure sound financial condition and compliance with applicable laws and regulations.

State-chartered credit unions operate under the supervision of the Division. The Division is empowered to approve applications to incorporate new state credit unions and to approve mergers between credit unions. State credit unions are subject to periodic examination by the Division staff.

The Division regulates certain financial activities of life care institutions, which provide long-term residence and care for the elderly. The Division may initiate enforcement action against violations of the law by life care providers.

The Division is empowered to consider applications for licensure of, grant licenses to, and periodically examine small business development credit corporations, which are designed to provide a variety of financing options to small businesses.

The Division also handles consumer complaints and information requests regarding the industries it regulates and has available, at a nominal cost, the annual *"Financial Report on Colorado State Chartered Savings and Loan Associations and Credit Unions"* as well as copies of the statute and regulations for the industries it regulates.

DIVISION OF INSURANCE

Commissioner: Joanne Hill
1560 Broadway, Suite 850, Denver, CO 80202, (303) 894-7499
The Division of Insurance has responsibility for the regulation of approximately 1800 insurance companies doing business in Colorado. Entities regulated by the Division include traditional insurance companies such as auto, health and workers' compensation carriers, as well as pre-need funeral companies, bail bonds companies, fraternal benefit societies, captive organizations and self insurance pools.
The Division's consumer protection mission includes:
- Resolving consumer complaints against insurers;
- Monitoring companies for financial solvency and compliance with the law;
- Licensing agents and brokers; and
- Investigating illegal activities.

Consumers who have complaints against a company or agent should put their complaint in writing and send it to the Division of Insurance at the above address. For general inquiries, call 894-7499.

PUBLIC UTILITIES COMMISSION

Commissioners: Robert E. Temmer, Chairman; Christine E. Mestas Alvarez; Vincent Majkowski
Director: Bruce N. Smith
1580 Logan Street, Office Level 2, Denver, CO 80203, (303) 894-2000
In-state WATTS Telephone:
1-800-888-0170—Transportation or General Issues
1-800-456-0858—Consumer Issues
The Public Utilities Commission achieves a regulatory environment that provides safe and reliable utility services to all on just and reliable terms. The Commission strives to assure that the public receives utility services at affordable prices. It also assures that utilities have the opportunity to receive a reasonable return on their investments. This return on investments allows Colorado utilities to obtain the necessary funds to build new facilities or to upgrade existing ones.

The Commission regulates investor-owned electric, gas, telephone, and water utilities, transportation companies, and some electric cooperatives. Municipal utilities are not regulated except for wholesale activities. Over the past few years, some types of telecommunications services and products and some types of transportation carriers have been deregulated.

The Commission holds public hearings to consider rate requests by large public utilities such as Public Service Company and US West Communications, as well as rate requests by smaller utility companies.

The Commission has established safety regulations and permit requirements for common and contract carriers, and has established safety regulations for the transportation of hazardous materials.

Commissioners are appointed for four-year terms by the Governor, and work full-time on Commission matters.

Commission consumer affairs specialists work to resolve complaints against regulated utilities and provide general information about utilities and the Commission. The Commission publishes many consumer brochures that are available to the public free of charge. Consumers should call 897-2070 or the Commission's instate WATTS line referenced above.

DIVISION OF REAL ESTATE

Director: Michael B. Gorham
1900 Grant Street, Suite 600, Denver, CO 80203, (303) 894-2166
The Division of Real Estate regulates real estate salespersons and brokers through licensure and discipline. Licensees must comply with established educational and experience requirements, and pass a test prior to licensure. A real estate broker must have served as a licensed salespersons for at least two years before he or she can become a broker. Earnest money deposits and escrow and trust funds are regulated by the Division.

The Division administers the real estate recovery fund, which can be used by persons to recover sums lost because of the actions of a licensee. Persons who obtain a final judgment against a broker or salespersons can regain their actual loss suffered in a transaction up to $15,000 per claimant and up to $50,000 in the aggregate against any one licensee.

The Division regulates all time share projects sold in Colorado, and regulates developers of subdivisions consisting of 10 or more residential sites, tracts or lots.

A five-member Commission meets monthly to conduct rule making hearings, make policy decisions, consider licensing matters, review complaints and take disciplinary action against licensees. Commission members serve three-year terms, and members are appointed as follows: three real estate brokers, one person with expertise in subdivision development, and one public member.

For information about whether a person is licensed and whether disciplinary action has been taken against a licensee call 894-2166. Persons wishing to file a complaint against a licensee should send a written complaint to the Division.

The Division also regulates real estate appraisers pursuant to the requirements of the federal Real Estate Appraisal Reform Amendments of the Financial Institutions Reform, Recovery, and Enforcement Act of 1989. The Board of Real Estate appraisers consists of seven members appointed by the Governor: four licensed or certified appraisers, one of whom must have expertise in eminent domain, a county assessor, an officer or employee of a commercial bank experienced in real estate lending, and one public member. Board members serve three-year terms.

DIVISION OF REGISTRATIONS

Director: Bruce M. Douglas
1560 Broadway, Suite 1300, Denver, CO 80202, (303) 894-7690
The Division of Registrations includes most of the professional and occupational licensing boards in Colorado. These boards have been created by the Colorado legislature to protect the public from unqualified and incompetent practitioners. Boards typically are empowered to determine the qualifications necessary to obtain a

license (including education and experience requirements); regulate the standards of conduct for the profession; review complaints against licensees; and take disciplinary action as they determine necessary. Boards can suspend or revoke licenses, but they cannot order a licensed individual to refund money or perform repairs.

Most of the boards in the Division meet on a monthly basis, and the public is invited to attend board meetings. For information on the time and location of a particular board meeting, contact the administrator for that board at the telephone number listed.

Although each board handles the disciplinary proceedings against its licensees, the Division has established a centralized complaint process for all the boards. Persons wishing to file a complaint may obtain a complaint form from the licensing board or from the Complaints and Investigations Section, 1560 Broadway, Suite 1300, Denver, CO 80202.

When complaints are received, they are ordinarily assigned to an investigator who notifies the licensee that a complaint has been filed against him and asks him to respond by letter, stating his side of the story. An investigation is then initiated to try to determine the facts of the situation. Staff of the Complaints and Investigations Section (894-7895) can answer general questions about the investigative process or specific questions about the status of the case (except where prohibited by law).

The Division has available a brochure entitled *"A Guide for Filing Consumer Complaints Against Licensed Professions and Occupations."* It also publishes a brochure for licensees entitled *"Questions and Answers Concerning the Complaint Against Your License."*

BOARD OF ACCOUNTANCY
(303) 894-7800
The Board regulates the profession of certified public accountants, both individuals and public accounting firms. The practice of public accounting includes issuance of reports on financial statements, management advisory or consulting services, preparation of tax returns, and furnishing advice on tax matters.

ACUPUNCTURISTS REGISTRATION
(303) 894-7690
The Division registers individuals providing acupuncture services, described as the insertion of needles into the human body by piercing the skin of the body at specific locations based on traditional oriental concepts of evaluation and treatment. The Division also registers individuals in training who are under the direct supervision of a registered acupuncturist.

BOARD OF EXAMINERS OF ARCHITECTS
(303) 894-7801
The Board licenses persons to practice architecture which means the planning and design of buildings, preparation of construction contract documents, observation of construction as agreed upon, and administration of construction contracts for the construction, but not the performance, of buildings.

CHAPTER TWO: THE POWERS THAT BE

BOARD OF BARBERS AND COSMETOLOGISTS

(303) 894-7772

The Board licenses barbers, cosmetologists, cosmeticians, and manicurists. The Board also registers locations at which any of the above professional services are provided. The Board investigates, upon written consumer complaint, all suspected or alleged violations relating to its area of responsibility.

BOARD OF CHIROPRACTIC EXAMINERS

(303) 894-7762

The Board licenses chiropractors. Chiropractors who wish to practice electrotherapy or acupuncture must provide the Board with proof of additional education in that area. The Board sets standards for unlicensed personnel who operate an x-ray machine or administer radiation for diagnostic purposes.

BOARD OF DENTAL EXAMINERS

(303) 894-7758

The Board licenses dentists and dental hygienists, and specifies the tasks that unlicensed dental auxiliaries may perform. Additionally, the Board administers a dentist peer assistance program.

STATE ELECTRICAL BOARD

(303) 894-2300

The Board licenses journeymen electricians, master electricians, electrical contractors and residential wiremen. Electrical apprentices are required to register with the Board. The Board also performs electrical inspections on new and remodeled facilities throughout the state in its areas of jurisdiction. The standard used by the Board is the National Electrical Code as may be amended.

BOARD OF REGISTRATION FOR PROFESSIONAL ENGINEERS AND PROFESSIONAL LAND SURVEYORS

(303) 894-7788

The Board licenses engineers and land surveyors, and certifies engineers-in-training and surveyors-in-training. The Board enforces minimum survey standards as set by law. Land surveyors are required to file monument records with the Board.

GRIEVANCE BOARD

(303) 894-7766

The Board hears disciplinary matters and can bring injunctive actions relating to licensed psychologists, clinical social workers, marriage and family therapists, and licensed professional counselors, and also relating to certified school psychologists and unlicensed psychotherapists. The Board maintains a database for licensed and unlicensed psychotherapists which includes information about their methods of practice and years of experience. For this information call 894-7771.

BOARD OF MARRIAGE AND FAMILY THERAPISTS EXAMINERS

(303) 894-7768

The Board licenses persons who practice psychotherapy and who are marriage and family therapists. Disciplinary matters are referred to the Grievance Board.

BOARD OF MEDICAL EXAMINERS

(303) 894-7690

The Board licenses qualified physicians and physician assistants. In addition, the Board reviews complaints in order to determine whether action is necessary to protect patients. The Board administers a physician's peer health assistance program.

MIDWIVES' REGISTRATION

(303) 894-2430

Effective July 1, 1993, the Division implemented a program to register direct-entry midwives, also known as "lay" midwives. Direct-entry midwifery means the advising, attending, or assisting of a woman during pregnancy, labor and natural childbirth at home, and during the postpartum period. This program administers examinations to graduates of educational programs that meet the standards established by the Division. The Division also establishes standards of practice and has authority to investigate complaints and take disciplinary action if necessary.

BOARD OF NURSING

(303) 894-2430

The Board licenses Registered Nurses, Licensed Practical Nurses, Psychiatric Technicians, and Certified Nurse Aides. The Board approves educational programs for all types of licenses. The Nurse Aide Advisory Committee assists the Board in their duties. Additionally, the Board administers a nursing peer health assistance diversion program to assist licensees experiencing impaired practice.

BOARD OF EXAMINERS OF NURSING AND ADMINISTRATORS

(303) 894-7760

The Board licenses nursing home administrators in an effort to ensure quality administration and sound management of nursing homes. Nursing home administrators are individuals who are responsible for planning, organizing, directing, and controlling the operations of a nursing home. The Board administers a nursing home administrator-in-training program.

BOARD OF OPTOMETRIC EXAMINERS

(303) 894-7755

The Board licenses optometrists and authorizes optometrists to prescribe and administer certain pharmaceutical agents upon meeting minimum educational and practical requirements.

OFFICE OF OUTFITTERS REGISTRATIONS

(303) 894-7778

The Office regulates outfitters who provide services for the purpose of hunting or fishing by requiring insurance, bonding and proficiency in first aid, and setting standards for operation. The Office works cooperatively with the Division of Wildlife, the Bureau of Land Management, the U.S. Forest Service, various District Attorneys throughout the state, and other state and federal game and land management agencies.

CHAPTER TWO: THE POWERS THAT BE

PASSENGER TRAMWAY SAFETY BOARD

(303) 894-7785

The Board regulates aerial tramways, surface lifts, and tows used for recreational purposes in Colorado. While the focus is ski-related equipment, the Board also licenses other types of tramways. The Board promulgates design, operation, and maintenance standards, reviews requests for variance from the rules, and investigates accidents related to the operation of tramways. Each licensed tramway is inspected at least twice annually.

BOARD OF PHARMACY

(303) 894-7750

The Board licenses pharmacists and pharmacy interns. Prescription and other drug outlets must be registered with the Board. The Board is responsible for the control and regulation of drugs, and administers the Controlled Substances Act with the Department of Health. It cooperates extensively with other state and federal agencies. Additionally, the Board's inspectors perform routine inspections of pharmacies and conduct special investigations.

PHYSICAL THERAPY REGISTRATION

(303) 894-2440

All persons practicing physical therapy or physiotherapy must register with the Division. An advisory committee appointed by the Director assists in registration. The rules also specify supervisory requirements for physical therapist assistants.

EXAMINING BOARD OF PLUMBERS

(303) 894-2319

The Board is responsible for the licensing of residential plumbers, journeyman plumbers and master plumbers. Plumbing apprentices who work for a plumbing contractor must register with the Board. The Board employs inspectors responsible for performing inspections in designated areas of the state. The Board establishes and administers the Colorado plumbing code, which represents the minimum standards for installation, alteration, and repair of plumbing equipment and systems.

PODIATRY BOARD

(303) 894-7690

The Board licenses qualified podiatrists. In addition, the Board reviews complaints in order to determine whether action is necessary to protect patients.

BOARD OF LICENSED PROFESSIONAL COUNSELOR EXAMINERS

(303) 894-7768

The Board licenses persons who practice psychotherapy and who are professional counselors. Disciplinary matters are referred to the Grievance Board.

BOARD OF PSYCHOLOGIST EXAMINERS

(303) 894-7769

The Board licenses persons who practice psychotherapy and who are psychologists. Disciplinary matters are referred to the Grievance Board.

BOARD OF SOCIAL WORK EXAMINERS
(303) 894-7769
The Board licenses persons who practice psychotherapy and who are clinical social workers. Disciplinary matters are referred to the Grievance Board.

BOARD OF VETERINARY MEDICINE
(303) 894-7755
The Board licenses veterinarians and specifies what tasks veterinary students may perform under the direct supervision of a licensed veterinarian. Veterinary medicine includes surgery, obstetrics, dentistry, and all other branches or specialties of animal medicine.

DIVISION OF SECURITIES
Commissioner: Philip A. Feigin
1580 Lincoln, Suite 420, Denver, CO 80203, (303) 894-2320
The Division registers securities and licenses people who distribute securities. The Division investigates complaints and monitors broker-dealer activities and sales promotions. The thrust of the Colorado regulation is to bring actions against fraudulent conduct; the Division enforcement staff works with local. state and federal law enforcement authorities. The Division performs broker-dealer field examinations of intrastate and NASD member firms.

The Division also administers and enforces the Colorado Commodity Code, enacted in 1989 to protect investors and to prevent and prosecute illegal and fraudulent schemes involving precious metals and other off-exchange commodities.

In addition, the Division regulates and monitors the issuance of certain kinds of municipal bonds in Colorado, and local government investment pool trust funds.

The Division has available a publication that lists the most common areas of investment schemes and the types of solicitation techniques used by promoters. Entitled *"How to protect your Savings Against Con Artist Hypnosis"*, the brochure is free of charge. The Division also has available a videotape cassette *entitled "Calling for Your Dollars"*, a consumer protection program about "boiler rooms", and a series of publications called *"Investor Alert"*, quarterly warnings to investors produced in cooperation with the Council of Better Business Bureaus.

CHAPTER THREE
SCHOOL'S OUT FOREVER

STATE SCHOOL SYSTEMS
Public, Private, Higher Education, Libraries

> The information in this chapter was compiled from various sources including, but not limited to, government reports and publications (Federal, State, and Local); materials provided by business and civic organizations; and books produced by independent Colorado publishers including:
>
> *The Guide to Metro Denver Public Schools, 1995-96 Edition,* and *Colorado Private and Elementary and Secondary Schools, 1995-96,* both by Magnolia Street Press
>
> For a complete description of the above books and related titles, please see the Publisher's listing in Appendix A.

AN OVERVIEW OF PUBLIC SCHOOLS

School Districts: In 1957, there were 239 non-operating districts in the state and 203 one-room school districts. Through the voluntary process of the School District Reorganization Act, the number of school districts was reduced to 176. Today 20 counties have only one school district, 17 counties have two school districts, and 12 counties have no more than three districts. County superintendents have been abolished.

The 176 school districts are not necessarily coterminous with any other political boundaries. Most districts maintain elementary, middle/junior high schools, and senior high schools.

Many elementary schools include kindergarten classes. A local board may establish and maintain a kindergarten; it is not mandated by law. Kindergartens may be paid for from the general school fund.

Entrance Age to School: Entrance age to school is determined by local board policy. The School Attendance Law entitles state residents between the ages of 6 and 21 to a free education, and requires persons between the ages of 7 and 16 to attend school. The Constitution entitles the legislature to require by law that children of sufficient physical and mental ability attend school during at least a three-year period between the ages of 6 and 18 years unless educated by other means.

The Exceptional Children's Educational Act defines a handicapped child as one between the ages of 5 and 21, and requires that administrative units serve every handicapped child. Thus, a handicapped child may enter school at age five. There are some programs for younger children. Over half of Colorado's school districts offer programs for 3-to-5-year-olds who are handicapped or "at risk".

Enrollment Requirements: Enrollment requirements (including entrance age for school) vary from district to district, but usually include legal proof of age (preferably a birth certificate) and various immunizations. Transfer students register in the district of prospective residence. Registration requirements and grade placement vary among school districts, but transcripts of the student's records from the school previously attended are usually required. In general, school authorities will send for transcripts.

Local Control of Instruction: The Constitution of the State of Colorado, Article IX, Section 15, states: "School districts—boards of education. The general assembly shall, by law, provide for organization of school districts of convenient size, in each of which shall be established a board of education . . . Said directors shall have control of instruction in the public schools of their respective districts." In 1993, the Colorado General Assembly enacted legislation aimed at bringing about coordinated improvement in the performance and accountability of the state's K-12 education system. House Bill 93-1313 requires local school districts to redesign curriculum, instruction, testing and teacher development around academic standards that spell out what students should know and be able to do, at various stages in their schooling, in 11 areas: math, science, reading, writing, history, geography, civics, art, music, physical education, and foreign language. The new system is to be fully in place statewide by 1999.

The law now requires that history and civil government of Colorado, as well as the history and civil government of the United States (incorporating history, culture, and contributions of minorities, including but not limited to Spanish-Americans and African-Americans) be taught in the public schools of the state. The federal Constitution is also to be taught, as well as the honor and use of the flag. In addition, students must be given information on the effect of use of alcohol and controlled substances.

Textbooks: In addition to curriculum, our Constitution states: "Textbooks in public schools: Neither the general assembly nor the state board of education shall have power to prescribe textbooks to be used in the public schools." We do not have statewide approved/mandated/adopted textbooks.

Local Boards of Education: Colorado Revised Statutes 22-32-109 and -110 enumerate local boards' powers and duties. Their curricula normally include general, college preparatory, business, and vocational-technical courses. Their high school graduation requirements usually include one or more units of English, math, social studies, science, and physical education.

Meetings of local boards of education are open to the public, however they may go into executive session.

Discipline: Local boards of education are required by law to adopt discipline codes as well as written policies, rules, and regulations which relate to the study, discipline, conduct, safety, and welfare of all pupils.

Accreditation: School districts are accredited by the Colorado Department of Education; additionally, some schools are accredited by the North Central Association. Districts are not ranked or rated as to which is best.

Home Study and Nonpublic Schools: The School Attendance Law distinguishes between non-public schools and home study. **Home study is permitted in Colorado under this law.** Non-public schools are required to provide a basic academic education, but are protected from untoward interference by any board of education, state or local.

SCHOOL CHOICES IN COLORADO

We know when it comes to education, one size does not fit all. Children learn in different ways and have different learning strengths and interests. Students are more excited about learning and learn more when they are in educational programs that suit their learning styles and special strengths, needs, and interests. To take the best advantage of public school opportunities now available, you need to know about the choices available to you:

Open Enrollment: Legislation enacted in 1994 creates open enrollment throughout Colorado. This means you may enroll your children in any public school in the state, assuming there is space available, without paying extra money.

Charter Schools: Colorado has 18 charter schools (some of them scheduled to open fall, 1995) and more are under development. Charter schools are public schools created by groups of parents, teachers, or community members to reflect different educational approaches or philosophies. These schools are self-governing, enjoy some independence from the local school district, and have a clear plan for how and what students should learn. They are open to all interested students on a space-available basis.

Magnet Schools: Many districts offer magnet schools—also called "focus" or "alternative" schools—that have specific educational approaches or philosophies. Examples include special emphasis schools in science or performing arts, as well as Montessori or Waldorf schools that reflect a particular educational philosophy. They range from highly structured schools to open schools. These schools are open to all interested students on a space-available basis. Admission is usually done by lottery.

College Classes: High school students have the opportunity to take college courses or to earn college credit for certain high school classes. These opportunities serve two important purposes: They provide challenging academic experiences for students, and they can help reduce the length and expense of college.

Finally, it's important to note you don't necessarily need to look outside your neighborhood school to have an impact on your children's educational program. You can discuss your child's learning style and special interests with his or her teacher. You can help set the direction for the educational approach in your child's school by getting involved in school committees that help make educational decisions. You also can have an impact on the educational philosophy of the district by voting in school board elections. You can attend and participate in school board meetings and share your ideas and concerns with teachers, principals, and school board members. There are many ways to make your neighborhood school your school of choice.

Excerpted *from A Parent's Guide to Colorado Public Schools,* published 1994 by Governor Romer's Office, for further information or a copy of the brochure call (303) 866-2471, or write to: Office of the Governor, 136 State Capitol, Denver, CO 80203

SELECTING THE RIGHT SCHOOL

When it comes time to select a school for your child or children, the responsibility for doing so falls squarely on your shoulders! Don't assume anything! Don't accept as fact any reputation a school may or may not have. Don't expect your realtor or local school administrator to "fill you in" on the down-side to any given school. Visit all prospective schools and check them out for yourself.

This chapter contains the basic information for you to do the necessary research. First and foremost, you must determine what is important to your child's education. Use the Parent Inventory of Educational Preferences below to clarify exactly what you are looking for in a school. Keeping in mind the various options available to Colorado residents, find the appropriate point of contact for your school district and start with some phone calls. After you get a feel for what's offered by the schools in your area, plan on spending an entire day making personal visits to your top choices. If you live in the greater Denver Metro area, I highly suggest you obtain a copy of *The Guide to Metro Denver Public Schools* published by Magnolia Street Press. If you are considering a private school anywhere in Colorado, the book you need is *Colorado Private Elementary and Secondary Schools,* also available from Magnolia Street Press. Both these books contain complete, accurate and up-to-date information on a school-by-school basis. See the publisher's listing in Appendix A for details.

While visiting the schools, make sure all your questions are answered by the administrators and if school is in session, stroll around and note the teacher/student ratio, the general atmosphere of the classrooms and things of special interest to you or your child. Many school systems have cut back or eliminated special classes like fine arts, music, etc., due to budget cuts. If you see temporary classrooms on the grounds, you can assume this means overcrowding. Many counties in Colorado are growing at such an explosive rate an adequate number of new school facilities may be years in the making. Check with the school district about future plans and budgets.

Finally, for the best possible inside information, visit with the parents of other children currently enrolled in the schools. The easiest way to do this is in front of the schools during normal drop-off/pick-up times or at designated bus stops.

Time spent doing this properly now can save you a lot of regrets years later.

The form below was taken from *The Guide to Metro Denver Public Schools* by Magnolia Street Press.

PARENT INVENTORY OF EDUCATIONAL PREFERENCES

What is important to you in a school for your children? Rank the following list of criteria or pick a few of greatest importance.

___Specific philosophy, curriculum or educational strategy_____

___Structured/unstructured environment (circle one)
___Small teacher/student ratio (state ideal number) _____
___College-preparatory/vocational emphasis of curriculum (circle one)
___School's capability to meet special needs_____
___Enrichment for gifted/talented children
___Enrichment for all children
___Handicap access
___High level of teacher experience and training
___Neighborhood school, close to home, walking distance
___On-site before- and after-school day care
___Other services such as transportation, lunch program, or boarding
___New building, modern facilities
___Older building, historical awareness
___Non-traditional school building and/or environment
___State-of-the-art technology and emphasis in curriculum
___High standardized test scores of other students
___No tuition or low tuition
___Religious instruction and environment
___Cultural, racial, ethnic, and/or economic diversity of students
___Small school enrollment (state ideal number) _____
___High level of involvement and input by parents or community
___Specific athletic offerings_____
___Specific extracurricular offerings_____

What educational goals do you have for your children? _____

What special needs do your children have which may require services beyond the "regular" classroom? _____

What expectations or desires do your children have for school programs in addition to or differing from yours? _____

INDEX OF CITIES AND SCHOOL DISTRICTS

CITY	DISTRICT	PHONE
AGATE	AGATE 300	719-764-2741
AGUILAR	AGUILAR REORGANIZED 6	719-941-4614
AKRON	AKRON R-1	970-345-2268
ALAMOSA	ALAMOSA RE-11J	719-589-6634
ANTON	ARICKAREE R-2	970-383-2202
ANTONITO	SOUTH CONEJOS RE-10	719-376-5512
ARVADA	JEFFERSON COUNTY R-1	303-273-6500
	WESTMINSTER 50	303-428-3511
ASPEN	ASPEN 1	970-925-3460
AULT	AULT-HIGHLAND RE-9	970-834-1345
AURORA	ADAMS-ARAPAHOE 28J	303-344-8060
	CHERRY CREEK 5	303-773-1184
AVON	EAGLE COUNTY RE 50	970-328-6321
AVONDALE	PUEBLO COUNTY RURAL 70	719-542-0220
BAILEY	JEFFERSON COUNTY R-1	303-273-6500
	PLATT CANYON 1	303-838-7666
BASALT	ROARING FORK RE-1	970-945-6558
BAYFIELD	BAYFIELD 10 JT-R	970-884-2496
BELLVUE	POUDRE R-1	970-482-7420
BENNETT	BENNETT 29J	303-644-3234
BERTHOUD	THOMPSON R-2J	970-669-3940
BETHUNE	BETHUNE R-5	719-346-7513
BEULAH	PUEBLO COUNTY RURAL 70	719-542-0220
BLACK HAWK	GILPIN COUNTY RE-1	303-582-0625
BLANCA	SIERRA GRANDE R-30	719-379-3259
BOULDER	BOULDER VALLEY RE-2	303-447-1010
BRANSON	BRANSON REORGANIZED 82	719-946-5531
BRECKENRIDGE	SUMMIT RE-1	970-668-3011
BRIGGSDALE	BRIGGSDALE RE-10	970-656-3417
BRIGHTON	BRIGHTON 27J	303-659-4820
	NORTHGLENN-THORNTON 12	303-451-1561
BROOMFIELD	BOULDER VALLEY RE-2	303-447-1010
	JEFFERSON COUNTY R-1	303-273-6500
	NORTHGLENN-THORNTON 12	303-451-1561
BRUSH	BRUSH RE-2(J)	970-842-5176
BUENA VISTA	BUENA VISTA R-31	719-395-8656
BURLINGTON	BURLINGTON RE-6J	719-346-8737
BYERS	BYERS 32J	303-822-5292
CALHAN	CALHAN RJ-1	719-347-2766
	ELLICOTT 22	719-683-2328
CAMPO	CAMPO RE-6	719-787-2226
CANON CITY	CANON CITY RE-1	719-275-0691
CARBONDALE	ROARING FORK RE-1	970-945-6558
CASTLE ROCK	DOUGLAS COUNTY RE 1	303-688-3195
CEDAREDGE	DELTA COUNTY 50(J)	970-874-4438
CENTER	CENTER 26 JT	719-754-3442
CHERAW	CHERAW 31	719-853-6655
CHEYENNE WELLS	CHEYENNE COUNTY RE-5	719-767-5866
CHIPITA PARK	MANITOU SPRINGS 14	719-685-1235
CLIFTON	MESA COUNTY 51	970-245-2422

COLLBRAN	PLATEAU VALLEY 50	970-487-3547
COLORADO CITY	PUEBLO COUNTY RURAL 70	719-542-0220
COLORADO SPRINGS	ACADEMY 20	719-598-2566
	CHEYENNE MOUNTAIN 12	719-475-6100
	COLORADO SPRINGS 11	719-520-2000
	FALCON 49	719-495-3601
	HANOVER 28	719-683-2247
	HARRISON 2	719-576-8360
	LEWIS-PALMER 38	719-488-4700
COLORADO SPRINGS	WIDEFIELD 3	719-392-3481
COMMERCE CITY	ADAMS COUNTY 14	303-289-3950
CONIFER	JEFFERSON COUNTY R-l	303-273-6500
CORTEZ	MONTEZUMA-CORTEZ RE-l	970-565-7282
COTOPAXI	COTOPAXI RE-3	719-942-4131
CRAIG	MOFFAT COUNTY RE:NO1	970-824-3268
CRAWFORD	DELTA COUNTY 50(J)	970-874-4438
CREEDE	CREED CONSOLIDATED 1	719-658-2220
CRESTED BUTTE	GUNNISON WATERSHED RE1J	970-641-7760
CRIPPLE CREEK	CRIPPLE CREEK-VICTOR RE-1	719-689-2685
DE BEQUE	DE BEQUE 49JT	970-283-5597
DEER TRAIL	DEAR TRAIL 26J	303-769-4421
DEL NORTE	DEL NORTE C-7	719-657-4040
DELTA	DELTA COUNTY 50(J)	970-874-4438
DENVER	CHERRY CREEK 5	303-773-1184
	DENVER COUNTY 1	303-764-3200
	MAPLETON 1	303-288-6681
	NORTHGLENN-THORNTON 12	303-451-1561
	WESTMINSTER 50	303-428-3511
DILLON	SUMMIT RE-1	970-668-3011
DINOSAUR	MOFFAT COUNTY RE:NO1	970-824-3268
DIVIDE	WOODLAND PARK RE 2	719-687-6048
DOLORES	DOLORES RE-4A	970-882-7255
DOVE CREEK	DOLORES COUNTY RE NO.2	970-677-2522
DURANGO	DURANGO 9-R	970-247-5411
EADS	EADS RE-1	719-438-2218
EAGLE	EAGLE COUNTY RE 50	970-328-6321
EASTLAKE	NORTHGLENN-THORNTON 12	303-451-1561
EATON	EATON RE-2	970-454-3402
EDGEWATER	JEFFERSON COUNTY R-1	303-273-6500
EDWARDS	EAGLE COUNTY RE 50	970-328-6321
EGNAR	DOLORES COUNTY RE NO.2	970-677-2522
ELBERT	ELBERT 200	303-648-3030
ELIZABETH	ELIZABETH C-1	303-646-4441
EMPIRE	CLEAR CREEK RE-l	303-567-4467
ENGLEWOOD	CHERRY CREEK 5	303-773-1184
	ENGLEWOOD 1	303-761-7050
	SHERIDAN 2	303-761-8640
ERIE	ST. VRAIN VALLEY RE 1J	303-776-6200
ESTES PARK	PARK (ESTES PARK) R-3	970-586-2361
EVANS	GREELEY 6	970-352-1543
EVERGREEN	CLEAR CREEK RE-1	303-567-4467
	JEFFERSON COUNTY R-1	303-273-6500
FAIRPLAY	PARK COUNTY RE-2	719-836-3114
FALCON	FALCON 49	719-495-3601

FLAGLER	ARRIBA-FLAGLER C-20	719-765-4684
FLEMING	FRENCHMAN RE-3	970-265-2111
FLORENCE	FLORENCE RE-2	719-784-6312
FORT CARSON	FOUNTAIN 8	719-382-5631
FORT COLLINS	POUDRE R-1	970-482-7420
FORT LUPTON	FORT LUPTON RE-8	970-857-6291
FORT MORGAN	FORT MORGAN RE-3	970-867-5633
FOUNTAIN	FOUNTAIN 8	719-382-5631
	WIDEFIELD 3	719-392-3481
FOWLER	FOWLER R-4J	719-263-4224
FRANKTOWN	DOUGLAS COUNTY RE 1	303-688-3195
FRASER	EAST GRAND 2	970-887-2581
FREDERICK	ST. VRAIN VALLEY RE 1J	303-776-6200
FRISCO	SUMMIT RE-1	970-668-3011
FRUITA	MESA COUNTY 51	970-245-2422
FT COLLINS	THOMPSON R-2J	970-669-3940
GALETON	EATON RE-2	970-454-3402
GARDNER	HUERFANO RE-1	719-738-1520
GATEWAY	MESA COUNTY 51	970-245-2422
GEORGETOWN	CLEAR CREEK RE-1	303-567-4467
GILCREST	GILCREST RE-1	970-737-2403
GLENWOOD SPRINGS	ROARING FORK RE-1	970-945-6558
JOLD HILL	BOULDER VALLEY RE-2	303-447-1010
JOLDEN	JEFFERSON COUNTY R-1	303-273-6500
GRANADA	GRANADA RE-1	719-734-5492
GRANBY	EAST GRAND 2	970-887-2581
GRAND JUNCTION	MESA COUNTY 51	970-245-2422
GRAND LAKE	EAST GRAND 2	970-887-2581
GREELEY	GREELEY 6	970-352-1543
GROVER	PAWNEE RE-12	970-895-2222
GUFFEY	PARK COUNTY RE-2	719-836-3114
GUNNISON	GUNNISON WATERSHED RE1J	970-641-7760
GYPSUM	EAGLE COUNTY RE 50	970-328-6321
HAXTUN	HAXTUN RE-2J	970-774-6111
HAYDEN	HAYDEN RE-1	970-276-3864
HENDERSON	BRIGHTON 27J	303-659-4820
HIGHLANDS RANGH	DOUGLAS COUNTY RE 1	303-688-3195
HOEHNE	HOEHNE REORGANIZED 3	719-846-4457
HOLLY	HOLLY RE-3	719-537-6616
HOLYOKE	HOLYOKE RE-1J	970-854-3634
HOOPER	SANGRE DE CRISTO RE 22J	719-378-2321
HOTCHKISS	DELTA COUNTY 50(J)	970-874-4438
HUDSON	KEENESBURG RE-3(J)	970-732-4844
HUGO	GENOA-HUGO C113	719-743-2428
HYGIENE	ST. VRAIN VALLEY RE IJ	303-776-6200
IDAHO SPRINGS	CLEAR CREEK RE-1	303-567-4467
IDALIA	EAST YUMA COUNTY RJ-2	970-332-5764
IGNACIO	IGNACIO 11 JT	970-563-4521
ILIFF	VALLEY RE-1	970-522-0792
INDIAN HILLS	JEFFERSON COUNTY R-1	303-273-6500
JAMESTOWN	BOULDER VALLEY RE-2	303-447-1010
JOES	WEST YUMA COUNTY RJ-1	970-848-5831
JOHNSTOWN	JOHNSTOWN-MILLIKEN RE-5J	970-587-2336
JULESBURG	JULESBURG RE-1	970-474-3365

CHAPTER THREE: SCHOOL'S OUT FOREVER

KARVAL	KARVAL RE-23	719-446-5311
KEENESBURG	KEENESBURG RE-3(J)	970-732-4844
KERSEY	PLATTE VALLEY RE-7	970-352-6177
KIM	KIM REORGANIZED 88	719-643-5295
KIOWA	KIOWA C-2	303-621-2115
KIT CARSON	KIT CARSON R-1	719-962-3219
KREMMLING	WEST GRAND 1-JT	970-724-3217
LA JARA	NORTH CONEJOS RE-1J	719-274-5174
LA JUNTA	EAST OTERO R-1	719-384-8141
LA PORTE	POUDRE R-1	970-482-7420
LA SALLE	GILCREST RE-1	970-737-2403
LA VETA	LA VETA RE-2	719-742-3662
LAFAYETTE	BOULDER VALLEY RE-2	303-447-1010
LAKE CITY	HINSDALE COUNTY RE-1	970-944-2314
LAKE GEORGE	PARK COUNTY RE-2	719-836-3114
LAKEWOOD	JEFFERSON COUNTY R-1	303-273-6500
LAMAR	LAMAR RE-2	719-336-3251
LARKSPUR	DOUGLAS COUNTY RE 1	303-688-3195
LAS ANIMAS	LAS ANIMAS RE-1	719-456-0161
LEADVILLE	LAKE COUNTY R-1	719-486-0160
LIMON	LIMON RE-4J	719-775-9052
LITTLETON	CHERRY CREEK 5	303-773-1184
	DOUGLAS COUNTY RE 1	303-688-3195
	JEFFERSON COUNTY R-1	303-273-6500
	LITTLETON 6	303-347-3300
LIVERMORE	POUDRE R-1	970-482-7420
LOMA	MESA COUNTY 51	970-245-2422
LONGMONT	ST. VRAIN VALLEY RE 1J	303-776-6200
LOUISVILLE	BOULDER VALLEY RE-2	303-447-1010
LOVELAND	THOMPSON R-2J	970-669-3940
LYONS	ST. VRAIN VALLEY RE 1J	303-776-6200
MANASSA	NORTH CONEJOS RE-1J	719-274-5174
MANCOS	MANCOS RE-6	970-533-7748
MANITOU SPRINGS	MANITOU SPRINGS 14	719-685-1235
MANZANOLA	MANZANOLA 3J	719-462-5527
MAYBELL	MOFFAT COUNTY RE:NO1	970-824-3268
MC CLAVE	MC CLAVE RE-2	719-829-4517
MEAD	ST. VRAIN VALLEY RE 1J	303-776-6200
MEEKER	MEEKER RE1	970-878-3701
MERINO	BUFFALO RE-4	970-522-7424
MILLIKEN	JOHNSTOWN-MILLIKEN RE-5J	970-587-2336
MINTURN	EAGLE COUNTY RE 50	970-328-6321
MOFFAT	MOFFAT 2	719-256-4710
MONTE VISTA	MONTE VISTA C-8	719-852-5996
	SARGENT RE-33J	719-852-4023
MONTROSE	MONTROSE COUNTY RE-1J	970-249-7726
MONUMENT	LEWIS-PALMER 38	719-488-4700
MORRISON	JEFFERSON COUNTY R-1	303-273-6500
MOSCA	SANGRE DE CRISTO RE-22J	719-589-6634
NATURITA	WEST END RE-2	970-865-2290
NEDERLAND	BOULDER VALLEY RE-2	303-447-1010
NEW CASTLE	GARFIELD RE-2	970-625-1595
NEW RAYMER	PRAIRIE RE-11	970-437-5386
NORTHGLENN	NORTHGLENN-THORNTON 12	303-451-1561

COLORADO: A Newcomer's Manual

NORWOOD	NORWOOD R-2J	970-327-4712
NUCLA	WEST END RE-2	970-865-2290
OAK CREEK	SOUTH ROUTT RE 3	970-736-2313
OLATHE	MONTROSE COUNTY RE-1J	970-249-7726
ORDWAY	CROWLEY COUNTY RE-1-J	719-267-3117
OTIS	LONE STAR 101	970-848-2778
	OTIS R-3	970-246-3755
OURAY	OURAY R-1	970-325-4218
OVID	PLATTE VALLEY RE-3	970-463-5414
PAGOSA SPRINGS	ARCHULETA COUNTY 50 JT	303-264-2228
PALISADE	MESA COUNTY 51	970-245-2422
PALMER LAKE	LEWIS-PALMER 38	719-488-4700
PAONIA	DELTA COUNTY 50(J)	970-874-4438
PARACHUTE	GARFIELD 16	970-285-7759
PARADOX	WEST END RE-2	970-865-2290
PARKER	DOUGLAS COUNTY RE 1	303-688-3195
PEETZ	PLATEAU RE-5	970-334-2435
PENROSE	FLORENCE RE-2	719-784-6312
PEYTON	PEYTON 23 JT	719-749-2330
PIERCE	AULT-HIGHLAND RE-9	970-834-1345
PINE	JEFFERSON COUNTY R-1	303-273-6500
PLATTEVILLE	GILCREST RE-1	970-737-2403
PRITCHETT	PRITCHETT RE-3	719-523-4045
PUEBLO	PEUBLO CITY 60	719-549-7100
PUEBLO	PUEBLO COUNTY RURAL 70	719-542-0220
PUEBLO WEST	PUEBLO COUNTY RURAL 70	719-542-0220
RANGELY	RANGELY RE-4	970-675-2207
RED FEATHER LAKES	POUDRE R-1	970-482-7420
RIDGWAY	RIDGWAY R-2	970-626-5468
RIFLE	GARFIELD RE-2	970-625-1595
ROCKY FORD	ROCKY FORD R-2	719-254-7423
RUSH	MIAMI/YODER 60 JT	719-478-2186
RYE	PUEBLO COUNTY RURAL 70	719-542-0220
SAGUACHE	MOUNTAIN VALLEY RE 1	719-655-2578
SALIDA	SALIDA R-32	719-539-4382
SAN LUIS	CENTENNIAL R-1	719-672-3691
SANFORD	SANFORD 6J	719-274-5167
SECURITY	WIDEFIELD 3	719-392-3481
SEDALIA	DOUGLAS COUNTY RE 1	303-688-3195
SEDGWICK	PLATTE VALLEY RE-3	970-463-5414
SEIBERT	HI-PLAINS R-23	970-664-2636
SHERIDAN LAKE	PLAINVIEW RE-2	719-727-4361
SILT	GARFIELD RE-2	970-625-1595
SILVERTHORNE	SUMMIT RE-1	970-668-3011
SILVERTON	SILVERTON 1	970-387-5543
SIMLA	BIG SANDY 100J	719-541-2291
SPRINGFIELD	SPRINGFIELD RE-4	719-523-6654
STEAMBOAT SPRINGS	STEAMBOAT SPRINGS RE-2	970-879-1530
STERLING	VALLEY RE-1	970-522-0792
STRASBURG	STRASBURG 31J	303-622-9211
STRATTON	STRATTON R-4	719-348-5369
SWINK	SWINK 33	719-384-8103
TELLURIDE	TELLURIDE R-1	970-728-6617
THORNTON	MAPLETON 1	303-288-6681

	NORTHGLENN-THORNTON 12	303-451-1561
TIMNATH	POUDRE R-1	970-482-7420
TRINIDAD	TRINIDAD 1	719-846-3324
USAF ACADEMY	ACADEMY 20	719-598-2566
VAIL	EAGLE COUNTY RE 50	970-328-6321
VILAS	VILAS RE-5	719-523-6738
VONA	HI-PLAINS R-23	970-664-2636
WALDEN	NORTH PARK R-1	970-723-4391
WALSENBURG	HUERFANO RE-1	719-738-1520
WALSH	WALSH RE-1	719-324-5632
WELDONA	WELDON VALLEY RE-20(J)	970-645-2411
WELLINGTON	POUDRE R-1	970-482-7420
WESTCLIFFE	CONSOLIDATED C-1	719-783-2357
WESTMINSTER	JEFFERSON COUNTY R-1	303-273-6500
	NORTHGLENN-THORNTON 12	303-451-1561
	WESTMINSTER 50	303-428-3511
WESTON	PRIMERO REORGANIZED 2	719-868-2715
WHEAT RIDGE	JEFFERSON COUNTY R-1	303-273-6500
WHEATRIDGE	JEFFERSON COUNTY R-1	303-273-6500
WIGGINS	WIGGINS RE-50(J)	970-483-7762
WILEY	WILEY RE-13 JT	719-829-4806
WINDSOR	WINDSOR RE-4	970-686-7411
WOODLAND PARK	WOODLAND PARK RE-2	719-687-6048
WOODROW	WOODLAN R-104	970-386-2223
WRAY	EAST YUMA COUNTY RJ-2	970-332-5764
YAMPA	SOUTH ROUTT RE 3	970-736-2313
YODER	EDISON 54 JT	719-478-2125
YUMA	WEST YUMA COUNTY RJ-1	970-848-5831

PRIVATE SCHOOLS

- Colorado has more than 300 private elementary and secondary schools
- 73 percent of those schools have a religious affiliation
- None of them are military schools
- A number of those schools focus on the special needs of children
- 43 percent of the schools offer foreign languages in the curriculum
- At least two schools provide support to home schoolers
- Many schools feature specialized curricula such as Montessori, Waldorf, British Primary, and Core Knowledge
- The Denver Metro area has 147 private schools
- Boulder has 19 private schools
- Colorado Springs has 29 private schools
- There are an additional 124 private schools scattered around Colorado from Aspen to Trinidad.

The information available about private schools in Colorado is vast. If you are considering enrolling your child(ren) in a private school it is highly recommended you obtain a copy of *Colorado Private Elementary and Secondary Schools* by Magnolia Street Press, described in Appendix A.

HIGHER EDUCATION
THE COLORADO COMMISION ON HIGHER EDUCATION

The Colorado Commission on Higher Education, (303) 866-2723, is a nine member lay board, appointed by the Governor and confirmed by the Senate, that acts as a central policy and coordinating board for Colorado public higher education. Commissioners are appointed from each congressional district and three are appointed at large. The mission of the Commission is to implement the directives of the General Assembly, and promote and preserve quality, access, accountability, diversity and efficiency within Colorado public higher education.

Commissioners serve staggered terms of four years. The Commission employs a professional staff of nineteen, and meets monthly, on campuses throughout the state, to discuss and act on statewide higher education policy. The Commission works in consultation with governing boards of higher education institutions in the development and implementation of legislative directives and statewide higher education policy. In addition, the Commission receives assistance from an advisory committee that includes legislative, faculty, student, and citizen representation. The responsibilities of the Commission are to:

- Develop long-range plans for an evolving state system of higher education
- Review and approve degree programs
- Establish the distribution formula for higher education funding; recommend statewide funding levels to the legislature
- Approve institutional capital construction requests; recommend capital construction priorities to the legislature
- Develop policies for institutional and facility master plans
- Administer statewide student financial assistance programs through policy development, program valuation, and allocation of funds
- Develop and administer a statewide off-campus (extended studies), community service, and continuing education program
- Determine institutional roles and missions
- Establish statewide enrollment policies and admission standards
- Conduct special studies as appropriate or directed, regarding statewide education policy, finance, or effective coordination.
- Provide the public with various publications concerning all aspects of higher education (see Additional Resources section)

FACTS ABOUT PUBLIC HIGHER EDUCATION

- The Colorado public higher education system includes: 13 colleges, 15 community/junior colleges, and 6 area vocational-technical schools
- 27% of Colorado residents 25 years or older have at least a bachelor's degree
- $531 million was appropriated by the Colorado legislature to higher education for fiscal year 1992-93
- 85% of the first-time freshmen enrolled for fall 1992 were from Colorado
- 30,000 Colorado students received nearly $35 million in state-funded student assistance in 1991-92

- Over 27,000 certificate, associate, bachelor's, master's, and doctoral degrees were awarded in 1991-92 from Colorado public institutions
- Over $393 million in government and private research funds were received by Colorado public institutions in 1992-93

STUDENT FINANCIAL ASSISTANCE PROGRAMS

Colorado student aid is appropriated by the state legislature and allocated by the Colorado Commission on Higher Education to eligible Colorado colleges and universities. Colorado student aid awards are made by institutions to students based upon state guidelines and according to institutional policies and procedures. Any aid received must be used for tuition, fees, room, board, books, and supplies or other expenses related to attendance at Colorado institutions.

General Student Eligibility Requirements:

Colorado residency for tuition purposes (A small percentage of Undergraduate Merit and Graduate Fellowship awards may be made to non-residents of Colorado at some institutions.)
Enrollment in an eligible program at an eligible Colorado post-secondary institution
Satisfactory progress toward completion of a course of study
No defaulted educational loans or grants.

Types of State Aid Available:

Colorado Diversity Grant: Available as part of a statewide effort to increase participation of under-represented groups in the Colorado public higher education system.

Colorado Nursing Scholarships: Designed to provide assistance to individuals seeking nursing education who agree to practice in Colorado. Applications are available from the Colorado Commission on Higher Education annually.

Colorado Part-time Grants: Need-based grants for less than full-time students attending eligible Colorado institutions.

Colorado Student Grants (CSG): Available to qualified undergraduates with documented financial need.

Colorado Student Incentive Grants (CSIG): Available to qualified undergraduates with substantial financial need. (Student grants under this program are comprised of both federal and state funds).

Colorado Work-Study: Part-time employment program designed to assist students with financial need or work experience.

Undergraduate Merit: Available to students who demonstrate superior scholarship or talent as defined by the college or university they attend.

Colorado Graduate Grants: Available to graduate students with financial need.

Colorado Graduate Fellowships: Provide merit based awards to graduate students.

Dependents Tuition Assistance Program: Pays tuition for dependents of Colorado law enforcement officers, fire or national guard personnel killed or disabled in the line of duty, and for dependents of prisoners of war or service personnel listed as missing in action. Dependents of disabled personnel must have demonstrated financial need for the assistance. Applications are available at the Colorado Commission on Higher Education.

Paul Douglas Teacher Scholarships: Federal program designed to encourage outstanding individuals to enter the teaching profession. Federal law stipulates that recipients must be (or have been) in the top ten percent of their high school graduating class, or have comparable GED scores.

Contact individual institutions for complete information and details about application procedures and deadlines. Information about other sources of financial aid may be obtained at many local libraries.

DEFINITION OF DEGREES

CERTIFICATES: Requires the completion of a program that would be completed in 30 to 120 credit hours. Includes 1, 2, and 4-year certificate programs, as well as post-bachelor's and postmaster's certificates.

ACADEMIC ASSOCIATE: Normally requires at least 2, but less than 4 years of full-time equivalent college work in an academic field of study.

VOCATIONAL ASSOCIATE: Normally requires at least 2, but less than 4 years of full-time equivalent college work whose expressed intent is to impart work-related knowledge and skills.

BACHELOR: Normally requires at least 4 but not more than 5 years of full-time equivalent college-level work. Includes all bachelor's degrees conferred in a Cooperative or Work-Study Plan or Program. Also includes bachelor's degrees in which the normal 4 years of work is completed in 3 years.

MASTER'S: Requires the successful completion of a program of study of at least the full-time equivalent of 1, but not more than 2 academic years of work beyond the bachelor's degree.

FIRST PROFESSIONAL: Requires completion of a program that meets all three of the following: (1) Completion of the academic requirements to begin practice in the profession; (2) At least 2 years of college work prior to entrance to the program; and (3) A total of at least 6 academic years of college work to complete the degree program, including prior required college work, plus the length of the professional program itself. The following fields are valid first-professional degrees in Colorado public institutions:

Dentistry (D.D.S. or D.M.D.); Medicine (M.D.); Veterinary Medicine (D.V.M.); Law (L.L.B. or J.D.); Nursing (N.D.); Pharmacy (D.Phar.); Osteopathic Medicine (D.O.); Podiatry (Pod. D. or D.P.); Optometry (O.D.); Chiropractic (D.C. or D.C.M.); Theology (m.Div., M.H.L., B.D., or Ordination)

COLORADO INSTITUTIONS OF HIGHER EDUCATION
2 Year Colleges and Vocational Schools

Aims Community College, P.O. Box 69, Greeley, CO 80632, 970-330-8008

CHAPTER THREE: SCHOOL'S OUT FOREVER

Arapahoe Community College, P.O. Box 9002, Littleton, CO 80160-9002, 303-794-1550
Boulder Valley Voc-Tech, 6600 Arapahoe, Boulder, CO 80303, 303-447- 5220
Colorado Mountain College:
CMC-Central Administration, P.O. Box 10001, Glenwood Springs, CO 81602, 970-945-8691
CMC-Alpine Campus, 1370 Bob Adams Drive, Steamboat Springs, CO 80477, 970-870-4444
CMC-Carbondale Center, 443 Main, Carbondale, CO 81623, 970-963-2172
CMC-Roaring Forks Campus-, Spring Valley Center, Glenwood Spgs, CO 81601, 970-945-7481
CMC-Timberline Campus, 901 South Highway 24, Leadville, CO 80461, 719-486-2015
Colorado N.W. Community College, 500 Kennedy Drive, Rangely, CO 81648, 970-675-2261
Community College of Aurora, 16000 E. Centretech Pkwy, Aurora, CO 80011, 303-360-4700
Community College of Denver, 1111 West Colfax Avenue, Denver, CO 80204, 303-556-2600
Delta-Montrose Voc-Tech, 1765 U.S. Highway 50, Delta, CO 81416, 970-874-7671
Emily Griffith Opportunity Center, 1250 Welton Street, Denver, CO 80204, 303-572-8218
Front Range Com. College, 3645 West 112th Avenue, Westminster, CO 80030, 303-466-8811
Front Range Com. College, Larimer Campus, Fort Collins, CO 80522, 970-226-2500
Lamar Community College, 2401 South Main Street, Lamar, CO 81052, 303-336-2248
Morgan Community College, 17800 County Road 20, Fort Morgan, CO 80701, 970-867-3081
Northeastern Junior College, 100 College Drive, Sterling, CO 80751, 970-522-6600
Otero Junior College, La Junta, CO 81050, 719-384-8721
Pikes Peak Com. College, 5675 S. Academy Boulevard, CO Spgs, CO 80906, 719-576-7711
Pueblo Community College, 900 West Orman Avenue, Pueblo, CO 81004, 719-549-3200
Red Rocks Community College, 13300 West 6th Avenue, Lakewood, CO 80401, 303-988-6160
San Juan Basin Voc-Tech, P.O. Box 970, Cortez, CO 81321, 970-565-8457
San Luis Valley Educational Center, 1011 Main Street, Alamosa, CO 81101, 719-589-5871
T. H. Pickens Voc-Tech, 500 Buckley Road, Aurora, CO 80011, 303-344-4910
Trinidad State Junior College, 600 Prospect Street, Trinidad, CO 81082, 719-846-5543

4 Year Colleges and Universities

Adams State College, Alamosa, CO 81102, 719-589-7936
Colorado School of Mines, Golden, CO 80401, 303-273-3000
Colorado State University, Fort Collins, CO 80523, 970-491-1101
Fort Lewis College, Durango, CO 81301, 970-247-7010
Lesley College, 2021 Clubhouse Drive, Greely, CO 80634, 970-654-1037
Mesa State College, P.O. Box 2647, Grand Junction, CO 81502, 970-248-1787
Metropolitan State College of Denver, Denver, CO, 303-556-6227
University of Colorado:, UC-Boulder, Boulder, CO 80309, 303-492-6937
UC-Colorado Springs, P.O. Box 7150, Colorado Springs, CO 80933-7150, 719-593-3000
UC-Denver, P.O. Box 173364, Denver, CO 80217-3364, 303-556-2844
UC-Health Sciences Center, 4200 East 9th Avenue, Denver, CO 80262, 303-399-1211
University of Northern Colorado, Greeley, CO 80639, 970-351-1890
University of Southern Colorado, 2200 North Bonforte, Pueblo, CO 81001, 719-549-2681
Western State College, Gunnison, CO 81230, 970-943-2030

Private Colleges And Universities

Chapman University, 7222 Commerce Center Dr #100, CO Spgs, CO 80919, 719-593-0970
Colorado Christian University, 180 S. Garrison Street, Lakewood, CO 80226, 303-238-5386
Colorado College, 14 E. Cache La Poudre, Colorado Springs, CO 80903, 719-389-6474
Regis University, 3333 Regis Boulevard, Denver, CO 80221-1099, 303-458-4135
University of Denver, 2301 S. Gaylord Street, Denver, CO 80208-0100, 303-871-2496
U. of Phoenix, Denver Campus, 7800 East Dorado Place, Englewood, CO 80111, 303-755-9090

Private Vocational Schools

American Diesel & Automotive, 1002 South Jason Street, Denver, CO 80223, 303-778-6772
Americana Beauty College I, 730 South Camino Del Rio, Durango, CO 81301, 970-247-9571
Americana Beauty College II, 3650 Austin Bluffs, Colorado Springs, CO 80907, 719-598-4188
Americana Beauty College III, 228 West 29th, Pueblo, CO 81008, 719-542-8290
Americana Beauty College VI, 1435 Main Street, Alamosa, CO 81101, 719-589-5892
Blair Junior College, 828 Wooten Road, Colorado Springs, CO 80915, 719-574-1082
Colorado Aero Tech, 10851 West 120th Avenue, Broomfield, CO 80020, 303-66-1714
Colorado Beauty College III, 2415 Fremont Drive, Canon City, CO 81212, 719-275-4116
Colorado Institute of Art, 200 East 9th Avenue, Denver, CO 80203, 303-837-0725
Colorado Technical College, 4435 N. Chestnut St., Colorado Springs, CO 80907, 719-598-0200
Columbine Beauty School I, 1225 Wadsworth Boulevard, Lakewood, CO 80215, 303-422-5219
Columbine Beauty School 11, 5801 44th Avenue, Denver, CO 80212, 303-451 -5808
Columbine Beauty School III, 3811 E. 120th Avenue, Thornton, CO 80229, 303-4512-5808
ConCorde Career Institute, 770 Grant, Denver, CO 80203, 303-861-1151
Denver Institute of Technology, 7350 North Broadway, Denver, CO 80221, 303-426-1808
Denver Technical College, 925 South Niagara, Denver, CO 80224, 303-329-3903
Glenwood Beauty Academy, W. Glenwood Plaza, Glenwood Spgs, CO 81601, 970-598-4188
Int' Beauty Academy, 1185 North Circle Drive, Colorado Springs, CO 80909, 719-598-4188
Parks Junior College, 9065 Grant Street, Denver, CO 80229, 303-457-2757
PPI Health Careers School, 820 Arcturus Avenue, Colorado Springs, CO 80906, 719-471-0814
Pueblo College of Business and Tech., 330 Lake Avenue, Pueblo, CO 81004, 719-545-3100
Rocky Mountain College of Art and Design, 6875 East Evans, Denver, CO 80224, 303-753-6046
Technical Trades Institute, 772 Horizon Drive, Grand Junction, CO 81506, 970-245-8101

LIBRARIES

Books are vehicles of ideas, instruments of education, vessels of literature and sources of entertainment.[1] The world of books is the most remarkable creation of man. Nothing else he builds ever lasts. Monuments fall, nations perish, civilizations die out. Yet books live on, still as fresh at the day they were written.[2] In the five and a half centuries since the invention of movable type, one thing hasn't changed—the ability of books to move mankind. The book is imagination. It is comfort and companionship. It is solace and inspiration. It is frivolity and formality. It is recipes and revelations. It is a tour down the Danube, a guide to the Louvre, an armchair adventure to the streams of the Rockies.

To learn a craft, professionals must devour huge amounts of information. To excel, they must continue to read. There is virtually nothing, from gardening to home-repairs to constructing an atomic bomb, that can not be learned from books. Anyone with average reading ability has the opportunity to learn, to improve and expand her or his base of knowledge, to find the answer to almost any question.

Today's modern libraries are a cross between repositories of books and the latest high-tech computer centers. The "information highway" is here and growing at a

---

[1] Based on remarks in *Book Printing, A Basic Introduction*, by John P. Dessauer, The Continuum Publishing Co., New York, 1989.
[2] From *To Advance Knowledge, A Handbook on American University Press Publishing*, by Gene R. Hawes, American University Press Service, Inc., New York, 1967

phenomenal rate. With the advent of the CD-ROM computer drive and on-line services, there exist no information which can not be located and studied.

One of the intentions for this chapter was to list every public library in Colorado. However, when I discovered there are over 300 such facilities, and because space in this book is limited, I decided to reduce the text presented to information not easily obtained through Directory Assistance or local phone books. Below you will find interesting facts about the newest and best equipped library in the county and a list of unique corporate and private libraries which house proprietary, technical, and research related material which may be difficult to find elsewhere.

THE NEW DENVER CENTRAL LIBRARY

In the Spring of 1995, Denver unveiled its newly renovated and expanded central library (see photograph on page 211) (phone: 303-640-6200). The new structure has seven floors above ground and three below for a total of 540,000 square feet. This new library has many special features which include:

Western History and Genealogy Department: Map room with 5,000 maps for browsing and study; Computer access to extensive, world-famous photo collection; Two-story seminar room; Manuscript reading room; Separate genealogy collection

Children's Library and Story Pavilion: Study rooms with word processors; Audiovisual study areas; Children's story pavilion for special programs; Enclosed patio and play area; Multi-cultural and foreign language book collections.

Technology: Touch-screen building directory; CD-ROM high-storage jukebox; CARL computerized public access catalog; Access to information highways of the world; On-line periodical delivery service; Digitized photographic imaging; Self-checkout systems; 24-hour dial-up access, by modem, to databases; Statewide network linking 120 academic and public library catalogs; Equipment for people with disabilities

General: Orientation theater; Bookstore and gift shop; Centralized reference service; Young adult reading room; Popular browsing collection; Two multipurpose rooms, seating 90 and 100; Ten study rooms; Seven public meeting rooms, each seating up to 30; Full accessibility to people with disabilities; Security systems and personnel; Four passenger elevators, plus escalators on first through fourth floors

CORPORATE, SPECIAL AND PRIVATE LIBRARIES

Many large corporations, hospitals, government agencies, and private foundations maintain their own libraries. These special libraries can be an unbelievable source of information not found in public libraries. Although not "public" in nature, most special libraries allow access to material by individuals for specific projects or purposes. This alphabetical list is presented because most special libraries are not listed in any phonebook.

A.T. & T. Gbcs. Library	Denver	303-538-1582
Adolph Coors Company Technical Library	Golden	303-277-3506
Amax Research And Development Center	Golden	303-273-7200
Amer. Humane Assoc. Ctr. On Child Abuse	Englewood	303-792-9900
American Legion Auxiliary Library,	Cheyenne Wells	719-727-4006
American Numismatic Association Library	Colorado Springs	719-632-2646

American Water Works Association Info. Services	Denver	303-795-7711
Amoco Production Company Library/Info. Center	Denver	303-830-5336
Arthur Andersen & Company Library	Denver	303-291-9444
Aspen Historical Society	Aspen	970-925-3721
Aspen Institute David Mayer Library	Aspen	970-925-7010
Assoc. Of Operating Room Nurses Library	Denver	303-755-6304
Augustana Lutheran Church Library	Denver	303-388-4678
Ball Aerospace Systems Division Library Service	Boulder	303-939-5755
Beet Sugar Development Foundation	Denver	303-321-1520
Bethesda Psychealth System Professional Library	Denver	303-758-1514
Boulder Community Hospital Medical Library	Boulder	303-440-2091
Boulder County Corrections Library	Boulder	303-441-4686
Brega & Winters PC Law Library	Denver	303-866-9400
Career Track Inc. Library/Info Center Resource	Boulder	303-447-2323
Cherry Creek Schools Educators Resource Center	Denver	303-341-6477
Children's Hospital Medical Library	Denver	303-861-6400
Cobe Bct. Inc. Library	Lakewood	303-231-4278
Colorado Dept. Of Education Resource Center	Denver	303-866-6618
Colorado Dept. Of Human Services Library	Denver	303-866-4086
CO Dept. Of Local Affairs State Planning Library	Denver	303-866-2156
Colorado Dept. Of Revenue Office Of Tax Analysis	Denver	303-866-3089
Colorado Dept. Of Transportation Tech. Library	Denver	303-757-9220
CO Developmental Disabilities Planning Council	Denver	303-894-2345
Colorado Div. Of State Archives And Public Records	Denver	303-866-2358
Colorado Div. Of Wildlife Library	Denver	303-297-1192
Colorado Div. Of Wildlife Research Library	Denver	303-484-2836
Colorado Historical Society Stephen H. Hart Library	Denver	303-866-2305
Colorado Legislative Council	Denver	303)866-3521
Colorado Mental Health Institute at Pueblo	Pueblo	719-546-4677
Colorado National Bank - Pueblo Law Library	Pueblo	719-543-1331
Colorado Springs Fine Arts Center Library	Colorado Springs	719-634-5581
CO Spgs Pioneer Museum Center For Local History	Colorado Springs	719-578-6650
Colorado State Bank Building Law Library	Denver	303-837-0287
Colorado State Veterans Center Library	Homelake	719-852-5118
Colorado Supreme Court Library	Denver	303-861-1111
Colorado Talking Book Library	Denver	303-727-9277
Community Living Alternatives Inc.	Denver	303-477-4500
Dames & Moore Library	Denver	303-299-7980
Defense Finance & Accounting / Denver Center	Denver	303-676-7566
Denver Art Museum Native Arts Dept. Library	Denver	303-640-1613
Denver Botanic Gardens Helen K. Fowler Library	Denver	303-370-8014
Denver General Hospital Medical Library	Denver	303-436-6360
Denver Medical Library	Denver	303-839-6670
Denver Museum Of Natural History Library	Denver	303-370-6362
Denver Post Newsroom Library	Denver	303-820-1443
Denver Public Schools Ed. Resource Services	Denver	303-764-3692
Denver Wildlife Research Center Library	Denver	303-236-7873
Digital Equipment Corp. Library/Info Center	Colorado Springs	719-548-2113
Econo-Clad Books American Bindery	Littleton	303-798-7063
EG&G Rocky Flats Plant Inc.	Golden	303-966-4809
El Paso Cnty Dept Of Health And Enviro.	Colorado Springs	719-578-3109
El Paso County Law Library	Colorado Springs	719-630-2880
First Presbyterian Church Library	Colorado Springs	719-471-3763
Ft Carson Hq & 4th Infantry Division Grant Library	Ft Carson	719-579-2842

CHAPTER THREE: SCHOOL'S OUT FOREVER

Gates Rubber Company The Information Center	Denver	303-744-4150
Great Sand Dunes National Monument Library	Mosca	719-378-2312
Healthone Aurora Presbyterian Hospital Library	Aurora	303-360-3105
Hebrew Educational Alliance Library	Denver	303-629-0410
Hewlett Packard Company Fort Collins Site Library	Fort Collins	970-229-3825
Hewlett Packard Company Library	Loveland	970-679-2460
Hewlett Packard S. Colorado Regional Library	Colorado Springs	719-590-2708
Holland And Hart Law Library	Denver	303-295-8096
Dolman Inc. Technical Services & Development Lab	Laporte	303-482-5600
Ntl Fed Of Petroleum & Chem Wkrs Library	Denver	303-333-1543
Efferson Center For Mental Health Library	Lakewood	303-425-0300
Kaman Sciences Corp. Technical Library	Colorado Springs	719-599-1777
Kirkland & Ellis Law Library	Denver	303-291-3045
KRMA-TV Channel 6 Educational Services	Denver	303-892-6666
Lakewood Environmental Library & Central Records	Lakewood	303-987-7678
Lutheran Church of The Master Library	Lakewood	303-988-6400
Lutheran Medical Center Medical Library	Wheat Ridge	303-425-8662
Marathon Oil Co. Production Technology Library	Littleton	303-347-5530
McClelland Center For Child Study	Pueblo	719-543-5271
Memorial Hospital Health Sciences Library	Colorado Springs	719-475-5182
Mental Health Center Of Boulder County Library	Boulder	303-443-8500
Mercy Behavioral Health Center	Durango	970-259-1110
Mercy Medical Center Library	Denver	303-393-3296
Mesa Verde Research Library Museum	Mesa Verda Park	719-529-4475
Metro Wastewater Reclamation District Library	Denver	303-286-3000
Metrum Information Storage Information Center	Littleton	303-773-4829
Mile High Center Law Library	Denver	303-832-3335
Montrose Memorial Hospital Medical Library	Montrose	970-240-7394
Morrison & Foerster Law Library	Denver	303-592-2259
Museum Of Western Colorado	Grand Junction	970-242-0971
National Archives and Records Adm.	Denver	303-236-0817
National Conference of State Legislatures	Denver	303-830-2200
National Indian Law Library	Boulder	303-447-8760
National Institute of Corrections Info. Center	Longmont	303-682-0213
Ntl. Jewish Center For Immun./Respiratory Medicine	Denver	303-398-1482
National Park Service Library	Denver	303-969-2716
National Renewable Energy Laboratory	Golden	303-275-4215
Natural Hazards Research & Applications Info Center	Boulder	303-492-6818
Parkview Episcopal Medical Center Medical Library	Pueblo	719-584-4582
Penrose St. Francis Healthcare System Library	Colorado Springs	719-630-5288
Platte River Power Authority Library	Fort Collins	970-229-5230
Porter Memorial Hospital Medical Library	Denver	303-778-5656
Poudre Valley Hospital Library	Fort Collins	970-495-7323
Raytheon Engineers & Constructors Inc.	Englewood	303-843-2256
Rocky Mountain News Editorial Library	Denver	303-892-2746
Rocky Mountain Resource & Training	Arvada	303-420-2942
Rose Medical Center Medical Library	Denver	303-320-2160
Schuller International Inc.	Littleton	303-978-5373
Science Apps International Corporate Library	Greenwood Village	303-773-6900
Second Judicial District Law Library	Denver	303-640-2233
Security Life Of Denver Corporate Library	Denver	303-860-2338
Shepard's/Mcgraw-Hill Library	Colorado Springs	719-481-7548
Sherman & Howard L.C.C. Law Library	Denver	303-299-8041
Sixth Judicial District Law Library	Durango	970-259-0258

COLORADO: A Newcomer's Manual

S. Metro Denver Small Business Development Center	Littleton	303-795-0142
Southeastern Colorado Area Health Education Center	Pueblo	719-544-7833
St. Anthony Hospital Central Medical Ref. Library	Denver	303-629-3790
St. John's Episcopal Cathedral Library	Denver	303-831-7115
St. Joseph Hospital Library	Denver	303-837-7188
St. Mary's Hospital & Medical Center Library	Grand Junction	970-244-2171
Stone & Webster Engineering Tech. Info. Center	Denver	303-741-7323
Storage Tech. Corporation Information Center	Louisville	303-673-5867
Swedish Medical Center Medical Library	Englewood	303-788-6616
Synergen Inc. Library & Information Center	Boulder	303-938-6214
Tri-County Health Department Library	Englewood	303-220-9200
U S West Inc. Corporate Library	Englewood	303-689-8877
U.S. Bureau Of Land Management Library	Denver	303-236-6649
U.S. Bureau Of Mines Library	Denver	303-236-0474
U.S. Bureau Of Reclamation Library	Denver	303-236-6963
U.S. Bureau Of Census Info. Services Program	Lakewood	303-969-7750
U.S. Court Of Appeals Tenth Circuit Library	Denver	303-844-3591
U.S. Dept. Of Veterans Admin. Med. Center Library	Denver	303-393-2821
U.S. Dept. Of Veterans Affairs Medical Library	Ft. Lyon	719-384-3130
U.S. Dept.Of Interior Geo. Survey Branch Library	Denver	303-236-5774
U.S. EPA Ntl. Enforcemement Investigations Ctr	Denver Co	303-236-5170
U S EPA Region VIII Library	Denver	303-293-1444
U.S. Geological Survey CO Water Resources Library	Denver Co	303-236-4882
U.S. National Biological Ecological Science Ctr.	Fort Collins	970-226-9403
U.S. Office Of Surface Mining Library	Denver	303-672-5538
U.S. Olympic Committee Info. Resources Center	Colorado Springs	719-578-4622
U.S. Veterans Affairs Medical Center Library	Grand Junction	970-242-0731
University Of Colorado Technical Reference Center	Boulder	303-492-8774
Ute Mountain Tribal Library	Towaoc	970-565-3751
Wayne Bond Memorial Technical Library	Denver	303-452-6111
Weld County District Court Law Library	Greeley	970-356-4000
Western Interstate Com. For Higher Educa. Library	Boulder	303-541-0285
YMCA Resource Center	Boulder	303-443-0419

ADDITIONAL RESOURCES

Colorado Department of Education, Communications Center, Room 500, 201 East Colfax Avenue, Denver, CO 80203-1799, (303) 866-6937. Call for prices and additional information about these selected publications:

1994-1995 Colorado Education and Library Directory. Lists every school and school administrator in Colorado. Also lists every public library and more. Updated annually.
State Report Card 1994, K - 12 Public Education in Colorado. Updated annually.
Newcomers' Packet, An Overview of Colorado's Public Education System.

Colorado Commission on Higher Education, 1300 Broadway, Second Floor, Denver, CO 80203 (303) 866-2723, offers numerous free reports on all aspects of Colorado's higher education system. Call for details.

Magnolia Street Press, 2600 Magnolia, Denver, CO 80207, (303) 322-2822. See Appendix A for complete description of titles.
The Guide to Metro Denver Public Schools, 1995-96 Edition
Colorado Private Elementary and Secondary Schools, 1995-96

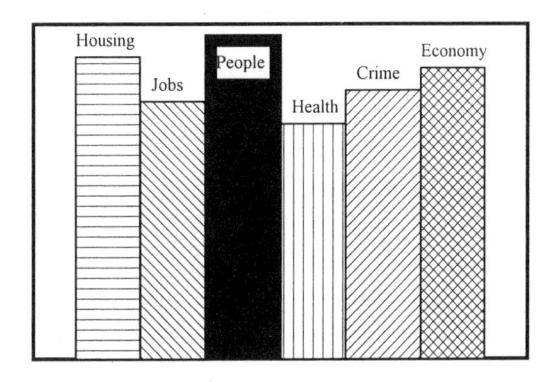

CHAPTER FOUR
THIS MUST BE THE PLACE

STATE-WIDE STATISTICS
General Statistics
Employment
Safest Communities
Health Care
Taxes

If you like reading books on world records, technical computer manuals, or actuarial charts, you're going to love this chapter. I have attempted to take a large hodgepodge of data and edit it into a small hodgepodge of data. I have also attempted to integrate narrative material so as not to put the average reader asleep. This chapter is loosely divided into the five sections shown above. You should keep in mind that many of the charts and figures are based on data which may be 1-3 years old and therefore may not provide an accurate picture. The data used are the most recent available from any source; however, due to the explosive growth Colorado has experienced during the last several years, the information provided should only be used as a basis for general trends or historical reference.

GENERAL STATISTICS
POPULATION GROWTH

Growth! From the smallest rural newspaper to the largest international magazines, the tremendous growth of Colorado is still making headlines. Regardless of which side of the debate you are on—that growth is a blessing or a curse—one thing is undeniable, the boom is not over. Recently released figures from the U.S. Census Bureau show that from 1990 to July 1994 the state's population grew 11 percent. Some counties experienced growth of more than 30 percent. Douglas County was in the lead with a total population increase of 45.8 percent. As a state, Colorado's population grew from 3,294,473 to 3,655,647. That is an additional 361,174 new residents. As of this writing, that figure is probably closer to 500,000!

Many lists of subjects like "The Fastest Growing Counties," "The Largest Counties," and related summaries are available from various sources. For the reasons stated in the beginning of this chapter, no such list should be considered definitive. In addition to the problem of "old" data concerning a rapidly changing subject, there is also the problem of statistical manipulation. This section contains three lists concerning the "Fastest Growing Counties in Colorado." One runs from 1990 to estimated July 1994 figures. The other two cover the same time period of 1990 through 1993; however one is based on percentage change and the other on numerical change. If one county had a numerical change of 37,000 new residents up from a base of 370,000 it would have a net 10% increase. However, if a small rural county with a base of 1,000 residents gained 110 new residents it would top the list with an 11% increase. You decide which has more growth.

10 LARGEST COUNTIES (1993)

County	Population 1993	Population 1990	Percentage Change 1990-1993
Denver	490,801	467,610	1.5
Jefferson	474,311	438,430	2.5
El Paso	432,752	397,014	2.7
Arapahoe	428,151	391,511	2.9
Adams	281,130	265,038	1.9
Boulder	247,510	225,339	3.0
Larimer	203,501	186,136	2.4
Weld	140,143	131,821	1.9
Pueblo	125,504	123,051	0.7
Mesa	99,340	93,145	2.1

(Population figures for 1994 are available but are still in the "challenge" period and thus have not been released as hard data)

20 FASTEST GROWING COUNTIES, 1990 - JULY 1994, (ESTIMATED)

County	94 Pop	% Change	County	94 Pop	% Change
Douglas	88,078	45.8	Teller	16,125	29.3
Elbert	13,016	34.9	Custer	2,481	28.8
Park	9,450	31.7	Hinsdale	598	28.1
San Miguel	4,796	31.3	Summit	16,278	26.4
			Eagle	27,371	24.8

CHAPTER FOUR: THIS MUST BE THE PLACE

County	94 Pop	% Change			
Ouray	2,860	24.6	Larimer	212,346	14.1
Archuleta	6,523	22.0	El Paso	452,416	14.0
Delta	24,120	15.0	Garfield	34,034	13.5
La Plata	36,996	14.6	Arapahoe	443,318	13.2
Routt	16,144	14.6	Montrose	27,605	13.0
			Gunnison	11,567	12.6

10 FASTEST GROWING COUNTIES BASED ON PERCENTAGE CHANGE
1990 - 1993, (CONFIRMED DATA)

County	93 Pop	90 Pop	% Change
Douglas	83,358	60,391	10.4
Lincoln	6,048	4,529	9.3
Custer	2,423	1,926	7.3
Park	8,835	7,174	6.6
San Miguel	4,400	3,653	5.9
Eagle	25,373	21,928	4.6
Archuleta	6,168	5,345	4.5
Ouray	2,624	2,295	4.2
Summit	14,631	12,881	4.0
Morgan	24,909	21,939	4.0

10 FASTEST GROWING COUNTIES BASED ON NUMERICAL CHANGE
1990 - 1993 (CONFIRMED DATA)

County	93 Pop	90 Pop	# Change
Arapahoe	428,966	391,511	37,455
Jefferson	475,214	438,430	36,784
El Paso	433,576	397,014	36,562
Denver	490,804	467,610	23,194
Boulder	248,353	225,339	23,014
Douglas	83,358	60,391	22,967
Adams	281,665	265,038	16,627
Larimer	200,782	186,136	14,646
Weld	140,057	131,821	8,236
Mesa	99,529	93,145	6,384

SUBSTATE POPULATION PROJECTIONS

Colorado is divided into 5 substate regions (see chart on page 24). The population projections below are an aggregation of all the counties within each region.

REGION	1996	2000	2005
Front Range	3,076,767	3,254,613	3,456,937
Western Slope	394,834	431,606	475,058
Eastern Plains	148,035	156,989	167,496
San Luis Valley	43,810	45,821	48,197
Eastern Mountains	121,335	129,280	138,623
Colorado Total	3,784,781	4,018,309	4,286,311

COLORADO: A Newcomer's Manual

80 SAFEST COMMUNITIES

The following statistics and information were provided by the KUSA (Channel) 9NEWS I-Team. They assembled statistics from the Colorado Bureau of Investigation and selected communities. The Statistics are the most current statistics available (1994) and one-year more current than those recently released by the FBI. Since Colorado has seen tremendous growth in the past three years, population projections were obtained from the State of Colorado and used in a database to compare crime rates in various communities.

Crime statistics fluctuate from year to year. The statistics for total crime also may appear abnormally high in communities such as ski areas or industrial centers, because their populations increase dramatically on business days. On the other hand, some large cities may appear to have abnormally low rates of larceny, because metropolitan police departments may decline to fill out paperwork for minor crimes.

The chart below ranks communities from the safest (#1) to the least safe (#80). It is based on the total number of crimes reported in the categories listed. You may wish to ignore the overall safety rating and focus on specific catagories depending on your situation. A single woman may be more concerned with how many rapes were reported; a male yuppie with a brand new BMW may care more about the number of auto thefts that took place in a particular county.

		Violent Crime H=Homicide RP=Rape RB=Robbery A=Agg. Assault				Property B=Burglary L=Larceny A=Auto Theft		
Community * = Unincorporated	Safety Rating	H	RP	RB	A	B	L	A
Washington County *	1	78		59	3	1	1	1
Arapahoe *	2	41		14	2	3	2	3
Windsor	3			4	29	2	4	2
Saguache County	4		35	3	19	5	7	17
Douglas County *	5	43	25	18	11	9	9	6
Morgan County*	6		51	6	33	4	10	7
Cherry Hills	7			45	5	19	8	18
Montrose County *	8	59	52	22	18	12	5	28
Mesa *	9		21	16	4	11	11	15
Evans	10	74	26	55	35	13	6	13
Routt County *	11			13	24	8	15	38
Fremont County *	12		19	2	12	24	14	21
Alamosa County *	13	75	45		1	14	17	19
Boulder *	14		61	15	23	37	12	33
Garfield County *	15	80		23	54	21	13	8

CHAPTER FOUR: THIS MUST BE THE PLACE

Community * = Unincorporated	Safety Rating	H	RP	RB	A	B	L	A
Logan County *	16		47	11	57	16	16	19
Louisville	17	55	15	5	32	10	21	12
Chaffee County *	18			26	20	31	19	14
El Paso County *	19	57	29	36	37	25	18	25
Jefferson County *	20	40	32	34	8	34	22	35
Larimer County *	21	45	70	20	9	15	23	24
Castle Rock	22		46	41	7	23	25	13
Englewood	23		53	72	55	68	3	70
Fountain	24		22	7	14	27	28	26
Montezuma County *	25		78	19	26	32	29	11
Broomfield	26	47	30	17	45	18	33	32
Salida	27		33	30	6	17	41	5
La Plata County *	28	52	79	10	66	44	20	37
Lafayette	29		38	17	38	34	34	
Pitkin County *	30			12	56	39	31	41
Weld County *	31	65	60	39	31	57	30	52
Golden	32		24	35	36	26	39	40
Fort Collins	33	42	44	43	41	35	37	36
Loveland	34		71	46	63	7	35	30
Steamboat Springs	35			8	10	52	43	29
Westminster	36	44	20	44	38	33	40	62
Arvada	37	60	56	56	39	53	38	51
Parker	38		18	63	16	46	46	10
Teller County	39		23	25	49	48	44	27
Trinidad	40	76	37	57	65	65	24	54
Sterling	41		17	42	27	30	47	39
Pueblo *	42	48	28	27	72	69	26	22
Wheat Ridge	43	58	27	52	25	29	50	45
Lakewood	44	53	48	65	46	42	45	63
Denver/Southeast	45	68	55	76	30	71	36	72
Denver/Montbello	46	72	65	74	61	75	27	73
Northglenn	47		42	60	40	36	55	58
Eagle County	48		16	9	67	6	57	4
Boulder	49	49	43	50	15	59	58	43
Pueblo	50	64	66	70	68	67	42	57
Federal Heights	51		36	68	22	40	60	60

COLORADO: A Newcomer's Manual

Community * = Unincorporated	Safety Rating	H	RP	RB	A	B	L	A
Denver/Southwest	52	69	59	75	52	76	32	77
La Junta	53		76	40	28	20	52	78
Longmont	54		41	51	13	43	67	46
Woodland Park	55			31	34	61	63	23
Adams County *	56	63	40	64	53	66	48	71
Manitou Springs	57			48	42	73	56	59
Craig	58	71	80	47	44	54	62	31
Lamar	59		39	21	59	50	51	74
Greeley	60	51	54	61	21	51	69	53
Colorado Springs	61	50	69	71	43	60	64	61
Brighton	62		64	54	71	56	54	47
Canon City	63	61	63	62	73	47	53	49
Thornton	64	46	49	66	62	55	59	64
Littleton	65		57	58	69	63	49	68
Fort Morgan	66		34	32	48	41	71	20
Fort Lupton	67		68	29	58	72	61	50
Cortez	68		58	49	47	28	72	44
Alamosa	69		74	67	78	62	65	55
Montrose	70	67	75	33	75	45	73	42
Aurora	71	54	62	77	76	70	66	69
Greenwood Village	72		38	73	51	49	74	67
Glenwood Springs	73	73		24	60	22	77	56
Denver/Northwest	74	77	72	79	64	79	70	79
Durango	75	62	50	53	79	58	78	76
Grand Junction	76	66	67	69	80	78	76	66
Commerce City	77	56	73	78	77	77	75	75
Denver/Northeast	78	79	77	80	74	80	68	80
Aspen	79			28	70	74	79	65
Summit County *	80	70		37	50	64	80	48

NOTE: Blank spaces in crime columns indicate no crimes of that type were reported to the Colorado Bureau of Investigation in 1994.

EMPLOYMENT

In February 1995, the Colorado Department of Labor and Employment released their report on Colorado Occupational Employment Outlook 1994-1999. This 35 page report contains data on the growth expected in virtually every occupation. This information is helpful for those contemplating a move to Colorado and to those deciding on educational and career goals. A summary of this report appears below.

Approximately 46% of the jobs created by growth from 1994-1999 is expected to come from two major occupational categories: Professional / Para-Professional / Technical, and Services. Job growth in the Sales, Clerical / Administrative Support, and Blue Collar positions should account for an additional 43% of total new job growth. The remaining 11% will occur in Managerial/Administrative, and Agriculture/Forestry/Fishing.

Professional/Para-Professional/Technical (including Education and Computer Sciences), and the Services Sector are anticipated to continue their dominance as the generator of the largest number of new positions. Although all subsectors with the exception of Hospitals and Legal Services are predicted to grow at a rapid pace, almost two-thirds of the new services positions are expected to be created by Business Services, Health Services, and Engineering, Accounting, Research, Management, and Related Services.

The Trade Sector is expected to produce jobs at just over half the rate of the Services sector. The largest increase will be in Restaurants and Bars, Building Materials and Mobile Home Dealers, Apparel and Accessory Stores, and Furniture and Home Furnishings. Declining employment is not foreseen in any of the Trade Sector Divisions.

Transportation, Communications, and Public Utilities are expected to have the third highest growth rate. Motor Freight Transportation and Warehousing will be the greatest contributor of new positions. Communications is expected to create 522 new jobs per year and the opening of Denver International Airport is expected to benefit both the Transportation by Air and Transportation Services.

The Finance, Insurance and Real Estate Sector has a predicted growth rate of 1.9% generating 2,080 positions annually. The highest rate is predicted for the Security and Commodity Brokers and Credit Agencies other than banks.

Although **Manufacturing** has been in decline in recent years and roughly one-third of its subsectors are expected to decline over the next five years, this sector, as a whole, is expected to grow at a rate of 2.4% from 1994-1999. The largest increases are projected in Lumber and Wood Products, Machinery, Electrical/Electronic Equipment, and Printing/Publishing. The six declining subsectors include Food Products, Textiles, Chemicals, Transportation Equipment, Instruments/Photographic Equipment, and Miscellaneous Manufacturing Industries.

Overall, the **Mining** industry will be declining at a rate of 1.4% annually with the exception of Bituminous Coal/Lignite Mining and Nonmetallic Minerals which will grow at an annual rate of 0.2% and 0.7% respectively.

The Construction Sector, although expected to incur losses over the next five years, will retain levels considerably higher than the majority of those seen over the past decade. Annual job loss for the entire industry is expected to be 1,160.

Local Government is expected to far exceed State and Federal Government in growth. Anticipated job growth at the local level is 2,680 positions per year. State Government will provide 980 positions annually while another 1,900 new positions are expected from the Federal Government level.

ADDITIONAL RESOURCES
Publications produced (including the one used for this section) by the Labor Market Information Section of the Colorado State Department of Labor and Employment, 1515 Arapahoe St., Denver, CO 80202, 303-620-4718:

Occupational Employment Survey; Occupational Supply/Demand Report; Occupational Employment Statistics Wage Survey; Job Bank Wage Listing; Colorado Labor Market Information Directory; Occupation Information System (on-line).

COLORADO LARGEST EMPLOYERS

I once interviewed for a high-paying position with an "International Corporation." The interview was conducted in an expensively furnished office and the offers were very generous—too generous. Listening to my intuition, I did some checking and discovered I was dealing with a "paper" corporation with questionable resources and intentions. If you are looking for a position and come across one with United Airlines, Hewlett Packard, UPS or another "household" name, you probably won't have doubts about the offer. Below is a list of many lesser known regional or state-wide companies which employ between 100-16,000 in Colorado. If you like the security of working for a "large and stable" company, this list may help you sort through the classifieds.

ACX Technologies	Exabyte Corp.	MDC Holdings Inc.
Adolph Coors Co	First Bank System	Mercantile Stores
Air Methods Corp.	First Federal Savings	Mewmont Gold Co.
ARA Services	Fischer Imaging Corp.	Neodata Services
Assoc. Natural Gas Corp.	Forest Oil Corp.	Newmont Mining Corp.
Ball Corp.	Gerrity Oil & Gas Corp.	Norwest Corp.
Basin Exploration	Goldenbanks of CO.	OEA Inc.
Bestop Inc.	Good Times Restaurants	PCL Construction
BI Incorporated	Grease Monkey	Public Service Co of CO
Big O Tires Inc.	Guaranty National Corp.	Random Access Inc.
Candy's Tortilla Factory	Hach Co.	Safeway
Comm. Bankcorp of CO.	Hauser Chem Research	Southland Corp.
CommNet Cellular Inc.	Hugh M. Woods	Storage Technology Corp.
ConAgra (Monfort)	Jones Intercable Inc.	Synergen Inc.
Confertech International	King Soopers	Tele-Communications Inc.
Cyprus Amax Minerals	KN Energy Inc.	Total Petroleum
Dayton/Hudson Corp.	Manville Corp.	U.S. West Inc.
Eastman Kodak	Marquest Medical Prods.	Vicorp Restaurants Inc.
EG&G (Rocky Flats)	May Co./Foley's	Western Gas Resources
Electromedics Inc.	MCI Communications	

HEALTH CARE

FACTS AT A GLANCE (1990 DATA)
PHYSICIANS: 202 per 100,000 population
HOSPITAL DAILY ROOM CHARGE: $262 (my recent stay cost $687 per day)
DENTISTS: 66 per 100,000 population
INFANT MORTALITY RATE, ALL RACES: 9.3 deaths per 1,000 live births
LEGAL ABORTIONS RATE: 335 per 1,000 live births
DEATHS, ACCIDENTS: 38.4 per 100,000 residents
DEATHS, CANCER: 133.4 per 100,000 residents
DEATHS, HEART DISEASE: 197.7 per 100,000 residents
DEATHS, HOMICIDE: 7.3 per 100,000 residents
DEATHS, LIVER DISEASE AND CIRRHOSIS: 9.5 per 100,000 residents
DEATHS, PNEUMONIA AND FLU: 26.4 per 100,000 residents
DEATHS, SUICIDE: 17.6 per 100,000 residents
AIDS CASES REPORTED, 1983-1989: 1,159
AIDS CASES REPORTED, 1989: 315
AIDS CASES REPORTED, 1989 (RATE): 11.54 per 100,000 residents
DEATHS AMONG AIDS CASES, 1983-1989: 649

HEALTH CARE FACILITIES

To describe every health care facility in Colorado would take 257, 8 1/2 x 11 pages. Suffice it to say, for most of us, having a hospital within an hour of home is good enough. Knowing most ski resorts have some type of emergency facilities and all but the most rugged mountain terrain can be reached by Air Rescue/Ambulance should ease our fears of injury or serious illness. But what if you or a family member have special medical needs or you are planning a rural move and would like to know what facilities are nearby? There are 20 separate directories available from the Colorado Department of Health and Environment, 4300 Cherry Creek Dr. S., #A200, Denver, CO 80222-1530, 303-692-2800, which contain complete data. Prices range from $1.25 for a 2-7 page report to $6.00 for the largest at 60 pages and include postage. Prices are less if picked-up and the maximum charge is $12.00 up to and including the entire set. Below is a list of the directories and respective page counts. Call the CDHE for the most current pricing and availability.

Alternative Care Facilities, 10	Mammography Facilities, 11
Ambulatory Surgical Centers, 5	Nursing Homes - Alphabetic, 24
Community Clinics, 7	Nursing Homes by City, 24
Community Mental Health Clinics, 4	Nursing Homes by County, 26
Elderly, Blind, Disabled Facilities, 13	Occupational Therapy Facilities, 3
End Stage Renal Dialysis Units, 3	Personal Care Boarding Homes, 60
Home Health Agencies, 19	Physical Therapy Facilities, 17
Hospices, 5	Portable X-Ray Units, 2
Hospitals - Alphabetic, 13	Rural Health Clinics, 4
Intermediate Care Facilities, 2	Swing Beds, 5

TAXES

Everyone's favorite subject. In addition to Federal Income Taxes, Colorado residents are subject to Colorado State Income Taxes, State Sales Tax, there are some County and City Sales Taxes and various Special Taxes.

STATE INCOME TAX

Colorado's personal income tax is 5% of what you claim as your federal taxable income (after all deductions and adjustments). If you work for someone else you will notice state withholding from every paycheck. If you are self-employed, you are responsible for estimated payments and collections just as with federal. This 5% also applies to corporations. Residency determines whether 100% or some lesser proportions is allocated to Colorado. Residents are allowed credit for tax payments to another state.

STATE/COUNTY/CITY SALES TAX

The State of Colorado has a flat 3% sales tax on the purchase price of retail sales of tangible personal property. This tax also applies to used vehicles and certain services such as telephone. Many counties and cities also have sales taxes which vary and can be as high as 4% for counties and 5% in cities. In addition, certain districts have Special Taxes for Public Transportation, the new Baseball Stadium, Cultural Facilities, Highway Construction and the like. The bottom line is this: in some counties you will pay only 3% sales tax on everything you buy and in others it can be three times that amount. But don't bother going to another county to buy your new $30,000 Range Rover to save the extra $2000 in taxes. Taxes on such purchases are based on your address of record, not where you purchase the vehicle. And if you buy all new furniture in a county without extra taxes and pick it up yourself you are fine. However, if you have it delivered to a county/city with extra taxes, and the retailer has a store there, you pay. The same applies to mail orders when the company has a store in your county/city. Real simple, eh?

HIDDEN TAXES

As mentioned above, you will pay the appropriate amount of sales tax on all vehicle purchases. However, you can also expect to pay additional taxes when you register and title your vehicle. This is better explained in Chapter Five. Every time you have an alcoholic beverage you are paying a hidden tax imposed on the manufacturer. This tax ranges from 8 cents a gallon on beer to 60.27 cents per liter on liquor. If you smoke you pay 20 cents tax per pack and 20% of list price on all other tobacco products. Every time you bet on a horse or tell the dealer to "hit me," you are paying special taxes. And let's not forget about the 22 cents per gallon on gasoline, etc., etc. Call the Department of Revenue with any specific questions.

CHAPTER FIVE
BEHIND THE WHEEL

VEHICLES
Registration/Titles, Tags, Insurance, Emissions, Drivers' Licenses

> The information in this chapter was compiled from various sources including, but not limited to, government reports and publications (Federal, State, and Local); materials provided by business and civic organizations; and books produced by independent Colorado publishers including:
>
> *Colorado Revised Statutes 1995, Vehicles and Traffic*, Bradford Publishing
>
> For a complete description of the above books and related titles, please see the Publisher's listing in Appendix A.

On April 25, 1901, New York became the first state to require automobile license plates; the fee was $1. Today, if you are a resident in the City and County of Denver and purchase a new sport utility vehicle (the vehicle of choice in Colorado) for around $25,000, it will cost you approximately $2,500 for title, taxes, and tags. In addition, you can expect to pay approximately $600 the following year to renew the tags. This fee is gradually reduced on the 3rd, 5th, and 10th year of ownership.

That is probably why I kept both my Florida driver's license and the Florida tags on my vehicle for almost 5 years after I moved to Denver (which, contrary to what I may state elsewhere in this book, was many, many years ago and I'm sure the Statute of Limitations for my heinous offense has since expired). I was lucky to get away with it as long as I did. But this was a time before the Department of Revenue initiated its violator Hotline. Recently, this Hotline was established so people could call and turnin anyone (noisy neighbors, ex-lovers, or anyone from California) who they believed where living in Colorado yet keeping out-of-state plates or DL's. The Hotline was flooded with reports and the dreaded "Truant Title and Tag Police" went into action.

It turns out many of the offenders were long-time Colorado residents who would register their $25,000 Chevy Blazer in another neighboring state where the whole shebang only cost about $10 per year. Shame! Shame!

All kidding and serious warnings aside, when I did finally decide (not by choice) to become an officially registered and tagged citizen of Colorado, I found the entire process very confusing and frustrating. I couldn't get my vehicle plates because I did not have an emissions test; I couldn't get an emissions test because my vehicle was titled and tagged in Florida. They wouldn't accept a bill of sale written on a vodka and tonic stained bar napkin and they told me when I went to trade in my Florida driver's License that someone with *my* name, height, weight, address, etc., already was in possession of a Colorado ID card (quite illegal you know). O.K., maybe it wasn't all that bad, but it can be a very frustrating process if you don't know everything "you should have known" before attempting the big switch-over.

Hopefully, this chapter will help prevent a great deal of aggravation by providing you with the basic information "you should have known."

NOTE: Everything in this chapter only applies to on-road vehicles. All off-road vehicles (3 or 4 wheel ATV's, Boats, Snowmobiles, etc.,) which are not required to have a tag, are required to have an annual registration sticker. This process is handled by the State Department of Resources, Division of Parks and Recreation, Registration Division. Many county offices carry the proper forms or the entire process can be completed through the mail. Write or call:

> Division of Parks & Recreation
> Registration Division
> P.O. Box 231
> Littleton, CO 80160
> 303-791-1920

REGISTRATIONS/TITLES

> Every citizen of Colorado who owns or drives a vehicle is required to have a Colorado Driver's License, Colorado Vehicle Title and Registration, and Colorado Vehicle License Plates. You become a citizen of the state at the first occurrence of the following: Working at any type of job, owning or operating a business in Colorado, or living here for more than 90 days. In other words, unless you are independently wealthy, this means almost immediately upon moving here. There are certain exceptions for special employment situations, military personnel and students. See the section on Drivers' Licenses.

A vehicle registration is that little piece of white paper you only see after you have been asked for it by a police officer. A vehicle title is the more official looking document which proves you do in fact own the vehicle (with or without liens).

CHAPTER FIVE: BEHIND THE WHEEL

Although these are two separate documents, the information, applications, and fees for both are combined into one process in Colorado.

In all counties except Denver, this process is handled by the County Clerk or Motor Vehicle Office. The end of this section provides a list of County Clerk's phone numbers for each county. Denver has several locations which are also listed. **You must register your vehicle in the county where you reside.**

Below, the requirements for registering and titling a vehicle are covered for three different contingencies: bringing a vehicle in from another state, buying a new or used vehicle from a dealer within Colorado, and buying a used vehicle from a private owner.

TRANSFERRING STATES

When transferring a vehicle from another state, you must have the following:

- Certificate of Title for the vehicle
- Current Registration
- Vehicle Identification Number (VIN) verification completed by a:
  - Licensed Vehicle Dealer
  - Emissions Testing Station
  - Law Enforcement Agency
- Emissions Test Certificate (where required, see Emissions Section)

BUYING FROM A DEALER

The process here depends on how you pay for your new/used vehicle. If you pay cash, the dealer will issue a temporary tag and hand you the rest of the paperwork. You then have to proceed to the proper office and go from there. Assuming, especially on new car purchases, you have some type of financing, the process is a little different. In this case, the dealer will send the proper information to the leinholder who will take care of the titling work. Once the county receives an O.K. from the leinholder, you will be notified by postcard and will then have to go to the proper office and apply for permanent tags.

Note: Most car dealers are authorized to collect state sales tax, some county and city taxes, and certain fees involved. It's best to make sure you know what taxes and fees are covered in the purchase price so you don't get a rude awakening when you go to apply for tags.

BUYING FROM A PRIVATE OWNER

Let's say you can't exactly afford the new $25,000 Jeep you want so you settle for another used vehicle from a private owner. In this situation, you will need the following:

- A signed (and possibly notarized, see note below) Vehicle Title.
- A recent (within 120 days) emission test (where required) provided by the Seller.
- A notarized bill of sale indicating purchase price (see note below).

Titles: All Colorado titles issued after January 1, 1990 no longer require a notary. There is a space on the back where the purchase price is entered. Titles issued before January 1, 1990 do require the seller(s) to sign the title in the presence of a notary public. If the vehicle has an out-of-state title you would be well advised to check with your county clerk to verify the requirements. Also, make sure the current title is in the name of the individual selling the car and that nothing has been filled-in or "whited-out" on the back. The powers that be frown upon third-party title transfers and white-out.

Bill of Sale: Although not required, especially for titles issued after January, 1990, it is well worth the effort to obtain a notarized bill of sale showing the vehicle make, model, year, and VIN number along with the purchase price. The amount of sales tax the state, county or city collects is based on your purchase price and they do have the option to collect taxes based on the current blue-book value of the vehicle if the purchase price you declare is in doubt and you do not have a notarized bill of sale as proof.

Taxes and fees: There are many taxes and fees involved in transferring a title and getting tags. These include title fee of $5.50, registration fee, license fee based on the weight of the vehicle, ownership taxes based on the age and original value, sales taxes (state and possibly county and city), and depending on your county, additional miscellaneous fees. When buying from a private owner, you will have to pay all this when you transfer and register.

PHONE LIST FOR COUNTY CLERKS

ADAMS	303-654-6010	HUERFANO	719-738-2380
ALAMOSA	719-589-6681	JACKSON	970-723-4334
ARAPAHOE	303-795-4500	KIOWA	719-438-5421
ARCHULETA	970-264-5633	KIT CARSON	719-346-8638
BACA	719-523-4372	LAKE	719-486-1410
BENT	719-456-2009	LA PLATA	970-259-4000
BOULDER	303-441-3510	LARIMER	970-498-7878
CHAFFEE	719-539-4004	LAS ANIMAS	719-846-3314
CHEYENNE	719-767-5685	LINCOLN	719-743-2444
CLEAR CREEK	303-569-3251	LOGAN	970-522-1544
CONEJOS	719-376-5422	MESA	970-244-1664
COSTILLA	719-672-3301	MINERAL	719-658-2440
CROWLEY	719-267-4643	MOFFAT	970-824-5484
CUSTER	719-783-2441	MONTEZUMA	970-565-3728
DELTA	970-874-2150	MONTROSE	970-249-3362
*DENVER	303-576-2882	MORGAN	970-867-5616
DOLORES	970-677-2381	OTERO	719-384-8701
DOUGLAS	303-660-7440	OURAY	970-325-4961
EAGLE	303-328-8710	PARK	719-836-2771
ELBERT	303-621-2341	PHILLIPS	970-854-3131
EL PASO	719-520-6240	PITKIN	970-920-5180
FREMONT	719-275-1522	PROWERS	719-336-4337
GARFIELD	970-945-2377	PUEBLO	719-583-6507
GILPIN	303-582-5321	RIO BLANCO	970-878-5068
GRAND	970-725-3347	RIO GRANDE	719-657-3334
GUNNISON	970-641-1602	ROUTT	970-879-1710
HINSDALE	970-944-2228	SAGUACHE	719-655-2512

CHAPTER FIVE: BEHIND THE WHEEL

SAN JUAN	970-387-5671	
SAN MIGUEL	970-728-3954	
SEDGWICK	970-474-4436	
SUMMIT	970-668-5623	
TELLER	719-689-2951	
WASHINGTON	970-345-6565	
WELD	970-353-3840	
YUMA	970-332-5809	

Denver Motor Vehicles Division
Office hours: 7:30 - 5:30
Southeast - Fairways Shopping Center, 10890 E. Dartmouth Ave.
Southwest - Bear Valley Shopping Center, 3100 S. Sheridan
Northwest - (by Safeway), 3698 W. 44th Ave.
Five Points - 2736 Welton, 2nd Fl.
Montbello - 4695 Peoria

LICENSE PLATES (TAGS)

The procedure for obtaining license plates is covered in the previous section, Registrations/Titles. This section provides information about the various types of plates available and the requirements for special plates.

There are 47 different types of plates issued in Colorado. 6 are for vehicle manufacturers or dealers, 6 are government-type plates issued to city, county, and state vehicles, with special plates for State Senators, State Representatives, members of Congress, U.S. Senators and members of the Honorary Consular Corps. Several more are issued to utility companies, farm vehicles, commercial fleets, and tractor/trailer rigs or heavy trucks.

For the rest of us, a wide choice of standard or custom versions is offered. The most common plate is the standard green mountains with white background. A second version, called DENIM, is white and blue and shows the Colorado "C". Both versions can be personalized with a 10 - 12 week waiting period. A third type is the "Always Buy Colorado" which is a limited edition of 1,000 plates. All the above come in two classes:

Passenger: Passenger vehicles, station wagons, hearses, ambulances (non-government), passenger vans, buses, and motor homes.

Light Trucks: Empty weight less than 16,000 pounds, body designed to transport property with special fees for tow trucks, wreckers, race horse vehicles, veterinary mobile trucks, and special use vehicles.

OTHER VEHICLE CLASSES:

Recreational Truck: Trucks which do not have an empty weight over 6,500 pounds and are not used exclusively for pleasure (non-commercial), plate configuration always begins with "3."

Trailer: Wheeled vehicle without motive power.

Motorcycle: Motor vehicle designed to travel on no more than 3 wheels.

Collector Series: Vehicles at least 25 years old, passenger and trucks, not for commercial use. Plates are issued for a 5 year period.

Street Rod: Issued to passenger and light trucks made in 1948 or earlier.

Horseless Carriage: Manufactured in 1942 or prior. Driving limited to/from auto club functions, to/from repair shops, occasional leisure drive.

OTHER CUSTOMS PLATES:

Special Organizational: "Naval Reserve"—to individuals in the Naval Reserve. "Honorably Discharged Veteran"—available to any person who has received an honorable discharge from any branch of the U.S. Armed Services. Issued to passenger and light trucks. One set only.

Disabled Veteran: One free set to qualifying applicant (50% or more permanent service connected disability occurring prior to 5/7/75). Issued to passenger, light truck, recreational truck, farm truck or motor home weighing less than 6,500 pounds.

Former Prisoner of War: One free set to qualifying applicant (on active duty with U.S. Armed Forces during a period of armed conflict and was incarcerated by an enemy of the U.S.). Issued to same vehicles as above.

Persons with Disability: Issued to passenger, light truck or mobile homes. Application must be signed by Colorado licensed physician.

Amateur Radio/Commercial Call Letters: Issued to passenger and light trucks with an empty weight of less than 5,000 pounds. One set per amateur call letter, up to 10 sets per commercial call letter.

For additional information concerning special or custom plates, call the State Motor Vehicle Division at 303-572-5607.

VEHICLE INSURANCE

Vehicle insurance is MANDATORY in Colorado. In fact, there are 41 Colorado Revised Statues under Article 7, Motor Vehicle Financial Responsibility Law. When you go to register your vehicles you must sign a sworn statement indicating you now carry and will continue to carry the proper insurances. The mandatory liability minimum is $25,000 bodily injury, $50,000 per accident, and $15,000 property damage. You are required to have proof of insurance with you at all times when driving and failure to do so can result in a mandatory court appearance and possible fines. The courts in this state tend to go ballistic on one involved in an accident without proper insurance coverage!

The only exception to the above are those who qualify for a certificate of self-insurance. Don't count on it. C.R.S. 42-7-501 reads as follows:

"Any person in whose name more than twenty-five motor vehicles are registered may qualify as a self-insurer. . . when the director [of motor vehicles] is satisfied that such person is possessed and will continue to be possessed of ability to pay all judgments which may be obtained against such person."

EMISSIONS TESTING

You can save yourself a lot of brain-damage by skipping this section unless you plan to, or currently live in **or work** in the following counties:

Enhanced Program Area: Adams, Arapahoe, Boulder, Denver, Douglas and Jefferson counties.

Basic Program Area: El Paso, Larimer, Pitkin and Weld counties.

Due to several factors (topography, heavy industry, and an increasing number of automobiles), the front-range of Colorado—especially the greater Denver metro region—suffers from what is known as the "Brown Cloud." When conditions are right, this cloud of pollutants can easily be seen from miles away. In an attempt to reduce the major source of pollutants (automobile emissions), the state's Air Care Colorado Program has recently intensified its effort to reduce emissions by instituting a more stringent testing program along with the older "tailpipe" test which has existed for years.

This effort has not been without its difficulties. The new test and testing facilities have been under attack since their inception from both consumers and some state legislators alike. Horror stories about invalid results, very costly vehicle repairs, and long-long lines abound. Regardless, if you live or work in any of the above listed counties (exceptions noted below), you MUST have a valid emissions test to register your vehicle and a valid emissions sticker on the windshield of your car or truck.

ENHANCED PROGRAM AREA

1981 and older vehicles: A tailpipe test is required each year at an Air Care Colorado Facility or an independent test-only station.

1982 and newer vehicles: An enhanced emissions test (on a dynamometer under actual driving conditions) is required at an Air Care Colorado facility every two years. Odd-year vehicles must be tested in 1995 and even-year vehicles in 1996.

Change of ownership: An emissions test is required when a vehicle is sold or its ownership changes. The seller is responsible for obtaining the test.

Commuters: Vehicles registered outside of the region but which are driven into the six county area 90 or more days a year must also undergo the tests.

Newly manufactured vehicles: Any new, never titled, vehicle is exempt from the emissions test for four years, or until a change of ownership. *(Like, if you sell a brand new car one day after you get it, somehow it magically becomes capable of polluting).*

Cost: $24.25 for 1982 and newer vehicles - 2 year sticker.
           $15.00 for 1981 and older vehicles - 1 year sticker.

Tips to ease the pain:

- Check your emissions sticker for the expiration date and have your vehicle tested promptly.
- Call the Air Care Colorado **Hotline at 303-456-7090** for the best time and most convenient locations (see map).
- Standard hours of operation are M-F, 7:00 a.m. to 7:30 p.m., and Sat., 8:00 a.m. to 3:00 p.m. Closed Sundays and State Holidays.
- Avoid the busiest times—the first three days and the last three days of each month, as well as any time during the noon hour.

- Make certain your vehicle has a gas cap.
- Cash and checks are accepted, but **NOT credit cards**.
- **Warm up your engine** thoroughly for at least 15 minutes before testing.
- All-Wheel and four-wheel drive vehicles must use specially marked testing lanes (make sure you don't wait in the wrong lanes).
- If your vehicle fails the test you can have it retested free after repairs within 10 days of the initial test.
- In the Enhanced Program Area, test and repairs **are not** done at the same facility.

Now, if that's not confusing enough, there are certain parts of Adams and Arapahoe counties that are completely exempt from any testing. In General, if you live east of Kiowa Creek you are exempt. However, as stated above, if you work west of Kiowa Creek, you need the test (see the map of enhanced testing stations on page 100). The same degree of confusion applies to the Basic Program Area covered next.

BASIC PROGRAM AREA

In the basic program area (El Paso, Larimer, Pitkin, and Weld counties), all vehicles, regardless of age (except new, never been titled) are required to have an annual tailpipe test only. There are independent inspection and repair facilities and inspections and repairs **can be** performed at the same facility.

The cost for this test is $15.00 and 1982 and newer vehicles receive a 2 year sticker and 1981 and older a 1 year.

Now, all of Pitkin county participates, most of El Paso out to and including Ellicot, a large portion of Larimer county including Loveland, Fort Collins and Poudre Park participates, yet Estes Park, Rustic and Virginia Dale areas are completely exempt. As far as Weld county is concerned, only the city of Greeley is involved, the remainder of the county is exempt from all testing. But remember the Commuters Regulation about working in a covered area. If in doubt, call the Air Care Colorado Hotline at 303-456-7090.

DRIVER'S LICENSE

In the event you skipped the previous sections of this chapter, Colorado laws state you must obtain a Colorado driver's license and vehicle plates immediately upon becoming a citizen. The state considers you a citizen upon the first occurrence of the following: you work at any type of gainful employment, you own or operate a business in Colorado, or you live here for 90 days or more.

The information presented in this section is intended as a guideline. For complete information please obtain a copy of the *Colorado Drivers' Manual and Supplemental Motorcycle Drivers' Manual.*

Any person 16 years of age or older who operates a motor vehicle or motor driven cycle (including MOPEDS) on the public streets and highways is required to have a valid license. The only exceptions to this are as follows:

Special Employment: Any resident who is employed in another state where the laws of that state require licensing to drive in order to engage in a regular trade or

CHAPTER FIVE: BEHIND THE WHEEL

profession, does not need a Colorado DL as long as such other license to drive is in force and the employment is not terminated. This exemption applies only if the other state is a member of the Interstate Driver License Compact Agreement.

Other Exemptions: The following need not obtain a Colorado license provided they are 16 years of age or older and possess a valid license from their home state or state of last assignment.

- **Military:** Anyone who is serving as a member of the Armed Forces of the U.S. on active duty including the spouse and children of such member.
- **Foreign Military:** On duty or assigned to temporary duty with the U.S. Armed Forces to include the spouse and children of such member.
- **Students:** Any non-resident who is temporarily residing in Colorado for the principal purpose of furthering his/her education and who is considered a non-resident for tuition purposes. If a student, regardless of the above, also works (even part-time) in Colorado, he/she needs both a Colorado DL and plates.
- **Trainees/Instructors:** Any employee of a Colorado licensed company, corporation, organization, school or business who is assigned temporarily in Colorado for the principle purpose of receiving or teaching special training relative to his trade, profession or employment.
- **Non-Resident Aliens:** Foreign tourists, instructors and business persons may drive up to one year with their own personal DL. Such foreign DL and/or permits issued by foreign countries are recognized when the holder has a valid U.S. Immigration Form 1-94, Arrival/Departure Record, and is driving any private (non-commercial) vehicle including rental vehicles.

Colorado issues five classifications of DL's.

The Class R (basic license) applies to any vehicle with a GVWR of less than 26,001 lbs., as a single unit or in combination, manufactured to transport 15 or fewer passengers including the driver, and not used to transport hazardous materials. The Class R license is valid for chauffeur purposes and for motorized bicycles (MOPEDS).

The Class M (motorcycle) license is valid for any vehicle designed to travel on not more than three wheels in contact with the ground except any such vehicle as may be included within the term farm vehicle or motorized bicycle.

Commercial Driver's License: There are 3 classes of CDL's which are covered in the Colorado Drivers' Manual.

NOTE: If you drive both automobiles and motorcycles, you do not need two licenses. For qualified applicants, a motorcycle endorsement is added to the Class R license.

NEW RESIDENTS WITH A VALID LICENSE

If you are 16 years of age or older and have a valid license in your possession which was issued by another U.S. state, territory or possession, you will normally not be required to take the road performance test nor written examination if the out-of-state license is similar to the Colorado classified driver's license and you surrender the valid out-of-state license.

The driver examiner has a responsibility to require a road performance test, even if you turn in a valid license, if there appears to be a problem with your Physical Aptitude Analysis (obvious disabilities), your Driving Record Analysis, or your Visual Screening (required in all cases).

Should you fail the road performance test, you will be issued an Instruction Permit. When you return to complete the test, both the Instruction Permit and any driver's license must be surrendered.

FEES: $15 for 5-year license, $16 if motorcycle endorsement was part of old license. Add $16 for new motorcycle endorsements.

NOTE: If you plan to drive a motorcycle in Colorado and you do not have a motorcycle endorsement on your previous license you will be required to take both the written and motorcycle driving skills test.

Renewal of A Colorado License or Instruction Permit: Once you obtain a Colorado Classified Driver's License or Instruction Permit, you will not normally have to repeat the written or driving test unless:

- You apply for a different class of license or endorsement
- You receive traffic tickets (8 or more points)
- The license or permit is canceled, revoked or denied
- You let the license or permit expire

You Can Lose Your License: All reports of traffic accidents and traffic law violations committed in Colorado are posted to your record. A poor record may be cause for suspension or revocation of your driving privilege. Suspension may be for any period up to one year. Revocation must be for at least one year.

POINTS ASSESSED

12 Points:	Leaving scene of accident, DWI or under the influence of drugs, Speed contests, Eluding or attempting to elude a police officer
8 Points:	Driving while ability is impaired by alcohol, Reckless driving
6 Points:	Failure to stop for a school bus
4 Points:	Careless driving or following too closely, Driving on wrong side of road, Improper passing, Failure to observe traffic sign or signal, Failure to yield to emergency vehicle, Failure to maintain or show proof of insurance
3 Points:	Failure to yield right-of-way, Improper turn, Driving through safety zone, Driving in wrong lane or direction on one-way street, Conviction of violations not listed
2 Points:	Failure to signal or improper signal, Improper backing, Failure to dim or turn on lights, Operating an unsafe vehicle
	Speeding over posted limit
1 Point	1 - 4 m.p.h.
3 Points	5 - 9 m.p.h.
4 Points	10 -19 m.p.h.
6 points	20 - or more m.p.h.

CHAPTER FIVE: BEHIND THE WHEEL

YOUR DRIVING PRIVILEGE MAY BE SUSPENDED/REVOKED/CANCELED IF YOU:
- Are convicted of DUI of alcohol or drugs
- Refuse to be tested for alcohol or drug content
- Leave the scene of an accident without stopping, exchanging information, and rendering aid
- Fail to report an accident to the Colorado Motor Vehicle Division according to the requirements of the financial responsibility law
- Give false information on your drivers' license application
- Fail to settle a judgment against you as a result of an accident while operating a vehicle
- Lend your license to someone else or misuse it in any way
- Alter or deface your license
- Fail to appear for a special reexamination requested by the Motor Vehicle Division
- Use a motor vehicle in committing a felony
- Are convicted of manslaughter as a result of a motor vehicle accident

If you are convicted of driving "while under suspension," your driving privilege will be suspended again effective for ONE YEAR FROM THE DATE YOU WOULD HAVE BEEN REINSTATED.

RE-EXAMINATION OF DRIVERS

You may be required to submit to a reexamination if the Motor Vehicle Division has good cause to believe you are incompetent or otherwise not qualified to be licensed. After you have taken the examination, your license may be returned, suspended, revoked, or you may be issued a restricted license. Refusal to submit to this test is grounds for suspension or revocation of your license.

COLORADO POINT SYSTEM

There is a specified number of points assigned for most traffic law violations. If you accumulate a certain number of points, your license may be suspended for up to one year. Points assessed against your record are not erased when you get a new license.

A driver's license may be classified as a chauffeur license; however, the vehicle must be a public or common carrier. To qualify for chauffeur points, all violations must have been received as a chauffeur of a motor vehicle in use as a public or common carrier of persons or property.

The point accumulations for suspension are as follows:

Minor Driver: More than 5 points in any 12 consecutive months or more than 6 points for period of license.
Provisional Driver: 9 points in any 12 consecutive months or 12 points in any 24 consecutive months or 14 points for the period of the license.
Regular Driver: 12 points in any 12 consecutive months or 18 points in any 24 consecutive months.
Chauffeur Points: 16 points in any 12 consecutive months or 24 points in any 24 consecutive months or 28 points in any 48 consecutive months.

EXPRESSED CONSENT LAW (ALCOHOL & DRUGS)

The Expressed Consent Law provides that if a law enforcement officer suspects that a person is driving under the influence of alcohol or other drug substance and the driver refuses to take the required test, or if the result of such test indicates a blood alcohol concentration (BAC) of .10 or more, the officer will confiscate the driver's license and issue a "Notice of Revocation or Denial" which becomes a seven-(7) day driving permit. If you desire a hearing, a request must be made at a drivers' license office, or in writing, within the seven days allotted on the driving permit or else the revocation of the license and driving privilege becomes effective automatically. If you do not have a valid driver's license the "Notice of Revocation or Denial" issued by the officer DOES NOT become a seven day driving permit and only allows the person to request a hearing within the seven day period.

IDENTIFICATION CARDS

To obtain a Colorado ID card you must appear in person at any drivers' license office. You must present at least two (2) documents of identification to support your true name and correct birthday, such as a state certified birth certificate, marriage certificate, or other legal documents. Documented proof of a Social Security number is required. If you are under 60 years of age you will be required to pay the ID card fee.

THE DRIVER EXAMINATION

In order to receive a driver's license, there are five separate tests you will undergo: Driving Record Analysis, Physical Aptitude Analysis, Vision Screening, Basic Written Test, Driving Test.

OFFICE LOCATIONS

EXPRESS OFFICES (NO TESTING)

Colorado Springs: Mall Hours, Chapel Hills Mall, 1520 Brairgate Blvd.
Denver (839-1829): 8:30 - 4:30, M-F, 1560 Broadway.
Denver (292-9310): 8:30 - 4:30, M-F, 2736 Welton St.
Littleton: Mall Hours, Southwest Plaza Mall, 8501 W. Bowles Ave.
Westminster: Mall Hours, Westminster Mall, 5433 W. 8th Ave.
Englewood: 10:00 - 6:00, Tue - Sat, Cinderella City Mall, 701 W. Hampden.
Aurora: Mall Hours, Buckingham Square Mall, 1307 Joliet.
Arvada: 8:00 - 5:00, M-F, 7450 W. 52nd Ave., Unit O, (offers written test).
Aurora S.E.: 8:00 - 5:00, M-F, 13736 E. Quincy Ave., (offers written test).

BRANCH OFFICES (HOURS/DAYS VARY, CALL FOR DETAILS AND LOCATION)
(location given if phone number unavailable)

Akron	345-2624	Brighton	659-5055
Alamosa	589-4274	Buena Vista	395-2060
Aurora	344-8400	Burlington	346-8638
Bailey	838-4441	Calhan	Fire Station
Basalt	927-3919	Canon City	275-5617
Boulder	442-3006	Castle Rock	688-4625

CHAPTER FIVE: BEHIND THE WHEEL

Center	754-3497	Lakewood	986-2742
Central City	595-0133	Lamar	336-2670
Cheyenne Wells	Co. Courthouse	Las Animas	Co. Courthouse
Colorado Springs	594-8701	Leadville	486-0888
Conejos	376-5919	Littleton	795-5954
Cortez	565-9779	Longmont	776-4073
Craig	824-5447	Loveland	667-6497
Creede	658-2440	Meeker	878-5548
Del Norte	657-2708	Minturn	827-5252
Delta	874-9795	Monte Vista	852-3362
Denver	937-9507	Montrose	249-5426
Dove Creek	677-2283	Norwood	327-4226
Durango	247-4591	Nucla	864-7351
Eads	438-5421	Ordway	267-3134
Eagle	328-7346	Ouray	325-4323
Estes Park	586-5331	Pagosa Springs	City Ext Blvd.
Evergreen	674-4152	Pueblo	543-5164
Fairplay	836-2771	Rangely	675-2881
Fowler	City Hall	Rifle	625-2044
Frisco	668-5015	Saguache	605 Christie
Ft. Collins	223-3648	Salida	539-2802
Ft. Morgan	867-2647	San Luis	672-3882
Georgetown	569-2005	Security-Widefield	392-6101
Glenwood Springs	945-8229	Silverton	387-5671
Granby	887-3875	Springfield	523-4372
Grand Junction	248-7010	Steamboat Springs	879-0715
Greeley	352-5845	Sterling	522-5982
Gunnison	641-1052	Strasburg	Adams Co Bg.
Holyoke	854-3131	Thornton	287-8033
Hotchkiss	872-3663	Trinidad	846-4348
Hugo	743-2796	Walden	723-4334
Julesburg	474-3346	Walsenburg	738-2807
Kiowa	Elbert Crthse	Westcliffe	Co. Courthouse
Kremmling	Public Library	Woodland Park	687-2447
La Junta	384-2801	Wray	332-5855
Lake City	Co. Courthouse	Yuma	848-3878

COLORADO: A Newcomer's Manual

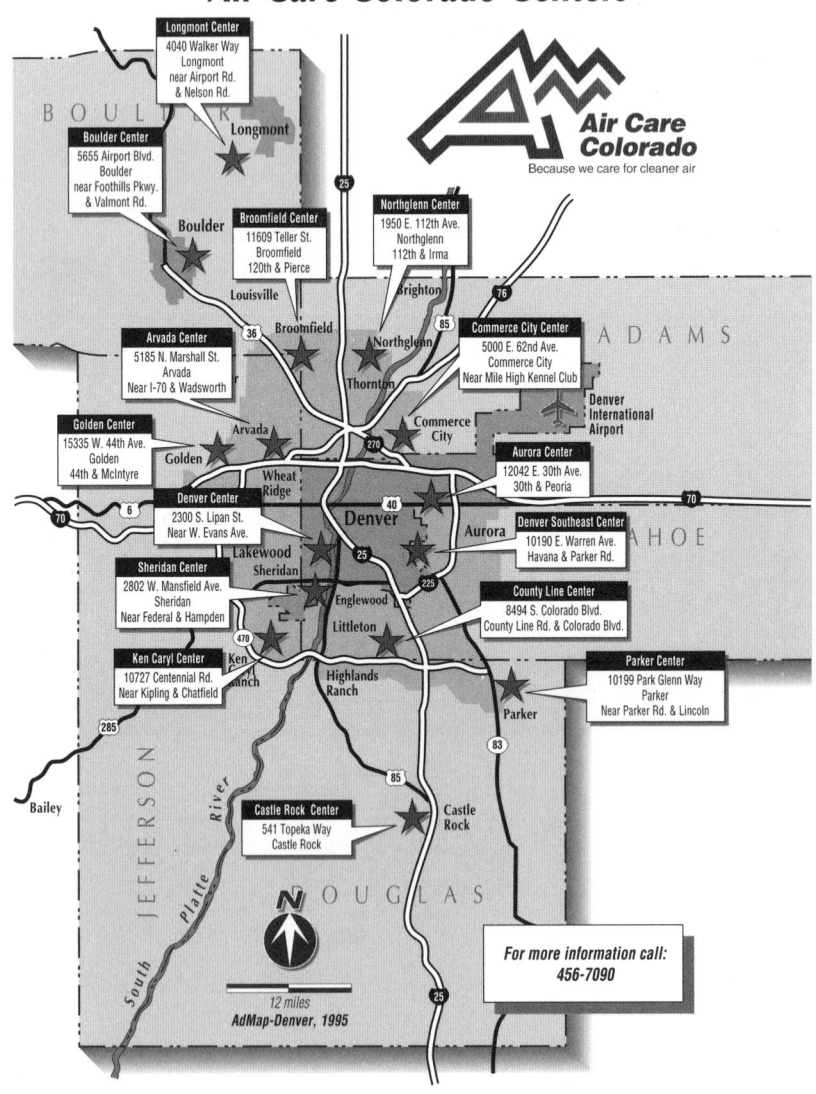

CHAPTER SIX
SEND LAWYERS, GUNS, AND MONEY

LAWS, RULES AND REGULATIONS

The information in this chapter was compiled from various sources including, but not limited to, government reports and publications (Federal, State, and Local); materials provided by business and civic organizations; and books produced by independent Colorado publishers including:

Colorado Revised Statues, 1995, Vehicles and Traffic;
Friendly Divorce Guidebook for Colorado;
Landlord & Tenant Guide to Colorado Evictions, all by Bradford Publishing
Discover The Good Life In Rural America, Communication Creativity

For a complete description of the above books and related titles, please see the Publisher's listing in Appendix A.

You just got married a month ago to your 15-year-old cousin who now wants a divorce and half of your winning Lotto ticket. So you go out to buy some liquor at the nearest drive-through using a check you know you can't cover and while having a few belts in the parking lot you get busted for DUI. On top of that, your landlord served you an eviction notice and the transaction on your new "For Sale by Owner" house is null and void because of bad paperwork. Maybe you should have read this chapter first. As the saying goes, "Ignorance of the law is no excuse."

DUI/DWAI

This section won't be a lecture on drinking and driving. However, a word of warning is warranted. In addition to the legal implications, DWI in Colorado can be quite hazardous to your health. A great number of people tend to drink and drive while on a weekend getaway to the mountains. DON'T! Imagine driving down unfamiliar, unlit, very narrow, very weavy, very slick mountain roads. Now imagine it after a couple of drinks.

In Colorado, a driver with a Blood Alcohol Content (BAC) between 0.05% and 0.09% is presumed to be driving with ability impaired (DWAI). If a driver's BAC is 0.10% or more, he is presumed to be driving under the influence (DUI). The penalties for DWAI/DUI are tough. If you drive with a BAC over .10% you will lose 100% of your driving privilege—no work license allowed—even if you will lose your job, you never had a ticket, or the court reduces or dismisses your DUI ticket. First offense DWAI can result in 8 points on your license, a $500 fine, up to 180 days in jail and 48 hours community service. You can be arrested for DWAI/DUI if you are in your car sitting in a parking lot, in an alley or parked on the street.

LIQUOR LAWS

Colorado has some strange liquor and beer codes. In California, I can walk into a 7-11 and buy liquor and munchies too. In Colorado, the only alcoholic beverage you can buy outside a liquor store or bar is 3.2% beer. Conversely, liquor stores can't sell food, snacks or anything else not directly related to the consumption of alcoholic beverages. The legal drinking age is 21; however, someone at least 18 years old can handle, dispense or sell drinks if acting as an employee for a liquor licensee.

Liquor and drug stores may sell from 8:00 a.m. until midnight but may not sell on Sundays or Christmas. All bars, restaurants and taverns may sell until 2:00 a.m., Mon - Sat, and until 8:00 p.m. on Sundays and Christmas unless they have an "extended hours license" which allows sales until midnight on those days. 3.2% beer may be sold from 5:00 a.m. until midnight, 365 day a year. When clocks are turned back for DST in October, licensees may remain open the "extra" hour.

It is illegal to consume spirits, wine, or malt liquor (all beer other than 3.2%) in public other than in a place which is licensed for that purpose. The consumption of 3.2% beer in public is not prohibited by state laws, however, many cities and counties have "open container" laws for all alcohol. It is illegal to bring any type of alcoholic beverage into any place which sells such. Alcoholic beverages may not be taken out of licensed establishments, except those places which sell for off-premise consumption.

BAD CHECKS

Colorado is not the place to write a bad check—intentionally or unintentionally. This is covered under statues 18-5-205 of the Colorado Criminal Code. In essence, the law states that if any person, knowing he has insufficient funds . . . issues a check for the payment of services, wages, rent, property, etc., that person commits fraud by check. Depending on the amount of the check, this can range from a class 3 misdemeanor to a class 6 felony. Even if you bounce a $5.00 check, you are subject to a fine of $100 or 3 times the amount of the check, whichever is greater.

CHAPTER SIX: SEND LAWYERS, GUNS AND MONEY

EVICTIONS

Colorado has very clear laws and procedures in regard to evictions, although technically, there is no such thing in the state. None of the courts or legal forms use the term "eviction." All such actions are referred to as "Unlawful Detainer," and are covered under the Forcible Entry and Detainer (FED) Statute (13-40-101 et seq. C.R.S.).

Whether you are a landlord or a tenant, it pays to know the laws concerning this matter if you are faced with a possible eviction. There are state statutes in place to protect the rights of both parties. Landlords need to know how to give proper notice, fill out, file and serve the necessary forms, and avoid violating any tenant rights. Tenants should know the legal defenses to an eviction, how to file an Answer or Counterclaim, and the laws regarding Security Deposits.

A written lease is of utmost importance to both parties. In almost all situations where there is a conflict between the common law and lease provisions, the lease will control. This is particularly important in regard to notice, security deposits and rental liability issues.

The factual and legal issues involved in an eviction are far too complicated to cover in this section. Before you lease property as a landlord, or, as a tenant, you find yourself on the receiving end of a possible eviction (for any reason), I recommend the *Guide to Colorado Evictions* by Bradford Publishing. I have seen cases won in court by a wrongful party simply because they knew the laws and the innocent party did not.

MARRIAGE

On the average day in Colorado there are 92 marriages. Unlike the federal speed limit, requirements for a legal marriage vary widely from state to state. Below are the basic requirements to become married in Colorado.

Marriages License Requirements: Licenses can be issued in any county seat and are valid throughout the state. There is no waiting period after the license is issued; however, the license must be used within 30 days of issuance. The fee for the license is $20 cash; checks are not accepted.

Age Requirements: The legal age without parental consent is 18 years of age. Ages 16-17 require a notarized consent form from either both parents, a parent having sole custody or a guardian having legal custody of the minor. If these do not apply then judicial approval is required. Applicants 15 and under must obtain a court-granted judicial approval in the county seat where residency has been established.

Identification: Acceptable forms of identification and proof of age are: Driver's License, Passport, Baptism Certificate, Military ID or a state issued ID card.

Blood Test: No blood test is required in Colorado.

Application Form: Both male and female applicants must appear in person to complete and sign the license application. If one party can not appear due to illness, travel or incarceration, he or she must obtain an absentee application in a county seat.

This form must be completed, notarized and returned before a license will be issued. Applicants do not need to be residents of Colorado.

Ceremonies: A marriage ceremony may be performed by a judge or public official who is authorized to perform such a ceremony. Also, a person in accordance with any mode of solemnization, recognized by a religious denomination, Indian tribe or nation, may perform the marriage. Clergy from out of state need not be registered in the state to perform the ceremony.

Prohibited Marriages: A person may not re-marry unless a divorce is absolutely final. Proof of divorce is required if it has been granted within 30 days prior to application. Marriage between ancestor, descendent, brother, sister, uncle, aunt, niece or nephews is prohibited, whether the relationship is by half or whole blood. Marriages between first cousins and further relations are permitted. Contact your county clerk for additional information.

DIVORCE

On the average day in Colorado there are 53 divorces. Although everyone would like to think their marriage was made in heaven and will last forever, statistics beg to differ. Almost 58% of all marriages end in divorce in Colorado. Depending on issues such as financial assets and children, divorces come in four basic varieties: friendly and simple, friendly yet complicated, nasty but simple, and plain old nasty (with complications). There are also four ways you can handle the process. You can do it all yourselves; do it yourselves with limited assistance from a legal center or attorney; do it yourselves with mediation; or have an attorney do it for you. Regardless of method, I recommend *The Friendly Divorce Guidebook* also by Bradford Publishing. In Colorado, whether and how you use a lawyer in your divorce is up to you, but having the proper information is invaluable.

Before running to the courthouse to file for a divorce, you may want to consider the various other options available in Colorado. Marriage counseling, marital mediation, physical or trial separation, legal separation, annulment, and finally the legal dissolution of marriage (divorce) are all available and legal.

For a legal separation or divorce the process begins by filing a petition with the clerk of the **district** court. You must have been domiciled in Colorado for at least 90 days before filing your first papers. A waiting period of 90 days, required by law, begins once you have filed the petition. The 90 day waiting period is mandatory as a "cooling off" time so both parties can give the action serious consideration before making it final.

Couples usually use the 90 days to work out their final divorce plan which, when written, is called the separation agreement. A separation agreement must cover all the following: property division, payment of debts, maintenance (alimony), custody and support of children, taxes and medical and life insurance. A separation agreement must be presented to the court at the time you ask for a final decree. A final decree can be obtained by affidavit without appearing before the court if no minor children are involved, or, if there are children, both parties must be represented by counsel. Those who do not qualify for divorce by affidavit, and those seeking a decree of legal separation, must appear at a final hearing in court.

After your divorce or legal separation has been granted, the court retains continuing jurisdiction over your children (custody, support, higher education costs).

One final note: Colorado recognizes common law marriages. You have a common law marriage if you have lived together while "holding yourselves out" as being married, meaning that you acted as though you were married. Typical proof of this is, you introduced each other as wife and husband, used the same last name, or filed married/joint tax returns AND neither of you was still married to someone else, either by a marriage license and a ceremony or by common law. A common law marriage and a marriage with a license and a ceremony are legally equal and subject to all the above.

REAL ESTATE

Almost all aspects of real estate transactions are regulated by the Division of Real Estate, 303-894-2166. The Division administers the real estate recovery fund, which can be used by persons to recover sums lost because of the actions of a licensee. Persons who obtain a final judgment against a broker or salesperson can regain their actual loss suffered in a transaction up to $15,000 per claimant and up to $50,000 in the aggregate against any one licensee. The Division also regulates all time-share projects sold in Colorado and regulates developers of subdivisions consisting of 10 or more residential sites, tracts or lots.

Real estate agents and brokers in Colorado are required to "declare their allegiance" in any transaction. In other words, they must state up front, and in writing, whether they are working for a seller or a buyer. This law was put in to place to protect consumers from being mislead by agents claiming to be on their side while they were actually looking out for the best interest of someone else.

Selling a home or property yourself is legal but not always well advised. The legalities involved can be quite complicated. However, if you want to give it a shot before committing to an agent, there are several excellent books available which walk you through the whole process.

Finally, if you are looking to buy rural property (acreage), there are many considerations which may not be apparent: water rights, well permits, test for septic permits, mineral rights (especially in Colorado), mining patents, legal access, road maintenance, zoning restrictions, utilities, and drastic changes in seasons to list a few. My wife and I recently looked at a beautiful 6 acre plot. The price was $36,000. However, it would have cost at least $10,000 to bring in electricity (only 900 feet away), $10,000 for well and septic, and $25,000 to re-grade the dirt road for construction. Now the price was over $80,000 before we laid the first brick. If you are serious (or just not sure) about moving out of the city, get copies of *Discover the Good Life In Rural America (The City Slicker's Guide To Buying Country Real Estate Without Losing Your Shirt),* and *Country Bound! (Trade Your Business Suit Blues for Blue Jean Dreams),* both by Communication Creativity. See Appendix A for details.

LOTTO

There are actually three "games of chance" run by the state. Lottery refers to the simple scratch and win cards available everywhere. Lotto is the twice-weekly drawing for the big bucks and Keno is a daily (Mon-Sat) drawing. The cash prizes for Keno are preset with a maximum of $50,000 for matching 10 out of 20 numbers. Lotto has a progressive pot which starts at $1.5 million. When you purchase a Lotto ticket you have a choice as to payment option which must be made at the time of purchase. You can chose either a 25 Year Annuity or the Cash Value (40% before taxes) option.

Keno drawings are held every Monday-Saturday and you can check your Lottery retailer for the previous day's drawing results. The Lotto drawings are on television every Wednesday and Saturday night at 10:00 p.m. The Lotto drawings can be seen on KCNC/Denver - Channel 4, KOAA/Colorado Springs & Pueblo - Channel 5/30, KREX/Grand Junction - Channel 5, KREY/Montrose - Channel 10, KREG/Glenwood Springs - Channel 3, and KREZ/Durango - Channel 6

Winning numbers for both games are available by calling the Lottery Luck Line at 759-LUCK (5825) in Denver, 542-LUCK in Pueblo and toll free at 1-800-283-LUCK anywhere else in Colorado. These numbers may also appear in local newspapers and are available at your Lottery retailer. You may begin claiming winning tickets the morning following the drawing.

If you win, immediately sign the back of your ticket if you haven't already done it. To claim prizes up to $150, simply present your ticket at any Keno/Lotto retailer within 180 days of the winning drawing. To claim prizes over $150, you must visit one of the Lottery offices in Pueblo, Denver, Ft. Collins or Grand Junction. Or mail the signed ticket and a filled out claim form available at all Lottery retailers to the Colorado Lottery, P.O. Box 7, Pueblo, CO 81002-0007 for payment by mail. Lotto jackpot winners (6 of 6) will be paid only at Denver or Pueblo Lottery offices.

Every time you play, Colorado wins. More than $629 million has been distributed for local and state park and recreation projects, the outdoors and wilderness projects and for state public buildings and facilities.

Be sure to check the numbers on your ticket to make sure they are the ones you asked for. You can correct or cancel your ticket within one hour of purchase during retailer's normal hours (before system cutoff) only at the place you bought the ticket. Sign the back of your ticket because Lotto and Keno tickers are bearer instruments.

You must be 18 or older to purchase tickets. Tickets may be given as gifts to anyone of any age, and they may win. All prize claims are subject to validation. Federal and State laws require a minimum 32% tax withholding on individual winnings over $5,000.

CHAPTER SEVEN
CHANGES IN LATITUDES, CHANGES IN ATTITUDES

THE TEN FASTEST GROWING COUNTIES IN COLORADO

> The information in this chapter was compiled from various sources including, but not limited to, government reports and publications (Federal, State, and Local); materials provided by business and civic organizations and The Colorado Economic and Demographic Information System (CEDIS) maintained by the Colorado Division of Local Government.

Explosive growth! I have used that term numerous times in this book. I can't think of a better way to describe it. Much like a bomb, the growth of Colorado has been sudden, unexpected, uncontainable and, in some respects, devastating to the state's resources (natural, economic and social).

I was drawn to Colorado almost a decade ago. The natural beauty, wide-open spaces, uncrowded cities (for the most part), and friendly, laid-back attitudes of the State's citizens were all factors in my move from Florida.

During the last ten years I have been an eye-witness to some dramatic changes in the state. When I arrived in the mid-eighties, the state was in an economic bust. Downtown Denver's business district was very vacant, LODO (Lower Downtown) was a place you did not want to be after dark, traffic in and out of Denver was only congested on rare occasions, mountain land could be had for a song, and there were distinct, natural divisions between one city and the next—all a memory now.

The state's population has increased by over 100,000 people a year for the last 3 years. Between 1990 and 1994 the population grew 11 percent. While most of the increase was centered in the six-county Denver metro area, many of the rural and mountain communities have also seen tremendous growth. There have been numerous news reports lately concerning the unwanted effects this growth has had in many areas. Several of the state's one-time "wildlife" areas are no longer have much wildlife due to a constant onslaught of hikers, campers, hunters and the like. The long-time residents of some smaller, rural areas are up in arms because the assets and beauty of their home-turf are being destroyed by newcomers. Many small areas have been populated by affluent new arrivals who, once situated, demand improvements in roads, utilities and conveniences so their new home will be more like the one they couldn't wait to get away from.

It was even suggested by a number of people that I put a coupon good for a one-way bus ticket back home in the front of this book. I have several friends here who were originally Californians. Most would never admit that in public.

Because they began to see the writing on the wall, a group of state leaders held a conference recently in an attempt to stop a disaster waiting to happen. On January 25-26, 1995, over one thousand Coloradans from different communities and backgrounds—elected officials, community, agricultural and business leaders, educators and students—met at the Colorado Leadership Summit on Smart Growth in Denver to tackle the tough issues raised by the state's explosive growth. Summit participants listened to a number of presentations and participated in small break-out groups to identify and discuss problems, opportunities, ideas, barriers and solutions related to growth and development issues. At the end of the conference, participants had developed 14 guiding principles or goals concerning Smart Growth and Development.

I would ask everyone who reads this book, newcomer and life-long citizen alike, to review the principles below and work together to keep Colorado the wonderful, beautiful, exciting, and prosperous state in which we all live.

GUIDING PRINCIPLES FROM THE COLORADO LEADERSHIP SUMMIT ON SMART GROWTH AND DEVELOPMENT

1. **Our vision and the process we take to get there should fully develop the human potential of all our citizens.** We must strive to make our communities places where all kids and adults can fully develop their human capacities—their minds and bodies. We should work together to ensure that strong families and communities, as well as great educational opportunities, cultural resources, good jobs, adequate food, clothing, and health care are available for all of our citizens. Colorado communities must sustain and enhance the lives of families and individuals today and for the future.

2. **We need to enhance the quality of our place.** We must identify and emphasize both the physical and the human elements of our communities that are important to us. We must make our communities more livable by keeping crime off our streets, making

all our neighborhoods attractive, protecting our natural resources and celebrating the magnificence of our setting. We also must cultivate an ethic of community, preserving towns and neighborhoods where we know and care for each other, where we respect cultural and ethnic diversity and the value of the environment, and where a child can grow up with a healthy body and healthy values.

3. **At the local and regional level, we should better coordinate growth planning with the provision of services such as schools, water, infrastructure and transportation.** A more cooperative effort between governments, communities and the private sector to make sure services accompany growth will guarantee the provision of services for new development, avoid duplication and inefficient use of services, allow for the fairer allocation of the cost of development, account for non-fiscal costs of development, help encourage urban in-fill and discourage sprawl, and allow us to preserve cherished areas we may not want to develop. Better coordination locally and regionally will also make it easier to plan for the long-term, increase citizen participation and enhance our sense of community.

4. **We need to expand the opportunities—such as better jobs, education, housing and health care—that result from growth, and help Coloradans take advantage of those opportunities.** Economic development can and should bring many benefits to Colorado. Clearly, affordable housing, improved education, better health and expanded job choices ought to be among the measurable results of growth in Colorado. Just as clearly, growth should generate increased cultural and recreational opportunities for Colorado citizens. To the extent possible, smart growth must strengthen the identity of Colorado's diverse neighborhoods, communities and regions. We must empower local governments to attract and help create "good" growth, and we must help Colorado residents—including low and moderate income residents-receive the benefits resulting from growth.

5. **We need to provide the structures so that we can effectively make the decisions that need to be made within each community, region and the state.** We must make decisions as locally as it is possible for them to be effective. Therefore, we need to identify more ways to support regional and local priorities while simultaneously assuring a positive response to the crucial statewide issues of air quality, transportation, telecommunications, and water quality. We need to foster collaborative and supportive relationships at every level of decision making, by making governmental structures more flexible, reducing institutional barriers to cooperation and input, creating more opportunities for citizens to be involved, cultivating partnerships between government and the private and non-profit sectors, empowering grass-roots activism, and taking into account overlapping areas of commercial and ecological interest.

6. **We must continuously reform our tax, revenue and regulatory framework.** Without creating an unpredictable regulatory environment, we must constantly rethink our tax and regulatory structure. Fees, licenses, permits, regulations such as zoning, taxes and tax revenue, should encourage and empower—not impede—state, regional and local efforts to provide services, as well as manage resources and plan for infrastructure, telecommunications and land use. We also must encourage non-regulatory approaches such as collaborative decision-making, facilitation and

negotiation to foster cooperation and dialogue among public, private sector and community groups regarding growth initiatives.

7. **We need to protect, enhance and promote the value of our public lands, our open spaces, our natural resources, our wildlife, our parks, our recreational opportunities and our historical facilities.** We must take personal and community responsibility for ensuring that growth supports and facilitates the protection and enhancement of Colorado's public assets. They enrich our lives. We need to cultivate improved relationships between state and federal land management and regulatory agencies, regional and local governments, community groups and the private sector in order to protoect assets that are valuable to our environment, our history and our communities.

8. **We need to foster a sustainable agricultural economy.** Agricultural lands are not merely open space. We must acknowledge the importance of Colorado's agriculture lands and communities to the state's economy, as well as the benefits that go beyond the primary purpose of farms and ranches, such as aesthetics, cultural contributions and wildlife habitat. Development of a sustainable agricultural economy should be given emphasis in state, regional and local growth strategies.

9. **We need to protect Colorado from pollution.** The health of our citizens and our environment is vital to our high quality of life and our economic strength. Individual citizens, community groups, government and the private sector must collaborate to reduce and prevent pollution and protect and conserve our natural resources, without disregarding local circumstances or disrespecting private property rights.

10. **We need to continue to develop economically.** We need a business climate that fosters quality jobs in stable or growing industries like telecommunications, promotes growth in areas that want it, and allows us to withstand boom and bust cycles. Smart growth is good business: long-range planning can help strike a balance between Colorado's "haves" and "have-nots," achieve economic diversity throughout the state and ensure a stable economy for many years into the future.

11. **We must always be conscious of the need for sustainability.** We must meet the economic, social and environmental demands of the present without compromising the ability of future generations to meet their needs. We must also work to mitigate the problems that have resulted from past actions.

12. **We need to foster a sustainable system of water management, in terms of treatment, storage and the regulation and determination of usage.** Water is the most important resource in Colorado, as it applies to growth and the environment. We also need to develop a conservation ethic as a state, within communities and as individuals.

13. **Smart growth must be an inclusive and cooperative process.** Direct citizen input at all levels of decision-making is crucial to viable growth management. Education and information about all the costs and benefits of growth as well as the needs and values of different communities around the state, must be available. We also must remember that the private and non-profit sectors can be very effective partners with government, and planning decisions should be made with as much input, support and collaboration

CHAPTER SEVEN: CHANGES IN LATITUDES/ATTITUDES

as possible. This is a cooperative venture, so we should share data and experiences, learn from each others' mistakes and share in each others' successes.

14. **We all must be conscious of our rights and responsibilities as individuals.** Planning decisions always must honor and respect private property rights and the need for compensation of all individuals, including business people, farmers and ranchers. At the same time, we all must take responsibility for the impacts our private actions and decisions have on other individuals, communities or shared resources. **For more information about the Summit contact the Colorado Department of Local Affairs at 1-800-899-GROW or 303-866-2817.**

For those considering a move, this chapter contains basic information about the ten fastest growing counties in the state. These counties were picked from two separate statistical lists (numerical and percentage changes). The counties appear alphabetically, not in order of growth (**Adams, Arapahoe, Boulder, Denver, Douglas**, El Paso, **Jefferson**, Larimer, Summit, and Weld), with the six counties of the Greater Metro Region being shown in Bold. You should keep in mind some data presented may be several years old (although it is the most recent available), and since the population of some counties has increased 20-45 percent since the release of the data, it should be used as a basic guide only. More recent (unreleased) figures may be available from the individual counties or agencies in question.

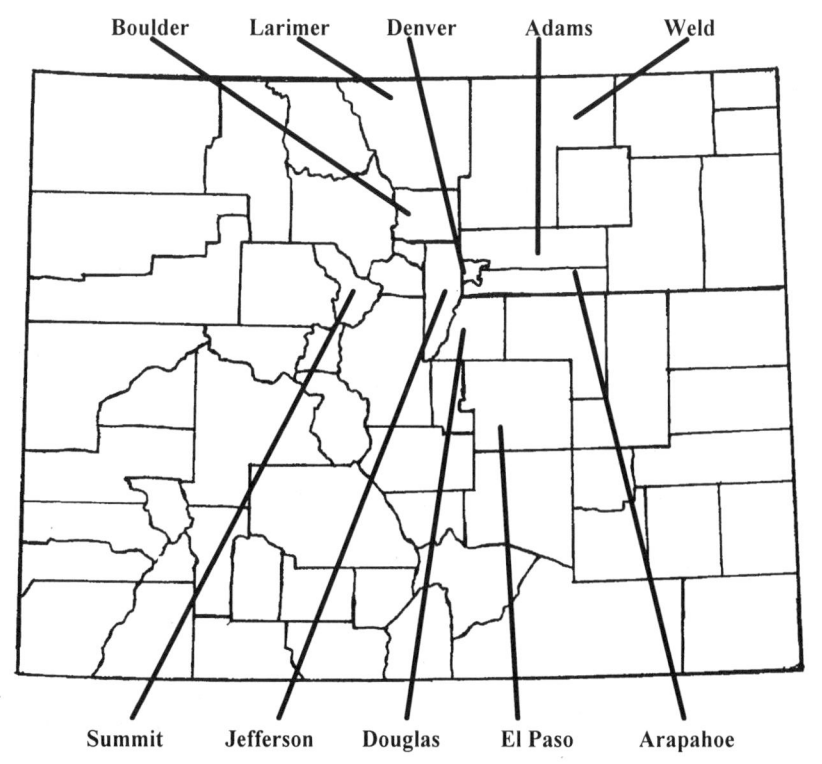

111

ADAMS COUNTY

LARGEST CITIES/TOWNS/COMMUNITIES

Aurora, Bennett, Brighton, Broomfield, Commerce City, Federal Heights, Northglenn, Thornton and Westminster (Current total population: 284,045)

POPULATION ESTIMATES BY AGE GROUPS, 1996-2005

AGE GROUP	1996	2000	2005
0 to 4 years old	24285	23392	23733
5 to 18	66351	71103	74738
19 to 34	65672	60887	64122
35 to 64	115617	134329	151662
65 to 89	24751	28860	33816
90 and over	515	565	745
Total	297191	319137	348816

LOCAL COMMUNITY DESCRIPTION

Adams County stretches from the foothills of the Rockies to the eastern Colorado plains, making up the northern tier of the six-county Denver metropolitan area. Western urbanized Adams County includes all or portions of the cities of Arvada, Aurora, Brighton, Broomfield, Commerce City, Federal Heights, Northglenn, Thornton and Westminster. Situated in a fast-growing area, Adams County is a diverse, cosmopolitan county supported by a broad base of business and industry. A wide price range of housing is available for the county's diverse work-force.

ADDRESS: 450 South 4th Avenue, Brighton, CO 80601, 303-659-2120
DATE OF INCORPORATION: 1901, COUNTY SEAT: City of Brighton

LOCAL EMERGENCY SERVICES

Aurora, Bennett, Brighton, Broomfield, Commerce City, Federal Heights, Northglenn, Thornton and Westminster are served by fire departments.

Staff - 288, Vehicles - 75, Phone: (303) 659-6400 x215

EMERGENCY MEDICAL SERVICE: 5 hospitals within Adams County.

LOCAL AMENITIES

HUMAN SERVICES: Adams County Social Services 303-287-8831 ext. 595, 7190 Colorado Blvd., Commerce City, CO 80022 **RECREATIONAL:** Barr Lake State Park, Adams County Regional Park and Fairgrounds, 3 Golf Courses, 6 Health Clubs, 7 Movie Theaters, Water World. The nearby Denver metropolitan area offers a wide variety of recreational facilities and attractions as well as all major hotel/motel chains.

CLIMATE

January Temperature (in degrees Fahrenheit) 30.0
July Temperature (in degrees Fahrenheit) 73.0

Annual Precipitation (in inches)	15.0
Annual Snowfall (in inches)	54.0
Elevation (in feet)	5300
Area (in square miles)	1197.8

TAXES

1993 PROPERTY TAXES: Mill Levy	26.779
1993 SALES TAXES: Adams County	.50%
Other (RTD, Stadium, Cultural Facilities, etc.)	.60%
State	3.00%

LOCAL ECONOMIC DEVELOPMENT CONTACTS

Major firms in area: **GOVERNMENT**: Adams County, Cities of Brighton, Commerce City, Westminster, Northglenn, and Thornton, School Districts, Front Range Community College **MANUFACTURING**: AT&T Info. Sys., Sundstrand Aviation, Whirlpool Kitchens, Fischer Imaging, Auto-trol Technology, Thompson Pipe and Steel **WHOLESALE TRADE**: APS, Associated Grocers, Silver Engineering Works **RETAIL TRADE**: Barber Poultry, ITT Continental Baking, JC Penney, K-Mart, King Soopers, Livtak Meat, NAPA, Peavey Conagra, Target **SERVICES**: Holiday Inn, Humana Valley View Hospital, Frederic Printing **HI-TECH**: Security Pacific Info. Sys., Melco Industries. Adams County has a diverse economy but major segments are services, manufacturing (electronics), government. Local banks have $592,500,000 in assets.

1994 PUBLIC SCHOOL INFORMATION

District Name	# of Students	# of Schools	# of Teachers	Students /Teacher
Mapleton 1	4,898	10	232	21.1
Northglenn-Thornton 12	23,373	38	1,212	19.3
Adams County 14	6,280	13	311	20.1
Brighton 27J	4,304	9	214	20.1
Bennett 29J	1,023	3	59	17.5
Strasburg 31J	475	3	58	17.5
Westminster 50	11,441	24	632	18.1

NEAREST FOUR-YEAR COLLEGE: Univ. of Northern Colorado (Greeley)
NEAREST COMMUNITY COLLEGE: Community College of Aurora
NEAREST VOCATIONAL CENTER: T.H. Pickens Voc-Tech (Aurora)

LOCAL TRANSPORTATION

NEAREST SCHEDULED AIR SERVICE: Denver International Airport
LOCAL BUSES, TRUCKS, AND TRAINS: Greyhound, Continental Trailways, RTD, Gray Line of Denver, Variety of trucklines providing local, interstate, and intrastate service. Freight: Colorado Southern, Denver & Rio Grande, Chicago Rock Is. Pacific, Union Pacific, Burlington Northern. Passenger: Amtrak.

COLORADO: A Newcomer's Manual

LOCAL UTILTIES (see page 206 for most Electric/Gas phone numbers)
LOCAL WATER INFORMATION: Lost Creek Groundwater Mgmt., Northgate & Shaw Heights Water, Central Colo. Water Conservancy, Central Colo. Groundwater Mgmt., N. Kiowa Bijou Groundwater Mgmt., Hazeltine Heights Water District.
LOCAL SEWER INFORMATION: Beebe Draw, Bennett Sanitation, Hi-land Acres, Himalaya, Metro Denver Sewage Disposal, Industrial Park, Berkeley, Box Elder, Central Adams County, Crestview, Eastlake, N. Pecos
LOCAL LANDFILL INFORMATION: 287-5249 x300. Adams County has 3 active landfills.
LOCAL GARBAGE INFORMATION: Arvada Rubbish, Commerce City Public Works, Eastlake, City of Thornton, Waste Management of Denver, Western Waste Industries.
LOCAL ELECTRICITY INFORMATION: Public Service Co., Intermountain Union Rural Electric Assn, United Power
LOCAL GAS INFORMATION: Public Service Co., Eastern Colorado Utility Co.

ARAPAHOE COUNTY

LARGEST CITIES/TOWNS/COMMUNITIES

Aurora, Englewood, Greenwood Village, Littleton (current total population: 415,475)

POPULATION ESTIMATES BY AGE GROUPS, 1996-2005

AGE GROUP	1996	2000	2005
0 to 4 years old	33136	31567	30114
5 to 18	93424	98095	99279
19 to 34	90776	81583	85956
35 to 64	192507	216021	227113
65 to 89	38056	42888	49912
90 and over	834	838	1120
Total	448733	470992	493494

LOCAL COMMUNITY DESCRIPTION

Arapahoe County is a rapidly growing area with several cities including Aurora, Englewood, Greenwood Village, and Littleton. It was one of the original 17 counties in the Colorado Territory and today has the highest number of up-scale communities in the greater metro area. Arapahoe county has its own business airport and encompasses a great portion of the Denver Technological Center.

ADDRESS: 5334 South Prince Street, Littleton, CO 80166, 303-795-4630
DATE OF INCORPORATION: 1901, COUNTY SEAT: City of Littleton

LOCAL EMERGENCY SERVICES

City and local fire districts: For details contact County.
Staff - 450, Vehicles - 190, Phone: Sheriff: Patrick J. Sullivan, Jr. - (303)795-4711.
Hospitals: 8 in area (see Healthcare below).

CHAPTER SEVEN: CHANGES IN LATITUDES/ATTITUDES

LOCAL AMENITIES

HUMAN SERVICES: Comitis, Arapahoe House, Social Services Department, Veterans Services, Child Care Food Program, Weatherization, Senior Transportation, Homemakers, Arapahoe Volunteers, Inter-Faith Task Force **ENTERTAINMENT:** Fiddlers Green Theater, Littleton Theater, River Front development; 23 Golf Courses, 14 Health Clubs, 18 Movie Theaters **HEALTHCARE:** Aurora Presbyterian, Aurora Regional Medical Center, Colorado Mental Health, Craig Hospital, Littleton Hospital/Porter, Porter Memorial Hospital, Spalding Hospital, Swedish Medical Center **LODGING:** Ramada, Heritage, Holiday Inn, Days Inn, Brock Residence Inn, Scanton Hotel & Conference Center **CHURCHES:** Episcopal, Baptist, Catholic, Lutheran, Methodist, Christian, Presbyterian, Congregational **ORGANIZATIONS:** Jaycees, Lions Club, Kiwanis, Rotary, Knights of Columbus, Sertoma, Optimists, Elks, Federated Women's Club, Junior League.

CLIMATE

January Temperature (in degrees Fahrenheit)	34.0
July Temperature (in degrees Fahrenheit)	79.0
Annual Precipitation (in inches)	15.0
Annual Snowfall (in inches)	52.0
Elevation (in feet)	5400
Area (in square miles) 805.5	

TAXES

1993 PROPERTY TAXES: Mill Levy	16.973
1993 SALES TAXES: Arapahoe County	0.00%
Other (RTD, Stadium, Cultural Facilities, etc.)	.60%
State 3.00%	

LOCAL ECONOMIC DEVELOPMENT CONTACTS

Major firms in area: **UTILITIES:** Mountain Bell, Public Service **SERVICES:** Stearns-Rogers, Inc., IBM, United Airlines, Honeywell, Inc., Amoco Product Co. **FINANCE, INSURANCE, REAL ESTATE:** Allstate Insurance. The leading source of income is Office/light-industrial centered around Centennial Airport.

1994 PUBLIC SCHOOL INFORMATION

District Name	# of Students	# of Schools	# of Teachers	Students /Teacher
Englewood 1	4,650	9	227	20.5
Sheridan 2	1,983	5	106	18.7
Cherry Creek 5	34,714	41	1,910	18.2
Littleton 6	15,751	22	869	18.1
Deer Trail 26J	182	2	18	10.3
Adams-Arapahoe 28J	27,421	40	1,492	18.4
Byers 32J	419	2	25	16.5

NEAREST FOUR-YEAR COLLEGE: Metro State, Univ. of Colorado (Auraria Campus - Denver)

NEAREST COMMUNITY COLLEGE: Community College of Aurora
NEAREST VOCATIONAL CENTER: T.H. Pickens Voc-Tech (Aurora)

LOCAL TRANSPORTATION

NEAREST SCHEDULED AIR SERVICE: Denver International Airport
LOCAL BUSES, TRUCKS, AND TRAINS Continental Trailways, Greyhound, RTD. All major trucklines serve Arapahoe County & the surrounding metropolitan area. Freight: Union Pacific, Denver & Rio Grande Western, Burlington-Northern. Passenger: Amtrak (in Denver).

LOCAL UTILTIES (see page 206 for most Electric/Gas phone numbers)

LOCAL WATER INFORMATION: INFORMATION Contact the Denver Water Department, 303-893-2444.

LOCAL SEWER INFORMATION: Contact the Denver Water Department.

LOCAL LANDFILL INFORMATION: Charles Bailey (303)373-0155.

LOCAL ELECTRICITY INFORMATION: Public Service Co., Intermountain Rural Electric Assoc.

LOCAL GAS INFORMATION: Public Service Co., Eastern Colorado Utility Co.

BOULDER COUNTY

LARGEST CITIES/TOWNS/COMMUNITIES

Boulder, Broomfield, Lafayette, Longmont, Louisville (current total population: 248,697).

POPULATION ESTIMATES BY AGE GROUPS, 1996-2005

AGE GROUP	1996	2000	2005
0 to 4 years old	18338	17330	16496
5 to 18	48646	53580	55809
19 to 34	65670	58396	60912
35 to 64	110450	126095	133568
65 to 89	19861	21959	25642
90 and over	725	768	862
Total	263690	278128	293290

LOCAL COMMUNITY DESCRIPTION

Boulder County houses the University of Colorado's main campus in Boulder, with an enrollment of 26,000 undergraduate, graduate, & professional students. In addition, the county is the center for research & high technology manufacturing. Nestled against the foothills of the front range, Boulder County is also a prime recreation area for activities including backpacking, hiking, cycling, water sports, & skiing. The territory within Boulder County first became part of the United States in 1803 with the Louisiana Purchase. Today Boulder County remains diversified, with both rural and

116

CHAPTER SEVEN: CHANGES IN LATITUDES/ATTITUDES

urban settings. Population of the county is approximately 248,697, with about 94,392 in the City of Boulder, another 56,065 in the City of Longmont, 26,296 in Broomfield, 15,995 in Lafayette, 14,356 in Louisville and the remainder dispersed throughout the smaller towns of Lyons, Nederland and Ward, Jamestown, Superior and Erie and unincorporated areas, including the communities of Niwot, Gunbarrel and Allenspark. The County encompasses 753 square miles and is situated on the eastern slope of the Rocky Mountains. Elevations within the boundaries of the County vary from the 5,000-foot level of the plains to the 14,000-foot peaks of the Continental Divide.

ADDRESS: P. O. Box 471, Boulder, CO 80306, 303-441-3500
DATE OF INCORPORATION: 1861, COUNTY SEAT: City of Boulder

LOCAL EMERGENCY SERVICES

All jurisdictions are served by fire departments - please contact them for details: 200 staff, 72 vehicles. Phone: (303)441-3636

EMERGENCY MEDICAL SERVICE: 5 hospitals in area.

LOCAL AMENITIES

AVAILABLE NEARBY: The Denver Metro Area has a variety of recreation areas/facilities, attractions & major hotels & motels available **CHURCHES:** All denominations of churches **HEALTHCARE:** Mental Health Center, Public Health, Developmental Disabilities Center **HUMAN SERVICES:** Housing Authority, Social Services **LODGING:** A great number of major hotels & motels exist in Boulder **ORGANIZATIONS:** Veterans, CAP **ENTERTAINMENT:** 8 Golf Courses, 23 Movie Theaters.

CLIMATE

January Temperature (in degrees Fahrenheit)	31.0
July Temperature (in degrees Fahrenheit)	73.0
Annual Precipitation (in inches)	16.0
Annual Snowfall (in inches)	93.0
Elevation (in feet)	6100
Area (in square miles)	751.4

TAXES

1993 PROPERTY TAXES: Mill Levy	22.245
1993 SALES TAXES: Boulder County	0.00%
Other (RTD, Stadium, Cultural Facilities, etc.)	.60%
State	3.00%

LOCAL ECONOMIC DEVELOPMENT CONTACTS

Major firms in area: **HI-TECH**: IBM, Rockwell, Storage Technology Corp., Ball Aerospace, Neodata, NBI, NCAR, Valley Lab, Syntex **MANUFACTURING**: Monsanto/Head, Dieterich Standard, Flatiron Co. **GOVERNMENT**: University of Colorado, St. Vrain Valley School District, Boulder County, US Department of Commerce, City of Boulder, City of Longmont, FAA **FOOD PROCESSING**:

Celestial Seasonings, Boulder Beer, Longmont Foods **SERVICES**: Boulder Community Hospital **UTILITIES**: Public Service, Mountain Bell. The leading source of income is Manufacturing, services, tourism.. Local banks have $ 1,421,560,000 in assets.

1994 PUBLIC SCHOOL INFORMATION

District Name	# of Students	# of Schools	# of Teachers	Students /Teacher
St. Vrain Valley RE 1J	16,482	31	872	18.9
Boulder Valley RE 2	24,658	45	1,417	17.4

NEAREST FOUR-YEAR COLLEGE: Univ. of Colorado (Boulder)
NEAREST COMMUNITY COLLEGE: Front Range Community College (Westminster)
NEAREST VOCATIONAL CENTER: Boulder Valley Voc-Tech (Boulder)

LOCAL TRANSPORTATION

NEAREST SCHEDULED AIR SERVICE: Fort Collins-Loveland Muni., Fred Anderson Jr., 4824 Earhart Road, Loveland, CO 80538, 970-669-7182
LOCAL BUSES, TRUCKS, AND TRAINS: Continental Trailways, RTD, BDT, Consolidated Freightways, Globe Truck Line, Yellow Freight, American Freight. Freight: Burlington Northern, Union Pacific. Passenger: Amtrak in Denver, CO (30 miles).

LOCAL UTILTIES (see page 206 for most Electric/Gas phone numbers)

LOCAL WATER INFORMATION Contact the Denver Water Department (303-893-2444) or the City of Boulder, 303-441-3260

LOCAL SEWER INFORMATION Contact the Denver Water Department (303-893-2444) or the City of Boulder, 303-441-3260

LOCAL LANDFILL INFORMATION: Debbie Fyffel (303) 441-3900.

LOCAL ELECTRICITY INFORMATION: Public Service Co., United Power

LOCAL GAS INFORMATION: Public Service Co.

CITY AND COUNTY OF DENVER

LARGEST CITIES/TOWNS/COMMUNITIES
Denver (current population: 486,596).

POPULATION ESTIMATES BY AGE GROUPS, 1996-2005

AGE GROUP	1996	2000	2005
0 to 4 years old	36653	35575	37672
5 to 18	90510	89325	87414
19 to 34	139426	144714	157235
35 to 64	172441	177779	173342
65 to 89	64038	62704	60773
90 and over	2851	3636	4053
Total	505918	513723	520490

LOCAL COMMUNITY DESCRIPTION
The heart of Colorado is the six-county Greater Metropolitan Area centered around the City and County of Denver (the only City and County in the State). Denver is a mix of the downtown business district, neighborhood businesses, residential areas, industrial parks and the new Denver International Airport. Being the capital city of Colorado with a very rich historical background, Denver is home to many amenities and recreational and cultural facilities including the Denver Center for the Performing Arts with nine theaters which seat nearly 100,000 people, the Denver Art Museum, the Denver Museum of Natural History, the Denver Zoo, and the Denver Botanical Gardens. Its newly revitalized LODO (lower downtown) area includes many restaurants, brew-pubs, Coors Field, and Elitch Gardens.

ADDRESS: 110 16th Street, Suite 400, Denver, CO 80202, 303-640-5555
DATE OF INCORPORATION: 1902, COUNTY SEAT: City & County of Denver

LOCAL EMERGENCY SERVICES
FIRE PROTECTION: This information was not provided by this community.
POLICE PROTECTION: Denver Police Department
EMERGENCY MEDICAL SERVICE: 15 hospitals in the area.

LOCAL AMENITIES
Denver is the largest city in Colorado and offers a full-range of amenities.

CLIMATE

January Temperature (in degrees Fahrenheit)	29.9
July Temperature (in degrees Fahrenheit)	73.0
Annual Precipitation (in inches)	15.5
Annual Snowfall (in inches)	59.9
Elevation (in feet)	5280
Area (in square miles)	154.9

TAXES

1993 PROPERTY TAXES: Mill Levy 33.088
1993 SALES TAXES: Denver 3.50%
Other (RTD, Stadium, Cultural Facilities, etc.) .60%
State 3.00%

LOCAL ECONOMIC DEVELOPMENT CONTACTS

The downtown business district alone has 7,000 employers.

1994 PUBLIC SCHOOL INFORMATION

District Name	# of Students	# of Schools	# of Teachers	Students /Teachers
Denver County 1	62,773	111	3,509	17.9

NEAREST FOUR-YEAR COLLEGE: MSC, UCD, CCD (Auraria Campus - Denver)
NEAREST COMMUNITY COLLEGE: Community College of Denver (Auraria Campus - Denver)
NEAREST VOCATIONAL CENTER: Several schools (Denver)

LOCAL TRANSPORTATION

NEAREST SCHEDULED AIR SERVICE: Denver International Airport
LOCAL BUSES, TRUCKS, AND TRAINS: All major carriers serve the greater Denver Metro Area.

LOCAL UTILTIES (see page 206 for most Electric/Gas phone numbers)

Denver Water Department, Public Service Company of Colorado, U.S. West

DOUGLAS COUNTY

LARGEST CITIES/TOWNS/COMMUNITIES

Castle Rock, Parker, Highlands Ranch (current population: 66,010)

POPULATION ESTIMATES BY AGE GROUPS, 1996-2005

AGE GROUP	1996	2000	2005
0 to 4 years old	9618	9470	10049
5 to 18	21677	29129	35759
19 to 34	20185	19260	22691
35 to 64	48185	64264	79285
65 to 89	4654	6726	9875
90 and over	70	86	166
Total	104390	128936	157824

CHAPTER SEVEN: CHANGES IN LATITUDES/ATTITUDES

LOCAL COMMUNITY DESCRIPTION

Located between the Denver & Colorado Springs metropolitan areas on Colorado's Front Range, Douglas County is experiencing significant development. In fact, from 1990 to 1994, Douglas County had a total population increase of 45.8 percent. Offering open terrain ranging from rolling grasslands on the east, to pine forests & rock canyons, the county has a wide potential for growth. There are 21 planned communities in the County offering a choice of lifestyle from remote rural to adult condominium & suburban neighborhoods. Elevation of the county ranges from 6300 to 9800 feet. One third of the county is in federal, state & local public lands.

ADDRESS: 101 Third Street, Castle Rock, CO 80104, 303-660-7400
COUNTY SEAT: Town of Castle Rock

LOCAL EMERGENCY SERVICES

All have service. For details please call Douglas Co. Fire Chiefs Assn. - (303) 770-3720. 80 staff, 40 vehicles, Phone: (303) 660-7505

EMERGENCY MEDICAL SERVICE: This information was not provided by this community.

LOCAL AMENITIES

CHURCHES: 30 churches **ENTERTAINMENT**: Douglas County Arts & Humanities Group, County Choir & Orchestra **FESTIVALS**: Renaissance Festival at Larkspur, Douglas County Fair at Castle Rock, Parker Days at Parker **GOLF TOURNAMENTS**: Senior Champions of Golf Tournament at Plum Creek, Tournament of Players Club, International PGA Tournament at Castle Pines, 7 PGA rated golf courses **HUMAN SERVICES**: County Extension Service, Senior Citizen Programs **ORGANIZATIONS**: Parker & Castle Rock Chambers of Commerce, Jaycees, Lions, Rotary, Civation, 4-H, Eagles **PARKS**: Pike National Forest, Castlewood Canyon State Park, Chatfield State Park, Roxborough State Park, Daniels Park.

CLIMATE

January Temperature (in degrees Fahrenheit)	28.0
July Temperature (in degrees Fahrenheit)	73.0
Annual Precipitation (in inches)	14.0
Annual Snowfall (in inches)	57.0
Elevation (in feet)	5900
Area (in square miles)	842.8

TAXES

1993 PROPERTY TAXES: Mill Levy	18.774
1993 SALES TAXES: Douglas County	0.00%
Other (RTD, Stadium, Cultural Facilities, etc.)	.60%
State	3.00%

LOCAL ECONOMIC DEVELOPMENT CONTACTS

Major firms in area: **GOVERNMENT**: Douglas County School District, Douglas County **MANUFACTURING**: Marquest Manufacturing, Racquet World-Inverness, Industrial Textiles, Moly Corp., Denver Brick, E.I. DuPont, Inventive Packaging, Saltzgitter Machinery, Inc., Ensign-Bickford, Toyota **HI-TECH**: Information Handling Systems, Honeywell, Hewlett-Packard, Tektronix **FINANCE, INSURANCE, REAL ESTATE**: Hartford Insurance, **SERVICES**: Mercy Medical Center, Tournament of Players **UTILITIES**: Intermountain Rural Electric Association, Mountain Bell. The leading source of income is Technology & communications services, construction. Local banks have $ 200,000,000 in assets.

1994 PUBLIC SCHOOL INFORMATION

District Name	# of Students	# of Schools	# of Teachers	Student /Teacher
Douglas County RE 1	20,041	28	1,042	19.2

NEAREST FOUR-YEAR COLLEGE: Metro State, Univ. of Colorado (Auraria Campus - Denver)
NEAREST COMMUNITY COLLEGE: Arapahoe Community College (Littleton)
NEAREST VOCATIONAL CENTER: Several schools (Denver)

LOCAL TRANSPORTATION

NEAREST SCHEDULED AIR SERVICE: Denver International Airport
LOCAL BUSES, TRUCKS, AND TRAINS Continental Trailways - 5 buses/day, RTD to Parker. All truck lines that service Denver & Colorado Springs. Santa Fe RR Piggyback Center in county. Freight: Santa Fe, Rio Grande, Burlington Northern. Passenger: Amtrak available in Denver CO (25 miles).

LOCAL UTILTIES (see page 206 for most Electric/Gas phone numbers)

LOCAL WATER INFORMATION: There are twenty different water and sanitation districts serving Douglas County.

LOCAL SEWER INFORMATION: There are twenty different water and sanitation districts serving Douglas County. Contact the Denver Water Dept., 303-893-2444.

LOCAL LANDFILL INFORMATION: County Highway Dept. (303) 660-7480. County managed waste transfer stations to regional landfills.

LOCAL ELECTRICITY INFORMATION: Public Service, Intermountain Rural Electric Assoc., Mountain View Electric Association.

LOCAL GAS INFORMATION: Public Service, People's Natural Gas

CHAPTER SEVEN: CHANGES IN LATITUDES/ATTITUDES

EL PASO COUNTY

LARGEST CITIES/TOWNS/COMMUNITIES

Colorado Springs, Manitou Springs, Fountain, Palmer Lake (Current population: 433,576)

POPULATION ESTIMATES BY AGE GROUPS, 1996-2005

AGE GROUP	1996	2000	2005
0 to 4 years old	38219	39228	40984
5 to 18	96366	101822	108000
19 to 34	119112	117910	127550
35 to 64	166658	186831	197431
65 to 89	39301	44619	50521
90 and over	1020	1128	1411
Total	460676	491538	525897

LOCAL COMMUNITY DESCRIPTION

Primarily rolling plains, El Paso County is located south of the Palmer Divide which separates it from Douglas County. The Federal Government owns most of the southwestern part of the county for use by the U.S. Army located at Fort Carson. The largest city in the county is Colorado Springs which also has the second largest population in the state.

ADDRESS: 27 East Vermijo, Colorado Springs, CO 80903, 719-520-6444
COUNTY SEAT: City of Colorado Springs

LOCAL EMERGENCY SERVICES

AF Academy, Peterson AFB, Calhan, Colorado Springs, Ft Carson, Manitou Springs, Fountain, Palmer Lake. Staff: 246, Vehicles: 94 + 6 fire units, Phone: (719) 520-7207

EMERGENCY MEDICAL SERVICE: This information was not provided by this community.

LOCAL AMENITIES

HUMAN SERVICES: More than forty-five organizations provide human services in this community **HEALTHCARE:** Ambicab, Brockhurst Ranch Adolescent Chemical Dependency Treatment Center, Cedar Springs Psychiatric Hospital, Hospice, Inc., Mental Health, Planned Parenthood, Rape Crisis Service, Visiting Nurses Association **ORGANIZATIONS:** More than fifty associations, organizations and clubs are active in the area; some are headquartered here **PROFESSIONAL SERVICES:** Institute for Business & Industrial Technology **ENTERAINMENT:** Imperial Hotel & Melodrama, Iron Springs Chateau Dinner Theater.

CLIMATE

January Temperature (in degrees Fahrenheit)   27.0
July Temperature (in degrees Fahrenheit)   78.0

Annual Precipitation (in inches) 16.0
Annual Snowfall (in inches) 59.0
Elevation (in feet) 6500
Area (in square miles) 2129.7

TAXES

1993 PROPERTY TAXES: Mill Levy 12.000
1993 SALES TAXES: El Paso County 1.00%
Other (RTD, Stadium, Cultural Facilities, etc.) 0.00%
State 3.00%

LOCAL ECONOMIC DEVELOPMENT CONTACTS

Major firms in area: **GOVERNMENT**: Ft. Carson, Peterson/NORAD/Space Command, Air Force Academy, City Governments, School District 11, County Governments, Harrison School District, US Postal Service, Academy School District, Widefield School District **HI-TECH**: Hewlett-Packard Co., Digital Equipment Corp., TRW Inc., Current Inc., Ampex Corp., Inmos Corp., Honeywell Inc., Ford Aerospace, Kaman Corp., Texas Instruments Inc. **SERVICES**: Penrose Hospitals, Broadmoor Hotel Inc., Memorial Hospital, St. Francis Hospital **RETAIL TRADE**: King Soopers, Safeway, Sears, Schoollage Lock Co. **FINANCE, INSURANCE, REAL ESTATE**: Farmers Insurance Group **UTILITIES**: Mountain Bell, Colorado Interstate Gas. The leading source of income is High Tech, Military.

1994 PUBLIC SCHOOL INFORMATION

District Name	# of Students	# of Schools	# of Teachers	Students /Teachers
Calhan RJ-1	479	3	26	18.3
Harrison 2	10,753	18	637	16.9
Widefield 3	8,279	14	427	19.4
Fountain 8 1	4,437	10	257	17.3
Colorado Springs 11	32,539	54	1,620	20.1
Cheyenne Mountain	2,907	6	151.9	19.1
Manitou Springs 14	1,368	4	73	18.8
Academy 20	13,529	19	731	18.5
Ellicott 22	604	2	35	17.1
Peyton 23 JT	396	3	25	15.8
Hanover 28	130	2	9	14.4
Lewis-Palmer 38	3,375	5	158	21.3
Falcon 49	3,269	6	182	18.0
Edison 54 JT	36	2	5	7.2
Miami/Yoder 60 JT	234	2	14	16.7

NEAREST FOUR-YEAR COLLEGE: Univ. of Colorado (Colorado Springs)
NEAREST COMMUNITY COLLEGE: Pikes Peak Community College (Colorado Springs)
NEAREST VOCATIONAL CENTER: Several schools (Colorado Springs)

CHAPTER SEVEN: CHANGES IN LATITUDES/ATTITUDES

LOCAL TRANSPORTATION

NEAREST SCHEDULED AIR SERVICE: Colorado Springs Municipal A/P, Gary Green, 719-596-0188
LOCAL BUSES, TRUCKS, AND TRAINS: Greyhound, Continental Trailways, A&A, ABF, ANR, American Freight, Consolidated Freightways, Edson, Ellis, McLean, Yellow Freight. Freight: Santa Fe, Rio Grande

LOCAL UTILITIES

LOCAL WATER INFORMATION City of Colo. Springs, 636-5300 - City of Fountain, 382-7591 - City of Manitou Springs, 685-5597 - Town of Calhan 347-2586, Denver Water Department, 893-2444.
LOCAL SEWER INFORMATION: City of Colorado Springs 636-5300 - Fountain Sanitation. 382-5719, Calhan Sewage District. 347-2338 - Monument Sewage District, Palmer Lake Sewage District - 481-2732
LOCAL LANDFILL INFORMATION See individual municipalities.
LOCAL ELECTRICITY INFORMATION Public Service Co., 623-1234, City of Colorado Springs, 636-5300 - City of Fountain, 392-9088, Mountain View Elec. Assn., 332-9881, Intermountain Rural Electric Assn., 688-3100
LOCAL GAS INFORMATION Public Service Co., 623-1234, City of Colorado Springs, 636-5300 - City of Fountain, 392-9088, People's Natural Gas, 688-3032

JEFFERSON COUNTY

LARGEST CITIES/TOWNS/COMMUNITIES

Mountain View, Wheat Ridge, Lakewood, Arvada, Bow Mar, Broomfield, Edgewater, Golden, Lakeside, Morrison (current population: 475,214).

POPULATION ESTIMATES BY AGE GROUPS, 1996-2005

AGE GROUP	1996	2000	2005
0 to 4 years old	35759	34553	33340
5 to 18	98664	103579	105929
19 to 34	98262	88933	92312
35 to 64	218642	241645	254723
65 to 89	45240	50703	58901
90 and over	1227	1337	1606
Total	497832	520749	546810

LOCAL COMMUNITY DESCRIPTION

Jefferson County is situated in the northcentral portion of the state where the eastern plains rise to meet the Rocky Mountains. The County forms the western & southwestern extension of Colorado's principle urban center, the six county Denver metropolitan area. Prairies, valleys, mountains & forests offer a varied physical appearance to the county whose chief landmark is the rock formation near Morrison which forms Red Rocks Amphitheater. Jefferson County's growth has led to increases in small business & professional services, the expansion of industrial operations, the creation of shopping centers & the enlargement of the regional operations of many federal government agencies. Economic expansion has created the opportunity for diverse lifestyles among the County's residents & has resulted in one of the nation's finest public education systems & a nationally acclaimed program for the preservation of open space. Golden, the countyseat, was the state's first capital.

ADDRESS: 100 Jefferson County Pkwy., Golden, CO 80419, 303-271-8525
DATE OF INCORPORATION: 1861, COUNTY SEAT: City of Golden

LOCAL EMERGENCY SERVICES

Mountain View, Wheat Ridge, Lakewood, Arvada, Bow Mar, Broomfield, Edgewater, Golden, Lakeside, Morrison are served by fire departments.
Staff: 465, Vehicles: 125, Phone: (303) 278-5310

LOCAL AMENITIES

HUMAN SERVICES: Jefferson County Social Services - Bill Hales 303-232-3632, JEFFCO Employment & Training Services, Jefferson Animal Shelter, Cooperative Extension Service, Prospect Recreation District **PUBLIC FACILITIES**: Public Library - 9 branches, bookmobile; CHURCHES: all denominations available **RECREATIONAL AREAS**: Pike National Forest, Arapahoe National Forest, Roosevelt National Forest, Red Rocks Park, Golden Gate State Park, Means Meadow, White Ranch Park, Mt. Falcon Historic Park, (16,000acres of open space park & recreational areas) **TOURIST ATTRACTIONS**: Hiwan Homestead Museum, Nature & Conference Center - Lookout Mountain, Buffalo Bills Grave, Coors Brewery, Heritage Square - amusement rides, craft & specialty shops, Jefferson County Fairgrounds - July 4th Festival of the West Celebration, Morrison - antique & craft shops **ACTIVITIES**: Swimming, Fishing, Boating, Camping, Windsailing, Hiking, Equestrian Trails **LODGING**: Denver West - Marriott Hotel, Motel 6, Comfort Inn, Holiday Inn, many others.

CLIMATE

January Temperature (in degrees Fahrenheit)	29.0
July Temperature (in degrees Fahrenheit)	75.0
Annual Precipitation (in inches)	16.0
Annual Snowfall (in inches)	50.0
Elevation (in feet)	5500
Area (in square miles)	778.2

TAXES

1993 PROPERTY TAXES: Mill Levy	25.584
1993 SALES TAXES: Jefferson County	.50%
Other (RTD, Stadium, Cultural Facilities, etc.)	.60%
State	3.00%

CHAPTER SEVEN: CHANGES IN LATITUDES/ATTITUDES

LOCAL ECONOMIC DEVELOPMENT CONTACTS

Major firms in area: **MANUFACTURING**: Martin Marietta, Rockwell International, Mannville Corp., Cobe Laboratories, Sunstrand, Ball Metal Container, IBM **ENERGY**: Rocky Mountain Energy, Amax Inc., Mobile Premix **FOOD PROCESSING**: Jolly Rancher, Adolph Coors Company **SERVICES**: General Cable, Mountain Bell, A T & T, Public Service Company **FINANCE, INSURANCE, REAL ESTATE**: Rocky Mountain Banknote **OTHER**: Statitrol **GOVERNMENT**: Federal Government, Jefferson County, R-1 School District., Federal Center **RETAIL TRADE**: King Soopers **TRANSPORTATION**: United Airlines. Local banks have $3,200,000,000 in assets.

1994 PUBLIC SCHOOL INFORMATION

District Name	# of Students	# of Schools	# of Teachers	Students /Teacher
Jefferson County R-1	84,018	88	3,935	21.4

NEAREST FOUR-YEAR COLLEGE: Colorado School of Mines (Golden)
NEAREST COMMUNITY COLLEGE: Arapahoe Community College (Littleton)
NEAREST VOCATIONAL CENTER: Columbine Beauty School, Mile Hi College (Lakewood)

LOCAL TRANSPORTATION

NEAREST SCHEDULED AIR SERVICE: Denver International Airport
LOCAL BUSES, TRUCKS, AND TRAINS Greyhound, Continental Trailways, RTD. A full array of truck lines serve the Denver Metro area & Jefferson County. Freight: Denver & Rio Grande Railway, Great Western Railway. Passenger: Amtrak

LOCAL UTILTIES (see page 206 for most Electric/Gas phone numbers)

LOCAL WATER INFORMATION: Contact the Denver Water Department, 303-893-2444.

LOCAL SEWER INFORMATION: Contact the Denver Water Department, 303-893-2444.

LOCAL LANDFILL INFORMATION: County residents using landfill in adjacent Boulder County. New landfill pending litigation.

LOCAL ELECTRICITY INFORMATION: Public Service Company, Intermountain Rural Electric Association, United Power

LOCAL GAS INFORMATION: Public Service Company.

LARIMER COUNTY

LARGEST CITIES/TOWNS/COMMUNITIES
Berthoud, Estes Park, Fort Collins, Loveland, Timnath, Wellington (current population: 200,782).

POPULATION ESTIMATES BY AGE GROUPS, 1996-2005

AGE GROUP	1996	2000	2005
0 to 4 years old	14581	15672	17024
5 to 18	43139	44801	46507
19 to 34	56952	58508	65203
35 to 64	82925	95534	104354
65 to 89	20401	21835	24155
90 and over	739	847	996
Total	218736	237197	258238

LOCAL COMMUNITY DESCRIPTION

Larimer County is located on the eastern edge of the Rocky Mountains in northern Colorado. Major urban areas in the county are arranged along scenic foothills, with a backdrop of spectacular mountain peaks. The county extends to the Continental Divide & includes several mountain communities & Rocky Mountain National Park. Lifestyle opportunities in Larimer County are as varied as the terrain & include sophisticated urban areas with established cultural facilities, productive agricultural lands, small-town environments & a wealth of outdoor recreation areas enjoyed by urban & rural residents alike. The area benefits from its proximity to the Denver metropolitan area, but has retained its own identity & unique quality of life. Colorado State University is located in Larimer County, which together with Colorado University in adjacent Boulder County has established the area as a center of advanced research & learning. The unique environment has attracted a variety of businesses, both large & small, which have generally prospered, so growth of existing business is a more important source of new jobs than those created by new industry. Still, the people of the county welcome the many new members of the community who wish to call Larimer County home.

ADDRESS: P. O. Box 1190, Fort Collins, CO 80522, 970-498-7000
DATE OF INCORPORATION: 1861, COUNTY SEAT: City of Fort Collins

LOCAL EMERGENCY SERVICES

Berthoud, Estes Park, Fort Collins, Loveland, Timnath, & Wellington are served by fire depts., Staff: 183, Vehicles: 78, Phone: (970) 221-7107

LOCAL AMENITIES

CHURCHES: 110 churches in the community **HEALTHCARE**: Foothills Gateway Rehabilitation Center, Hospice, Inc., Human Development, Mental Health, Public Health **ORGANIZATIONS**: Boy Scouts, Camp Fire, Girl Scouts, Multiple Sclerosis Society of Colorado, Neighbor to Neighbor, United Service Organization, Right to

CHAPTER SEVEN: CHANGES IN LATITUDES/ATTITUDES

Life, Birthright, AA, Al Anon **HUMAN SERVICES**: More than thirty organizations provide human services in the area **ADDITIONAL INFORMATION**: contact Larimer County Parks & Recreation at 970-669-4077; **LODGING**: several major hotels in major municipalities

CLIMATE

January Temperature (in degrees Fahrenheit)	23.0
July Temperature (in degrees Fahrenheit)	71.0
Annual Precipitation (in inches)	14.0
Annual Snowfall (in inches)	58.0
Elevation (in feet)	5400
Area (in square miles)	2634.0

TAXES

1993 PROPERTY TAXES: Mill Levy	21.723
1993 SALES TAXES: Larimer County	0.00%
Other (RTD, Stadium, Cultural Facilities, etc.)	0.00%
State	3.00%

LOCAL ECONOMIC DEVELOPMENT CONTACTS

Major firms in area: **MANUFACTURING**: Woodward Governor, Teledyne Water Pik, Hewlett Packard, Eastman Kodak, Anheuser Busch **GOVERNMENT**: Colorado State University, Poudre Valley Schools, Larimer County, City of Fort Collins **SERVICES**: Poudre Valley Hospital **UTILITIES**: Mountain Bell, **PLEASE NOTE:** All of the above employers have more than 500 employees. The leading source of income is high tech manufacturing.

1994 PUBLIC SCHOOL INFORMATION

District Name	# of Students	# of Schools	# of Teachers	Students /Teacher
Poudre R-1	21,183	41	996	21.3
Thompson R-2J	13,137	26	19.5	
Park (Estes Park) R-3	1,399	3	70	20.0

NEAREST FOUR-YEAR COLLEGE: Colorado State Univ. (Fort Collins)
NEAREST COMMUNITY COLLEGE: Aims Community College (Greeley)
NEAREST VOCATIONAL CENTER: Larimer County Voc-Tech (Fort Collins)

LOCAL TRANSPORTATION

NEAREST SCHEDULED AIR SERVICE: Fort Collins-Loveland Muni., Fred Anderton Jr., 4824 Earhart Road, Loveland, CO 80538, 970-669-7182

LOCAL BUSES, TRUCKS, AND TRAINS: Continental Trailways, TWX, American Freight Systems, Consolidated Freightways, CH&W Transportation Co., Ryder. Freight: Union Pacific, Colorado & Southern

LOCAL UTILTIES (see page 206 for most Electric/Gas phone numbers)

LOCAL WATER INFORMATION: Arkins Water Association, Inc., Bald Mountain Water Assn., East Larimer Co. Water (ELCO), Ft. Collins-Loveland Water, Laporte Water, Sunset Water, Little Thompson Water

LOCAL SEWER INFORMATION Boxelder Sanitation, Cherry Hills Sanitation, Estes Park Sanitation, Laporte Sanitation, Mountain View Sanitation, S. Ft. Collins Sanitation

LOCAL LANDFILL INFORMATION Frank Lancaster (303) 221-7712.

LOCAL ELECTRICITY INFORMATION Poudre Valley REA, Public Service Co.

LOCAL GAS INFORMATION Poudre Valley REA, Public Service Co.

SUMMIT COUNTY

LARGEST CITIES/TOWNS/COMMUNITIES

Breckenridge, Silverthorne, Dillon, Frisco, Blue River, Montezuma (current population: 14,631)

POPULATION ESTIMATES BY AGE GROUPS, 1996-2005

AGE GROUP	1996	2000	2005
0 to 4 years old	1029	943	909
5 to 18	2466	2804	2965
19 to 34	4605	4405	4568
35 to 64	7517	8719	9681
65 to 89	737	1039	1414
90 and over	8	18	34
Total	16362	17927	19571

LOCAL COMMUNITY DESCRIPTION

In the heart of the Rockies, Summit County has the highest average elevation of any county in the nation. It spans 383,260 acres, 73% of which is public land, made up of jagged mountain peaks & beautiful valleys. The Eisenhower Tunnel provides the east entrance to the county & Vail Pass the west. On the north, Summit County is bounded by Kremmling & on the south by Hoosier Pass. Summit County has been identified as a hot spot of US Growth. From the 1980 census to the 1990 census, this County was the fifth fastest growing of any in the State with respect to population. The permanent population soared from 8,848 in 1980 to 12,881 in 1990, a 46% increase. Summit County offers a variety of activities year-round, from skiing to white water rafting, from World Cup skiing competition to hiking, horseback riding & fishing & from theater to music & film festivals. The County offers a variety of commercial & industrial zoned parcels, both in the incorporated & unincorporated areas. The entire County is only approximately 45% built-out. Through the master planning processes of the Towns & County, growth is expected to take place in a regular, directed pattern.

CHAPTER SEVEN: CHANGES IN LATITUDES/ATTITUDES

Summit County truly is an area with high amenities, good climate, recreational opportunities, attractive scenery & even more growth potential.

ADDRESS: P. O. Box 68, Breckenridge, CO 80424, 970-453-2561
DATE OF INCORPORATION: 1861, COUNTY SEAT: Breckenridge

LOCAL EMERGENCY SERVICES

Breckenridge, Silverthorne, Dillon, Frisco, Blue River, Montezuma have Fire Protection. Joe Morales, sheriff's office, Phone: 970-453-2232

LOCAL AMENITIES

HUMAN SERVICES: Contact Bob Taylor, Director of Social Services 303-453-2561 **HEALTHCARE FACILITIES**: Frisco Medical Center, Breckenridge Medical Center, Copper Medical Center, Snake River Health Services **CHURCHES**: Episcopal, Catholic, Mormon, Jehovah, Methodist, Community, Church of Christ, Bible **ORGANIZATIONS**: Elks, Masons, Rotary, PEO **RECREATION AREAS**: Arapaho Basin, Copper Mountain, Keystone, Breckenridge ski areas. National Rep. Orchestra festival.

CLIMATE

January Temperature (in degrees Fahrenheit)	16.0
July Temperature (in degrees Fahrenheit)	61.0
Annual Precipitation (in inches)	16.0
Annual Snowfall (in inches)	***** (Lots)
Elevation (in feet)	9500
Area (in square miles)	619.3

TAXES

1993 PROPERTY TAXES: Mill Levy	13.210
1993 SALES TAXES: Summit County	2.50%
Other (RTD, Stadium, Cultural Facilities, etc.)	0.00%
State	3.00%

LOCAL ECONOMIC DEVELOPMENT CONTACTS

Major firms in area: **SERVICES**: Keystone, Breckenridge Ski Area, Copper Mountain, Beaver Run, Village at Breckenridge **UTILITIES**: Public Service **RETAIL TRADE**: City Market, Walmart **GOVERNMENT**: Summit County School District, Summit County, State of Colorado **MINING**: Climax/Henderson, AMAX. The leading source of income is Ski Industry/Resort.

1994 PUBLIC SCHOOL INFORMATION

District Name	# of Students	# of Schools	# of Teachers	Students /Teacher
Summit RE-1	2,157	6	144	15.5

NEAREST FOUR-YEAR COLLEGE: Colorado School of Mines (Golden)
NEAREST COMMUNITY COLLEGE: Colorado Mountain College (Leadville)
NEAREST VOCATIONAL CENTER: Boulder Valley Voc-Tech (Boulder)

LOCAL TRANSPORTATION

NEAREST SCHEDULED AIR SERVICE: Eagle County Airport, Dan Reynolds, Box 850, Eagle, CO 81631, 970-524-9490
LOCAL BUSES, TRUCKS, AND TRAINS Summit stage, Continental Trailways, DSL & RAC, Rider P.I.E

LOCAL UTILTIES (see page 206 for most Electric/Gas phone numbers)

LOCAL WATER INFORMATION: Municipal districts
LOCAL SEWER INFORMATION: Municipal districts: 970-468-5794
LOCAL LANDFILL INFORMATION: Bill Schmidt, 970-468-2475
LOCAL ELECTRICITY INFORMATION: Public Service Co: 970-468-0613
LOCAL GAS INFORMATION: Public Service Co: 970-468-0613

WELD COUNTY

LARGEST CITIES/TOWNS/COMMUNITIES

Greeley, Evans, Platteville, Fort Lupton (current population: 140,057)

POPULATION ESTIMATES BY AGE GROUPS, 1996-2005

AGE GROUP	1996	2000	2005
0 to 4 years old	11309	11413	12403
5 to 18	32435	33543	34191
19 to 34	38282	40016	43940
35 to 64	53969	61026	67076
65 to 89	14794	15724	17321
90 and over	540	639	719
Total	15130	162361	175651

LOCAL COMMUNITY DESCRIPTION

Weld County represents a highly diversified economy with excellent growth potential. Within the last 3 years 2,100 new manufacturing jobs have been added in the county. Weld County offers an outstanding quality of life. Within a 60-mile radius are located 4 major universities with their attendant cultural & athletic events. The Denver metro-area forms the county's southern boundary & 6 major ski areas are located within a 2

CHAPTER SEVEN: CHANGES IN LATITUDES/ATTITUDES

hour drive and the county will soon be home to the largest performing arts center in Northern Colorado.

ADDRESS: P. O. Box 758, Greeley, CO 80632, 970-356-4000
DATE OF INCORPORATION: 1861, COUNTY SEAT: City of Greeley

LOCAL EMERGENCY SERVICES

See individual municipalities. Staff: 149, Vehicles: 34, Phone: 970-356-4000 x4631, Contact Ed Jordan. Weld Ambulance Service

LOCAL AMENITIES

ORGANIZATIONS: American Cancer Society, Cystic Fibrosis Foundation, Leukemia Society of America, Multiple Sclerosis Society, National Kidney Foundation, National Association of Sickle Cell Disease **HEALTHCARE**: Crisis Pregnancy of Weld County, North Colorado Medical Center, Weld County Health Department, Island Grove Regional Treatment Center, Northern Colorado Center on Deafness, Rape Crisis Team, Schaefer Rehabilitation Center, Weld Mental Health Center, Patient Advocacy Team, Northeast Home Health Care Service **HUMAN SERVICES**: Battered Women's Helpline, Catholic Community Services, Chemical Families Support Services, Child Abuse Resource & Education, Parent Child Learning Center, Partners, Inc., SAVE, Salvation Army, The Sycamore Tree, United Way of Weld County, Women's Place, Weld County Community Center Foundation, Weld County Social Services, Weld County Human Services, Weld County Health Department, Weld Information & Referral Service, Colorado Christian Services, Colorado Civil Rights Commission, Volunteer Resource Bureau; **CHURCHES**: All major denominations **LODGING**: Holiday Inn, Raintree Hotel & Conference Center, Heritage Hotel **PERFORMING ARTS CENTER** (soon to be completed); **PHILHARMONIC ORCHESTRA** (oldest philharmonic orchestra west of the Mississippi River).

CLIMATE

January Temperature (in degrees Fahrenheit)	29.0
July Temperature (in degrees Fahrenheit)	75.0
Annual Precipitation (in inches)	13.0
Annual Snowfall (in inches)	37.0
Elevation (in feet)	4900
Area (in square miles)	4021.8

TAXES

1993 PROPERTY TAXES: Mill Levy	22.457
1993 SALES TAXES: Weld County	0.00%
Other (RTD, Stadium, Cultural Facilities, etc.)	0.00%
State	3.00%

LOCAL ECONOMIC DEVELOPMENT CONTACTS

Major firms in area: **MANUFACTURING**: Eastman Kodak, Monfort of Colorado, Hewlett Packard, ConAgra, Electronic Fab **GOVERNMENT**: School District #6,

University of Northern Colorado, Aims College, Weld County, City of Greeley, Federal Government, State of Colorado, School District #8, School District #4 **SERVICES**: North Colorado Medical Center, Mountain Bell, Golden Recycling (Coors) **FINANCE, INSURANCE, REAL ESTATE**: State Farm Insurance **RETAIL TRADE**: Safeway, Toddys, K-Mart **CONSTRUCTION**: Hensel Phelps (contractor) **TRANSPORTATION**: Steinbecker Brothers (motor freight transport.) **OTHER**: Northwest Publishing, Greeley Publishing. The leading source of income is Agriculture, Oil & Gas, Meat Products, Film, Computers. Local banks have $497,330,000 in assets.

1994 PUBLIC SCHOOL INFORMATION

District Name	# of Students	# of Schools	# of Teachers	Students /Teacher
Gilcrest RE-1	1,866	6	126	14.8
Eaton RE-2	1,289	4	73	17.6
Keenesburg RE-3(J)	1,343	4	82	16.5
Windsor RE-4	1,890	5	112	16.9
Johnstown-Milliken RE-5J	1,230	4	78	15.7
Greeley 6	12,931	22	715	18.1
Platte Valley RE-7	975	2	59	16.5
Fort Lupton RE-8	2,583	4	141	18.3
Ault-Highland RE-9	863	3	63	13.7
Briggsdale RE-10	89	2	11	7.7
Prairie RE-11	128	2	15	8.3
Pawnee RE-12	115	2	15	7.9

NEAREST FOUR-YEAR COLLEGE: Univ. of Northern Colorado (Greeley)
NEAREST COMMUNITY COLLEGE: Aims Community College (Greeley)
NEAREST VOCATIONAL CENTER: Larimer County Voc-Tech (Fort Collins)

LOCAL TRANSPORTATION

NEAREST SCHEDULED AIR SERVICE: Fort Collins-Loveland Muni.
LOCAL BUSES, TRUCKS, AND TRAINS: Greyhound, Estes Park Bus Company, Greeley Bus, Weld County Mini-Van System, Continental Trailway, Airport Shuttle. MOST MAJOR TRUCKLINES. Freight: Great Western, Union Pacific, Burlington Northern. Passenger: AMTRAK.

LOCAL UTILTIES (see page 206 for most Electric/Gas phone numbers)

LOCAL WATER / SEWER INFORMATION: Contact city or town
LOCAL ELECTRICITY INFORMATION: Home Light & Power Service Company, Union REA
LOCAL GAS INFORMATION: Greeley Gas

CHAPTER EIGHT
MONEY FOR NOTHING

SMALL AND HOME-BASED BUSINESS START-UP

The information in this chapter was compiled from various sources including, but not limited to, government reports and publications (Federal, State, and Local); material provided by business and civic organizations; and books produced by independent Colorado publishers including:

Big Ideas For Small Service Businesses and *Country Bound! Trade Your Business Suit Blues for Blue Jean Dreams,* Communication Creativity

For a complete description of the above books and related titles, please see the Publisher's listing in Appendix A.

So you want to be your own boss? Be self-employed or own your own business? There are 21.5 million small businesses in the United States which employ 54 percent of the private workforce. Of the 1.9 million new jobs created in 1993, small businesses produced an estimated 71 percent of those jobs. In the United States, small businesses account for 52 percent of all sales. In Colorado, during 1993 and 1994, there were 31,000 new businesses created. However, a full 17 percent—or 2,644—of the 15,425 for-profit businesses started in 1993 are no longer in business.

I have been self-employed since I turned in my parachute, beret, and uniform and became a civilian again in 1979. I can tell you from experience the "American Dream" of owning your own business is not always what it's cracked-up to be. It takes a special type of person to make it successfully. There is the hard work, the uncertain financial returns, the responsibilities, and the ever increasing burden of rules, regulations and laws.

This chapter is designed to help you determine if starting your own small or home-based business is really what you want to do and to give you as much information and resources as space permits. While all federal laws concerning this subject are uniform throughout the country, most states have unique laws, rules and regulations of which you need to be aware. The simple self-quiz below should help you decide whether to skip this chapter or not.

SO YOU WANT TO BE AN ENTREPRENEUR?

There is no way to eliminate all the risks associated with starting a small business. However, you can improve your chances of success with good planning and preparation. A good starting place is to evaluate your strengths and weaknesses as the owner and manager of a small business. Carefully consider each of the following questions.

Are you a self-starter? It will be up to you, not someone else telling you, to develop projects, organize your time, follow through on details.

How well do you get along with different personalities? Business owners need to develop working relationships with a variety of people including customers, vendors, staff, bankers and professionals such as lawyers, accountants or consultants. Can you deal with a demanding client, an unreliable vendor or cranky staff person in the best interests of your business?

How good are you at making decisions? Small business owners are required to make decisions constantly, often quickly, under pressure and independently.

Do you have the physical and emotional stamina to run a business? Business ownership can be challenging, fun and exciting. But it's also a lot of work. Can you face 12-hour work days six or seven days a week? How well do you plan and organize? Research indicates many business failures could have been avoided through better planning. Good organization—of financial inventory, schedules, production—can help avoid many potential pitfalls.

Is your drive strong enough to maintain your motivation? Running a business can wear you down. Some business owners feel burned out by having to carry all the responsibility on their shoulders. Strong motivation to make the business succeed will help you survive slowdowns as well as periods of burnout.

How will the business affect my family? The first few years of business start up can be hard on family life. The strain of an un-supportive spouse may be hard to balance against the demands of starting a business. There also may be financial difficulties until the business becomes profitable, which could take months or even years. You may have to adjust to a lower standard of living or put family assets at risk.

Is it worth it? For many, yes! While there are numerous reasons not to start your own business, there are many advantages which, for the right person, far outweigh the risks. For starters, you get to be your own boss. Your hard work and long hours directly benefit you, rather than increasing profits for someone else. Your earnings and growth potential are far less limited. A new venture—your new venture is exciting

CHAPTER EIGHT: MONEY FOR NOTHING

and running a business will provide endless variety and challenge and won't settle into a dull routine.

Assuming you have seriously considered each of these questions and have decided to go for it, the next step is to plan your new venture using the check-list below.

CHECK-LIST FOR NEW BUSINESS START-UP

You should be fully aware of the implications of owning your own business. The best advice for anyone starting or operating a business is to EDUCATE YOURSELF. This chapter is only a first step. It outlines only the basic information you will need to start your business. To obtain complete information, there are dozens of books available, many specific to Colorado business operation. Highly recommended is the Colorado Business Start-up Kit available free of charge from the Colorado Business Assistance Center, (303) 592-5920 or 1-800-333-7798

- Decide upon the legal structure of your business and register your business and tradename with the appropriate State and/or federal agencies. **If you plan to open a business checking account you must have a tradename registration.** Refer to the Legal Structure and Registration section of this chapter.

- If your business will have employees, you must open federal, state and local wage withholding and payroll tax accounts. See the Employers Responsibilities section of this chapter.

- If your business will be selling, renting or leasing tangible personal property, obtain state and local sales tax licenses. If you rent accommodations for less than 30 days, a sales tax license is also required. Refer to the Colorado Sales Tax Licenses section.

- Be aware of the personal and business tax implications of starting your own business. Refer to the Income and Property Taxes section.

- Define the products or services you will provide. **Is there actually a need for what you will provide in today's marketplace. Is the demand great enough to be profitable! What is your competitive advantage? Develop your marketing strategy first!**

- Are there any special licenses required for the business you are starting? The Colorado Business Assistance Center, (303) 592-5920 or 1-800-333-7798, has information on federal, state, and local business licensing.

- Find the best location for your business. The Colorado Department of Transportation, 4201 E. Arkansas Ave., Denver. CO 80222: (303) 757-9488, has information on traffic patterns on state highways. Some local governments have information on city and county roads. They may also have information on local population demographics. Observe pedestrian movement during business hours to estimate walk-in potential.

- Check with the local city and county government regarding any special business regulations, sales taxes, personal property taxes and zoning restrictions.

- Seek management advice and counseling. Assemble your team of professional advisors, e.g., an accountant, an attorney, an insurance broker, a real estate agent, etc. Business organizations, business consultants, your local Small Business Development Center, the Small Business Administration, trade associations, and your local chamber of commerce are good resources. Refer to the Additional Resources section.

- **Develop a sound business plan with specific goals and objectives. A business plan should show where you are, where you want to go and how you will get there.** There are numerous books and software packages designed to assist you in every step of formulating a business plan—well worth the investment!

- Develop a financial plan. Include profit and loss projections, cash flow analysis and capitol requirements.

- Obtain adequate insurance coverage. Protect your business activities for enough in advance to cover your growth. See the Business Insurance section.

- **Protect your ideas, products, symbols and logos through the proper registration and maintenance.** The Colorado Business Assistance Center, (303) 592-5920 or 1-800-333-7798, has information on Trademarks, Patents, and Copyrights.

NEW, ESTABLISHED, OR FRANCHISE

There are typically three avenues available to start a new business: starting a new venture from scratch, buying an existing business, or buying a franchise.

Starting a New Venture: A new start up is typically pursued when you have a unique idea that requires special equipment, specialized talents or a new way of doing things. A new venture may also be pursued when there is a customer base you can serve, or you are aware of an unfilled market. Factors you need to consider when forming a new venture include: legal structure, location, facilities, equipment, employees, taxes, marketing and advertising, a records system, and capital. **Be warned: recent estimates suggest investors lose $500 million annually in franchise and work-at-home schemes.** There are several free brochures available from the Federal Trade Commission including, "Job Ads, Job Scams and '900' Numbers," "Work At Home Schemes," and "Telemarketing Fraud." Call (202) 326-2222.

Buying an Established Business: Buying an existing business can have its advantages. By purchasing a business that is already established, you may eliminate some of the problems associated with starting a brand new business. However, when you acquire an existing business, you may also acquire the business's debts. Purchasing an existing business can be fairly complex. The following is a brief summary of some of the concerns of which you should be aware:

AVOIDING COMMERCIAL FRAUD

- Do you know why the seller is selling the business? If the business has not been profitable, find out why. Do you have a plan to make it profitable?

CHAPTER EIGHT: MONEY FOR NOTHING

- Does your purchase agreement include the sale of the business name? The property? The equipment and inventory? The debts? Be sure the exact terms of the sale are explained clearly before you buy. It is highly recommended you have your own attorney review all parts of the agreement.

- Ask the seller about outstanding claims on inventory, equipment and fixtures. Whose responsibility will it be to settle these claims? Are there liens against the property you are buying? Check with the seller and the county clerk and recorder's office in the county where the business and the seller are located. Also check with the Colorado Secretary of State, Uniform Commercial Code Section, 1560 Broadway, Suite 200, Denver, CO 80202. (303) 894-2251, for records of any security interests that may have been filed as liens against the property or assets of the business.

- Will the owner of the building transfer the lease to you? What are the terms and restrictions of the lease?

- Review the business's past and current financial statements. Are they in good order? Also, examine any existing contracts that affect the business's operations.

- Can you transfer the existing phone number(s)? The phone service may require information from both you and the seller. See the U.S. West heading under the Additional Resources Section.

If there are employees in the business, you will be responsible for withholding tax, unemployment insurance, workers' compensation and social security (FICA). You must open new employee payroll accounts unless you buy out the stock of an existing corporation and do not set up a new corporation. In every case the unemployment history established under the former owners will transfer to your account. When you purchase the business, the former owner should file form UILT-2 to report the change in ownership. For more information on payroll tax requirements see the Employer Responsibilities section.

Tax Liabilities: If you purchase a retail business you may be liable for sales tax debts of the business. As a precaution, you should get a tax status letter from the Department of Revenue before buying. The tax status letter must be requested by the current owner using form DR0096. Tax status letters may be requested on all state collected tax accounts including sales tax, wage withholding and corporate income tax accounts. There is a $10 charge for each tax requested. If you purchase a corporation, you may have the option of keeping the same sales tax account with the Department of Revenue. If you purchase a sole proprietorship or a partnership, you are required to open a new sales tax account.

When you purchase tangible property as part of a business, such as furniture, fixtures or equipment (new or used) for which you have not paid sales tax, you must pay a state use tax. For further information about state tax liabilities when purchasing a business contact the Colorado Department of Revenue, (303) 534-1208.

Many cities and counties also collect a use tax. All county use taxes and most city use taxes are collected by the state. Large "home rule" cities may collect use taxes directly. There may be additional liabilities for personal property taxes imposed by the county.

Contact the local city clerk, the county assessor and/or the county treasurer's offices for more information regarding local use and personal property taxes.

Buying a Franchise: Franchising offers a unique opportunity for individuals interested in operating a business. It allows you to both own and operate a business while drawing from the resources of the parent company. This arrangement may reduce some of the risks of going into business for yourself depending upon the quality and stability of the franchiser. It should be noted that while a franchise is a method for going into business it is NOT a form of legal structure. The franchiser—the business with the plan and structure—and the franchisee—you—must determine the appropriate form of legal structure. See the next section on Legal Structure and Registration for more information.

Once you have decided you are able to meet the requirements for purchasing a franchise, you may want to shop around for the best investment. There are various publications and franchise directories available from bookstores and public libraries. Many times the classified sections of your local newspaper or magazines have listings of franchise offers.

Exercise Caution: Before you agree to invest in a company that promises you large financial returns, you should exercise some caution. **Colorado lacks specific laws to protect you should you need recourse.** There are, however, general provisions governing "good business practices." These protections against deceptive and unfair trade practices are stated in the *Colorado Consumer Protection Act* and the *Uniform Consumer Credit Code.* The Federal Trade Commission's Franchise Rule requires franchisers to provide prospective buyers with a detailed disclosure statement regarding the company's history, background and operations. This document should also describe the costs and responsibilities of both the franchiser and the franchisee and must be made available to you at least ten days before any agreements are signed, or at the first face to face meeting, whichever comes first.

"The Franchise Opportunities Handbook," published by the US Department of Commerce is available for $16.00 from the Government Printing Office Bookstore, Federal Building, 1961 Stout St., Room 117, Denver, CO 80204, (303) 844-3964.

"Disclosure Requirements and Prohibitions Concerning Franchising and Business Opportunity Ventures" (The Franchise Rule), is available free from the Federal Trade Commission, 1405 Curates St., Suite 2900, Denver, CO 80202, (303) 844-2271.

LEGAL STRUCTURE AND REGISTRATION

Choosing The Right Legal Structure: When starting your own business, you must carefully choose the appropriate legal structure for your business. You should examine the characteristics of each structure along with the needs of and desires you have for your business.

A Sole Proprietor is a single individual who owns and operates the business. There is no legal separation between the individual and the business. She or he benefits from 100% of the profits and is personally responsible for 100% of all the debts and liabilities of the business.

A General Partnership is very similar to a sole proprietorship except there are two or more individuals who own the business. A general partnership offers the means for pooling all resources and sharing control of a business. There is relatively little formality required to establish and run the business, and control remains with the partners. However, all partners remain 100% responsible for all the debts and liabilities of the business, regardless of any partnership agreement outlining work responsibilities and shares of profit.

A Limited Partnership provides the ability to acquire additional capital while avoiding the need to borrow while the general partner(s) maintain(s) control of the day to day operations of your business. The *general partner(s)* is/are 100% responsible for all the debts and liabilities of the business. The *limited partner's* liability does not exceed her/his investment in the business. However, the *limited partner* cannot be involved in the operations or management of the business.

A Corporation is a legal entity separate from the owners of the business. There are significant formalities that must be observed to properly operate a corporation. The corporation provides a wall of liability protection between the business and the owners. It has the ability to raise capital by issuing stock.

While the limited liability enjoyed by shareholders may appear attractive, most creditors will probably require a personal guarantee as collateral anyway. The corporation must pay its own taxes, and the owners and owners who work in the business are normally classified as employees. A corporation may become an S corporation through application to the IRS. A corporation must comply with the Colorado Corporation Code. Among the requirements of the Code are the following:

- "Articles of Incorporation" must be filed with the Secretary of State
- The corporation must adopt bylaws
- A corporation must adhere to certain corporate formalities including procedures for shareholder meetings, the election of the board of directors, maintenance of corporate records and proper filings with the Secretary of State

An S Corporation is not actually a separate form of legal structure, but rather a special tax status granted by the IRS to tax business's income more like that of a partnership or a sole proprietorship. While an S corporation is not subject to double taxation as is a regular corporation, it may lose the ability to deduct the full cost of medical insurance as a business and business losses are treated differently. A competent tax advisor should be consulted before applying for S Corporation tax status. It is important to note the corporation must file the "Articles of Incorporation" with the Secretary of State before it can apply to the IRS for S status.

For more specific information about qualifying and applying for filing as an S Corporation, contact the IRS at 600 17th Street, The Dominion Plaza, 12th Floor, South Tower, Denver, CO 80202-2490, (303) 825-7041 or 1-800-829-1040.

Non-Profit Corporations: Non-Profit Organizations (NPO's) are not covered in this chapter. If you are interested in forming an NPO, all information can be obtained through the office of the Secretary of State, (303) 894-2251. It should be noted, a Not-for-Profit Corporation can be formed in Colorado by a single person for approximately $10.

A Limited Liability Company (LLC) combines the benefits of liability protection such as a corporation provides with the more simplified tax structure that a partnership can employ. However, limited liability companies are a new form of business structure which is not recognized throughout the US and many tax, legal and liability questions have not yet been completely clarified.

A **Limited Liability Partnership** (LLP) was approved for use in Colorado in mid-1995. It is basically the same as a LLC except it is for use by partnerships.

As you decide upon your legal structure, you should carefully evaluate both your present and future needs for operating your business. To avoid duplication of legal expenses, licensing and paperwork, analyze your various options and choose the business structure that will meet your long term needs rather than choosing a business structure solely for its short term convenience.

WHERE TO REGISTER YOUR NEW BUSINESS

Department Of Revenue: If you are a sole proprietor or general partnership and will be doing business under a name other than your own legal name(s), you must register a trade name with the Department of Revenue. Registration of the trade name does not grant exclusive rights to the use of the trade name. Sole proprietors and general partnerships gain exclusive rights to the use of a trade name only through the use of the name over a period of time. If you want to find out if a name is already being used, call the Department of Revenue, (303) 534-1208.

There are two forms which you may use to register a trade name. If your business will not have any sale of tangible products or any employees, you may use form DR0592, "Trade Name Registration." If you will have sales or employees, you should use the "Colorado Business Registration" form. This form will register your trade name as well as open your sales tax license, state wage withholding and unemployment insurance accounts. The appropriate form can be obtained from the Department of Revenue, (303) 534-1208, or through the Small Business Hotline, (303) 592-5920 or 1-800-333-7798. Completed forms may be filed via mail. Department of Revenue, 1375 Sherman Street, Denver, CO 80261, or in person at one of the local service centers: **Colorado Springs**, 3650 Austin Bluffs Parkway / **Denver**, 1560 Broadway, Suite 1530 / **Fort Collins**, 300 E. Foothills Road / **Grand Junction**, 222 S. Sixth St., Room 208 / **Pueblo**, 310 E. Abriendo Ave.

NOTE: Via mail, you will receive confirmation in approximately 4-6 weeks. In person, accounts will be established immediately.

Secretary Of State: If your business will be a Limited Partnership, Limited Liability Company or Corporation, you must file with the Secretary of State,. 1560 Broadway, Suite 200, Denver, CO 80202, (303) 894-2251. You should not register trade names for these businesses with the Department of Revenue. If you do business under an additional name, you must file a "Certificate of Assumed or Trade Name" with the Secretary of State. If you are outside the Denver metro area, you can obtain the original filing paperwork and trade name forms for the Secretary of State through the Small Business Hotline, 1-800-333-7798.

Internal Revenue Service: All forms of legal structure, except sole proprietors with no employees, must obtain a Federal Employer Identification Number (FEIN). The FEIN is your federal tax ID number. You can obtain your FEIN by filing the SS-4 form with the IRS, Ogden, UT 84201. If it is necessary to obtain your FEIN immediately, fill out the form, then call (801) 620-7645. This form can be obtained

CHAPTER EIGHT: MONEY FOR NOTHING

from the IRS, (303) 825-7041 or 1-800-829-1040 or through the Small Business Hotline, (303) 592-5920 or 1-800-333-7798. The SS-4 may also be faxed to the IRS 24 hours a day, (801) 620-7115. If you fax your form, you will receive your FEIN in approximately 10-14 days. If you are a sole proprietor. with no employees, you may use your social security number as your federal tax ID number or file form SS-4 at your option.

COLORADO SALES TAX LICENSES

If you sell, rent or lease tangible personal property in Colorado, you must obtain a sales tax license. The type of license you need and the amount of tax you are required to collect depends upon who you are selling to and where and how you are doing business. A license is also required to rent accommodations for periods of less than 30 days.

Retailer License: A retailer license is required if you are selling, renting or leasing your product to the end user of the product. If you will be doing wholesale and retail sales. you only need a retailer license. A retailer license costs $16 for a two-year period plus a one time $50 deposit. The deposit will be automatically refunded to you once you have collected and remitted a total of $50 in state sales tax to the Department of Revenue. 501(c)(3) charitable organizations are not required to pay the $50 deposit when they obtain their license.

Wholesaler License: A wholesaler license is required if you are selling your product to another business that will resell your product or use it as an ingredient in another product to be resold. A wholesaler license costs $16 for a two year period. If your business is primarily wholesale, you may have up to $1,000 in retail sales per year and will not be required to obtain a retailer license. If you will have more than $1,000 in retail sales per year, you should get a retailer license and record your wholesale sales under your retail license.

Single Event: If you plan to attend a single event as a vendor at a location other than your regular business location, you must obtain a single event license. A single event license costs $8. unless you already have a wholesaler or retailer license; then there is no charge.

Multiple Event License: If you attend more than one event during a two-year period, you should obtain a multiple event license. A multiple event license costs $16, unless you already have a wholesaler or retailer license, and then there is no charge.

Local License: Most city sales taxes are collected for the city by the state. However, there are 43 home rule cities in Colorado that have their own city sales tax license for retail sales conducted within their jurisdiction (see Collecting Sales Taxes below).

Fees: All state sales tax licenses are $16 and are issued for the same two year period. Each two year period is divided into four six month "quarters." The actual cost of your initial license will be pro-rated depending upon the quarter in which you start your business.

COLLECTING SALES TAXES

If you will be selling a product to the end user, you must collect sales tax. The amount of sales tax you collect depends upon the taxing districts where your business is located, the type of business you are in and how the transaction is completed. To determine the amount of tax you must collect, you need to add together the various rates that apply to your business. The 3.0% state sales tax must be collected by all businesses selling tangible, personal property located in Colorado.

In addition, you may be required to collect county, city, RTD/CD/BD, and special taxes. You should obtain a retail sales tax license to collect all state taxes and you may need several city sales tax licenses from the home rule cities where you do business. Department of Revenue Publication DRP1002, Colorado Sales/Use Tax Rates, lists all state, county and city sales tax rates as well as addresses and phone numbers for home rule cites with separate licensing and collection procedures. Also note special situations below:

Mail Order and Delivery: When you have a mail order business or you sell a product contingent upon delivery to another location within the state, you must collect the taxes you have in common with the delivery location. Check with the Department of Revenue for details.

Mobile Businesses: If your business involves sales at your client's address or is mobile, you must collect the appropriate tax for each sales location. This applies to such businesses as mobile locksmiths, mobile dog-groomers, interior decorators and the like. If this situation applies to you, you will not have a principle place of business and must collect the appropriate tax for each point of sale.

Craft Shows: If you will be selling at events you must have a state multiple events license. If the event is held in a city that collects its own city sales tax, you may be required to obtain an additional city sales tax license.

Flea Markets: Flea markets which operate more than three times per year are considered to be a retail location. If you sell at a flea market, you may not use an event license. All vendors should obtain retail licenses.

Multiple Permanent Business Locations: If your business has multiple permanent branch locations, each branch must have its own license and collect the appropriate tax. Exception: vending machine operators are only required to have one state license and report the appropriate tax collection under a single license. Although, each machine is required to display a sales tax decal and may still be subject to local licensing requirements.

Small Home Businesses: If you operate a small business from your home and your total annual sales are less than $1,000 per year, you do not have to obtain a state sales tax license. However, you must collect all applicable sales taxes and file a "Combined Annual Retail Sales Tax Return," DRO100A, at the end of each year. In addition, you will not be able to purchase inventory or supplies at wholesale without a license. If you are located in a home rule city, contact your city officials regarding your local sales tax requirements.

EMPLOYER RESPONSIBILITIES

As your business grows you may ask, "Should I hire full or part-time employees or should I hire subcontractors to perform specific jobs on an as-needed basis?" If you hire contract labor, your paper work is much easier. But just calling someone contract labor doesn't make her/him so and if you incorrectly classify those working for you,

CHAPTER EIGHT: MONEY FOR NOTHING

you may end up paying substantial penalties and back taxes to the IRS and the State of Colorado.

Most individuals who work for you will be considered either common law employees or independent contractors. Unfortunately, there are many state and federal laws which are used to define an employment relationship and to determine whether an individual who performs services for you is an "employee" or an "independent contractor." The following are general definitions for common law employees and independent contractors.

Common Law Employees: Common law employees are individuals who perform services subject to the control of an employer, regarding what, where, when and how something must be done. It does not matter if the employer gives the employee substantial discretion and freedom to act, so long as the employer has the legal right to control both the method and results of service. Employers are responsible for withholding all state and federal taxes and all common law employees must be covered by workers' compensation insurance.

Independent Contractors: Persons who follow a trade, business or profession such as lawyers, accountants, or construction contractors who offer their services to the general public are usually considered independent contractors. The single most important characteristics of independent contractors are freedom from control and financial risk. An independent contractor is responsible for her or his own self-employment taxes and any necessary insurances.

The IRS uses a list of 20 factors to determine whether a worker is a common law employee or an independent contractor. The Colorado Unemployment Insurance - Liability Unit and the Division of Workers' Compensation use similar guidelines.

If you are not sure whether your workers are employees or independent contractors, you will need to contact the IRS, (303) 825-7041 or 1-800-829-1040, the Colorado Division of Workers Compensation, (303) 764-2929, and the Unemployment Insurance Tax Liability Unit (303) 839-4922, for a determination of an actual employer-employee relationship.

Statutory Employees: Commissioned delivery drivers, insurance agents, full-time commissioned sales agents and individuals who do piece work with materials supplied by the employer are considered to be statutory employees by the IRS. The employer is not required to withhold federal income tax from payments. However, if the contract states an individual must perform the services personally, that the individual will perform the service on a continuing basis and that the equipment will be supplied by the employer, then the payments are subject to FICA. Payments to commissioned delivery drivers and sales agents are subject to unemployment insurance tax. Because statutory employees are similar in some respects to both common-law employees and independent contractors, you should contact the Colorado Division of Workers' Compensation directly regarding your workers' compensation liability.

Children And Spouses: If your business is a sole proprietorship, your children who work for your business are not considered to be employees by the IRS and are not subject to FICA and Medicare taxes until age 18. If a child is paid for domestic work in the parent's home, wages are not subject to social security and Medicare taxes until the child reaches age 21. Federal unemployment does not cover services performed by children under the age of 21 who work for their parents. It is not necessary for the children to be claimed as dependents. All wages paid to children may still be subject to income tax withholdings. Wages paid by a sole proprietor to a spouse are subject to income tax withholding and social security taxes (FICA), but not to federal unemployment insurance taxes. All wages paid to a child or a spouse are subject to withholding taxes, FICA and state and federal unemployment insurance taxes if the parent/spouse's business is a partnership or a corporation, unless each partner is parent of a child. Workers' Compensation insurance must be provided for family member/employees.

Corporate Officers: Generally, working corporate officers are considered employees by the IRS and may not be paid through a distribution of dividends only. They must be paid a "reasonable wage or salary." All wages are subject to federal and state wage withholding, FICA, and unemployment insurance taxes. Corporate officers who own more than a ten percent share of the business may elect to reject workers' compensation coverage. These rules apply to the corporate officers in both C and S corporations.

Leased Employees: An alternative to hiring your own employees is to contract for workers from a temporary employment agency or an employee leasing agency. You pay the agency a fee to provide the number and type of employees you need and specify the conditions they must work under, but the individual workers remain employees of the agency. The agency is responsible for all payroll taxes, unemployment insurance, and workers' compensation. However, if a leasing company defaults in payment of unemployment insurance, the client company is then responsible for payment of unemployment insurance. A temporary agency is used when workers are needed for a "short" period of time. Leasing agencies provide employees under contract on a permanent basis.

Household Employees: If you hire someone to work in your own home, you may have responsibilities as a household employer. If the employee earns over $50 during a quarter, you are responsible for social security and Medicare taxes. If the employee earns over $1,000 during a quarter, you will also be responsible for unemployment insurance. The law does not require that you withhold federal or state income taxes for your employee; however, you may do so voluntarily if requested by your employee and she or he completes Form W-4. Workers' compensation insurance must be obtained for household employees who work 40 or more hours per week or 5 or more days per week. For additional information regarding your responsibilities as a household employer, call the IRS, (303) 825-8041 or 1-800-829-1040, and request Publication 926, "Employment Taxes for Household Employers." NOTE: The rules regarding household employees are under consideration for revision by congress and subject to change.

PAYROLL TAX FILING REQUIREMENTS AND FORMS

Wage Withholding And Social Security/Medicare Taxes: If you have employees, you will be responsible for withholding income taxes and social security/Medicare taxes from your employees' wages. As the employer, you must pay an equal share of social security/Medicare taxes. Also, you must withhold Colorado withholding tax from all employees working in Colorado, including non-residents.

CHAPTER EIGHT: MONEY FOR NOTHING

Unemployment Insurance: Unemployment insurance is a fund established by law to provide benefits to employees who lose their jobs through no fault of their own. As an employer, you will be required to pay both state and federal unemployment insurance taxes.

Employee W-2s: At the end of the year, you are responsible to report wage and tax withholding information with W-2 forms. Copies of the W-2 must be sent to your employee no later than January 31. Copy A of form W-2 must be sent to the Social Security Administration (SSA) by February 28 with form W-3. For your Colorado employees, you must file DR 1093, Transmittal of State W-2s.

Independent Contractor 1099s: If you have determined your workers are independent contractors, you are not required to withhold or pay any taxes on their behalf. However, you must keep track of how much you pay them and file form 1099 for each person to whom you paid over $600 during the year. The independent contractor must be sent her/his form 1099 by January 31. Copy A of form 1099 must be sent to the IRS by February 28 with form 1096.

Payroll Records And Audits: It is important to keep complete and accurate employee/payroll records and to retain the records for at least five years. The IRS, the Immigration and Naturalization Service, the Colorado Department of Revenue and the Colorado Department of Labor & Employment all have the authority to audit your records. Remember, your liabilities begin as soon as you hire an employee.

Workers' Compensation: Workers' compensation is mandatory insurance that provides coverage for medical expenses and lost wages due to a job-related injury or occupational disease. The cost of coverage for employees must be paid by the employer. All employees must be covered beginning with the very first employee. Corporate officers who actively work in a Corporation and members who work in a Limited Liability Company must be covered unless they own at least ten percent of the business and they formally elect in writing to reject coverage. The election to reject coverage is filed with the insurance carrier. If there are no other employees, the election to reject coverage should be filed using form WC43 with the Division of Workers' Compensation. According to state law, sole proprietors and partners in a partnership have the option of electing coverage for themselves although it may be required by a prime contractor. However, this election may significantly affect health insurance coverage. Carefully discuss this election with your insurance agent before making your decision.

You can obtain workers' compensation insurance from an insurance agent or the Colorado Compensation Insurance Authority (CCIA), 720 South Colorado Blvd., Suite 100 N, Denver, CO 80203, (303) 782-4000 or 1-800-873-7242. CCIA is NOT a state agency. It is a quasi-independent nonprofit insurance company established by state law that sells workers' Compensation insurance at cost.

BUSINESS INSURANCE

Before starting your business, you should be aware of the potential liabilities which may be incurred when operating a business. You should look into what types of insurance may be required or may be in your best interest. Insurance companies can put together a specialized package to meet your specific needs.

General Business Liability: General Business Liability is the broadest form of coverage which can protect you against losses when injury, damage or even death result to another person or her/his property because of business negligence. Your obligations may even extend beyond the general liability for which you assume you are responsible. Read the terms of the insurance contract carefully.

Product Liability Insurance: If you manufacture a product, product liability insurance can also cover the goods you produce. Insurance coverage typically relates to the product itself, but may also protect you as the manufacturer should someone experience personal injury or property damage from the use of your product.

Completed Operations Insurance: If you are a contractor, you can become insured for events that may occur after you leave the job site. Problems which may be covered include personal injuries or damage to someone's property due to something on which you worked going wrong. This is called Completed Operations Liability Insurance.

Health Insurance: Employers are not required by federal or state law to provide health coverage to their employees. However, if you do provide health benefits, certain laws will determine the nature of the plan and how it is administered. Effective January 1995, Colorado health insurers in the small group (employers with 2-50 employees) market must at least provide a basic or standard health benefit plan to an entire small group, regardless of the health status of its employees. Other consumer protections that apply to small group policies include guaranteed renewability, underwriting restrictions, and stringent premium rating rules. Starting in January 1996, all of the above will apply to even one-person businesses. **"Shopping the market" can help you find the best plan for your employees at the least cost.** I would highly recommend contacting the Cooperative for Health Insurance Purchasing (CHIP) at 800-996-CHIP. This cooperative can offer small businesses a wide choice of HMO and POS health plans at reduced rates. If you need assistance with issues concerning employee health insurance and state insurance laws, you may contact the Consumer Section of the Colorado Division of Insurance at (303) 894-7490.

Property Insurance: This coverage is especially important if you own the property or building where your business is located. As the mortgagee, you can be protected against losses and a loss of income in the event your business experiences damage as a result of natural disaster, fire, burglary or vandalism that may destroy all or part of your property.

Business Interruption Insurance: (Also referred to as "Specific Time Element Coverage") can pay losses of income as a result of personal property damage that might occur to your business from either environmental factors, natural disasters or destruction by others until you are able to begin operating again.

Errors And Omission/Professional Liability Insurance: E & O insurance is often recommended for employees, owners and directors of the business. Errors and omissions and professional liability coverage offer protection for employees and owners of the business against lawsuits that many arise as a result of their actions or failure to act for duties performed during the course of business.

Bonding: Bonding is not an insurance contract; however, there are several types of surety bonds you can purchase which cover a wide range of losses. Fidelity bonds are designed to protect a business or employer from losses due to the dishonesty of employees, partners or officers in the business. Performance bonds guarantee a business' performance because of an obligation or contractual agreement. Colorado Law requires certain occupations (such as construction work or motor vehicle dealers) post a bond before they can be licensed or before they are awarded a state contract. Bonding is usually not a mandatory requirement; however, many companies do require that you post a bond before beginning work.

INCOME AND PROPERTY TAX

This section outlines the general income tax laws you will encounter when you own your own business. For more specific information you should contact the Internal Revenue Service, (303) 825-7041 or 1-800-829-1040 and the Colorado Department of Revenue, (303) 534-1209.

Corporations: If your business is a corporation located in or "doing business" in Colorado, it is subject to state and federal corporate income taxes. If you will be filing as an S corporation, your business's income will be taxed as a partnership and will be exempt from corporate income taxes, although a corporate income tax return must still be filed. Working corporate officers are still treated as employees, even in an S corporation, and must be paid a reasonable wage which is subject to all payroll taxes.

Every corporation, including S corporations, "doing business" in Colorado or deriving income from Colorado sources, must file a corporate income tax return with Colorado. Colorado taxable income is determined by adding and/or subtracting various adjustments to your federal taxable income. Contact the Colorado Department of Revenue for more information. (303) 534-1209.

If you expect your federal tax liability to be $500 or more and/or your state tax liability to be $5,000 or more, you are required to file and pay estimated taxes during the year. A corporation that owes more than $500 in federal income tax or $5,000 in state income tax may be subject to penalties and interest.

Partnerships: If your business is a partnership, you must file state and federal partnership income tax returns. The partnership as a whole is not required to pay income tax. Each partner in the partnership is responsible for her or his own self-employment taxes as an individual. If you and your spouse run your business together and share in the profits, your business may be considered a partnership. You should record your respective shares of partnership income or loss separately for self-employment taxes. Doing this will usually not increase your total tax, but will give each spouse credit for social security earnings on which retirement benefits are based. IRS Publication, *Tax on Partnerships*, is a useful guide regarding partnership filing requirements and the allocation of income to the partners.

Self-Employment Taxes: If you are a sole proprietor or a partner in a partnership, you must file your own estimated self-employment taxes. When you work for others as an employee, your employer withholds your taxes from your paycheck. As an employee, your employer pays half of your social security taxes and you pay half. When you are self-employed, you must pay the entire amount. Estimated taxes are normally paid quarterly on actual income. If you do not have taxable income, you do not have to pay estimated taxes. If you expect to owe the IRS more than $500 in federal taxes, you must make federal estimated tax payments. IRS Publication 533, *Self-Employment Tax,* is a useful guide in determining your estimated federal tax liability. If you expect to owe Colorado more than $1,000 in state taxes, you must pay state estimated tax payments. Estimated payments are made using federal form 1040-ES and Colorado form 104-ES.

Property Taxes: Property taxes are assessed on any real and/or personal property (land, buildings, furniture, equipment, etc.) which directly or indirectly produce income within your business. The County Assessor will mail a declaration schedule for property taxes after January 1st. Taxes must be paid by April 15th unless an extension has been obtained. The County Treasurer is responsible for mailing and collecting the actual property tax bill. Agricultural and natural resources are treated somewhat differently. **You should contact your local County Assessor regarding property taxes, personal and real estate, whenever you start a new business.**

Enterprise Zones: An Enterprise Zone is defined as an economically depressed area of Colorado in which special tax incentives are offered to businesses that expand or locate in the zone. You should call the Department of Revenue at (303) 866-2421 for more information regarding tax credits.

There are currently 16 Colorado enterprise zones. An individual zone may include all of several counties in rural areas or small portions of a single county in urban areas. Businesses should contact the Department of Local Affairs. 1313 Sherman St., Room 518, Denver, CO 80203, (303) 866-2771.

ADDITIONAL RESOURCES

The Office of Regulatory Reform (ORR) was established to serve as an ombudsman for the small business community in Colorado. The office is charged with identifying and working to eliminate unnecessary, duplicative, and burdensome regulation. If you have concerns regarding burdensome state regulations, contact ORR, 1560 Broadway, Suite 1530, Denver, CO 80202, (303) 894-7839.

The office maintains a database of comprehensive (federal, state and local) regulatory requirements. In conjunction with the Office of Business Development and the Department of Revenue, ORR operates the Small Business Hotline, (303) 592-5820 or 1-800-333-7798, and the Colorado Business Assistance Center, 1560 Broadway, Suite 1530, Denver, CO, which together assist over 6,000 new, expanding and existing Colorado businesses each month.

DBE Certification: An additional service provided by ORR is Disadvantaged Business Enterprise (DBE) certification. The certification process determines the eligibility of minority and women owned businesses to participate as DBEs on projects for the Colorado Department of Transportation, the Regional Transportation Distinct and the Denver Water Board. For more information call (303) 894-2355.

The Office of Business Development (OBD) works with companies starting, expanding or relocating in Colorado. OBD offers a wide range of services to assist new and existing businesses of every size. The Colorado First training program provides job training assistance as an incentive for companies to expand within Colorado or relocate to the state. OBD manages a Revolving Loan Fund which serves existing businesses in rural areas.

The Small Business Office coordinates start-up and existing small business programs and activities, including the Colorado Leading Edge Training Program and the

CHAPTER EIGHT: MONEY FOR NOTHING

Women's Program Coordinator. The Colorado Leading Edge training program teaches new and existing businesses how to develop a comprehensive business plan during a 10-12 week intensive education program. The Women's Program Coordinator acts as a liaison between state government and the women's business community.

The Minority Business Office provides assistance to ethnic minority-owned businesses in areas of procurement, marketing, training and technical assistance programs. The office works as an advocate for minority businesses and is a point of contact for current bid information and maintains a database of ethnic minority-owned businesses.

Small Business Development Centers (SBDC) offer free one-on-one counseling services in the areas of business financing information, research and marketing, business plan preparation and other small business subjects, as well as specialized seminars on many small business topics. There are twenty-one community-based SBDC branches co-sponsored by OBD. Services are provided for new and existing businesses. In addition to general services listed above, local SBDCs also specialize in international trade, government procurement, home-based business and technology resources. The SBDCs are a cooperative venture of the US Small Business Administration, the State of Colorado Community Colleges and Chamber of Commerce.

Local Small Business Development Centers:

Alamosa	719-589-7372	Glenwood Springs	970-928-0120
Aurora	303-341-4849	Grand Junction	970-243-5242
Boulder	303-442-1475	Greeley	970-352-3661
Cañon City	719-275-5335	Lakewood	303-987-0710
Colorado Springs	719-471-4836	Lamar	719-336-8141
Craig	970-824-7078	Littleton	303-795-5855
Delta	970-874-8772	Pueblo	719-549-3224
Denver	303-620-8076	Stratton	719-348-5596
Durango	970-247-9634	Trinidad	719-846-5645
Fort Collins	970-226-0881	Westminster	303-460-1032
Fort Morgan	970-867-4424		

For more information regarding the programs administered by the Office of Business Development, the Small Business Office, the Minority Business Office or state coordination of the SBDC program, contact each office at 1625 Broadway, Suite 1710, Denver, CO 80202, (303) 892-3840.

Colorado Community Colleges and Occupational Educational System: Colorado offers a wide variety of education and training programs for youth and adults through the Colorado Community College and Occupational Education System. The system provides training in more than 400 specific occupations ranging from basic entry level skills to highly technical positions and develops industry specific training programs for employers for entry level employees or upgrading of current employees. In addition to the Small Business Development Centers, assistance is available from:

Alms Community College	Greeley	970-330-8008 x251
Boulder Valley Vo/Tech Center	Boulder	303-447-1010 x632
Colorado N.W. Community College	Rangely	970-675-2261
Emily Griffith Opportunity School	Denver	303-572-8218
Larimer County Vo/Tech Center	Ft. Collins	970-226-2500

Mesa College Area Vo/Tech School	Grand Junction	970-248-1514
Northeastern Junior College	Sterling	970-522-6600 x683
Otero Junior College	La Junta	719-384-8721

Access Colorado Library and Information Network (ACLIN) is a project of the Colorado library community in partnership with Colorado Supernet—a Colorado access point to the information superhighway. ACLIN provides access to the information resources of the libraries in the state to support education, business, health, social services, and personal growth activities of the residents of Colorado. It creates a statewide library computer network that links the automated systems and on-line catalogs of participating libraries in a single network which includes academic, public, private and specialized (medical, legal, etc.) library participants. The service also provides free access to over 130 library catalogs, which list over 11 million books, as well as over 35 other information databases. ACLIN connects users via a single phone call, local or toll-free, using a computer and a modem from home, office, school or library. For additional information about ACLIN, contact your local public library.

To access ACLIN, use the local access number for your area or if outside a local calling area, use the 800 number. NOTE: if you attempt to use the 800 number from an area with a local number, your call will be blocked. At the first two prompts (user name and annex) type "ac" then follow the on-line instructions.

ACLIN Phone Numbers: Toll Free within Colorado   1-800-748-0888

Alamosa	719-589-0505	Glenwood Spgs	970-928-0055
Boulder	303-440-9969	Grand Junction	970-243-4441
Colorado Springs	719-575-0200	Greeley	970-353-2225
Denver	303-786-8700	Gunnison	970-641-4446
Durango	970-385-4949	Pueblo	719-543-8811
Fort Collins	970-498-9199	Telluride	970-728-4448

The Small Business Administration (SBA) is a federal agency which offers a wide variety of services for new and expanding businesses, including an all-day business seminar on advertising/marketing, financial sources, record keeping, insurance needs, legal Considerations and computers. Reservations may be required for SBA classes and there is usually a nominal charge. The SBA also offers free counseling to small businesses through SCORE (Service Corps of Retired Executives) and ACE (Active Corps of Executives) (303) 534-7518. For more information on these and other programs offered by the SBA, please Contract: US Small Business Administration, 721 19th Street, Denver, CO 80202, (303) 844-3985

Local SCORE offices:

Boulder	303-442-1044	Gunnison	970-641-1501
Colorado Springs	719-636-3074	Longmont	303-776-5295
Durango	970-247-4389	Loveland	970-667-6311
Fort Collins	970-663-7583	Montrose	970-249-5515
Grand Junction	970-242-3214	Pueblo	719-542-1784
Greeley	970-352-3566		

Colorado Department of Labor & Employment (DOLE) operates a statewide network of Job Service Centers (JCSs) providing a number of employer services including: Screening and Referral, Mass Recruitment, Affirmative Action Hiring, Layoff Assistance, and the Interstate Job Bank.

CHAPTER EIGHT: MONEY FOR NOTHING

Local Job Service Centers:

Alamosa	719-589-5118	Hot Suphur Spgs	970-725-3317
Aurora	303-695-1660	Lakewood	303-937-2490
Boulder	303-441-3985	Lamar	719-336-2256
Brighton	303-659-4250	Leadville	719-486-2428
Burlington	719-346-5331	Limon	303-775-2387
Canon City	719-275-7408	Littleton	303-797-5603
Colorado Spgs	719-473-6220	Longmont	303-449-6637
Cortez	970-565-3759	Loveland	970-667-4261
Craig	970-824-3246	Minturn	970-827-5766
Delta	970-874-5781	Monte Vista	719-852-5171
Denver	303-830-3000	Montrose	970-249-7783
Durango	970-247-4308	Pueblo	719-546-5627
Fort Collins	970-223-2470	Rocky Ford	719-254-3397
Fort Morgan	970-867-9401	Salida	719-539-6523
Frisco	970-668-5360	Steamboat Spgs	970-879-3075
Glenwood Spgs	970-945-8638	Sterling	970-522-9342
Golden	303-271-4850	Trinidad	719-846-9221
Grand Junction	970-248-7350	Walsenburg	719-738-3004
Greeley	970-353-3815	Westminster	303-429-0039
Gunnison	970-641-0031		

The Governor's Job Training Office (GJTO) provides opportunities for both employees and employers by offering programs through the Job Training Partnership Act. The goal is to prepare unemployed individuals, both youth and adult, for entry into the labor force and to assist with job training for those individuals who require this assistance to prepare them for productive employment. To achieve this goal, local service areas develop training programs that meet the needs of local employers as well as eligible clients. Employers may receive financial reimbursement for hiring and helping train eligible participants.

Local GJTO service areas:

Adams County	303-289-6500	El Paso County	719-578-6916
Arapahoe County	303-752-5820	Jefferson County	303-271-4600
Boulder County	303-441-3985	Larimer County	970-223-2470
Denver County	303-893-3382	Weld County	970-353-3800

Office of Rural Job Training: 303-894-7410

Local Economic Development Offices provide variety of different services to the businesses in their area, including permitting assistance; relocation, demographics, and site location information; and counseling and support services. A few offices administer small loan programs. Some are agencies of local city or county governments. Some are independent, non-profit organizations that receive funding from local governments and/or chambers of commerce.

Local Economic Development Agencies:

Adams County	303-450-5106	Broomfield	303-469-7645
Archuleta	970-264-4722	Chaffee County	719-539-2218
Arvada	303-431-3000	City of Sterling	970-522-9700
Aurora	303-340-2101	CO Sprgs	719-578-6132
Boulder	303-442-1044	CO Sprgs EDC	719-471-8183
Brighton	303-659-5713	Commerce City	303-289-3620

COLORADO: A Newcomer's Manual

Crowley County	719-267-3718	Mesa County	970-245-4332
Delta	970-874-7566	Montezuma Cty	970-565-8227
Delta County	970-874-7595	Montrose	970-249-9438
Denver	303-640-7100	Morgan County	970-867-6256
Douglas County	303-795-9447	Northglenn	303-450-8743
Dtn Denver Ptrsh	303-534-6161	Parker	303-841-8683
El Paso County	719-520-6480	Prowers County	719-336-2384
Englewood	303-762-2353	Pueblo	719-546-1133
Evans	970-339-5345	Region 10	970-249-2436
Fort Collins Inc.	970-221-0861	Rocky Ford	719-254-7414
Fountain	719-382-8521	San Juan Basin	970-247-9634
Fremont County	719-275-8601	San Luis Valley	719-589-7925
Golden	303-279-3331	South Colorado	719-545-8680
Greeley/Weld	970-356-4565	Thornton	303-538-7295
Jefferson County	303-271-6982	Town of Fowler	719-263-4461
La Junta	719-384-7711	Town of Rangely	970-675-8469
Lakewood	303-987-7730	Trinidad	719-846-9412
Littleton	303-795-3748	Washington Cty	970-345-6395
Longmont	303-651-0128	Westminster	303-430-2400
Loveland	970-667-0905	Wheat Ridge	303-235-2844
Mead	970-535-4477	Yuma County	970-332-3200

Chambers of Commerce: Chambers of Commerce provide a number of opportunities for business owners. Primarily your local chamber of commerce is where you can meet and "network" with other business owners from your community.

Minority Chambers of Commerce:

Asian	303-595-9737	Hispanic - CO Springs	719-635-7506
Black	303-341-1296	Indian (East)	303-446-2422
Black - CO Springs	719-260-9535	Korean/American	719-554-1411
Chinese	303-236-5902	Latino Pueblo	719-542-1704
Gay & Lesbian	303-595-8042	Native American	303-665-3476
Hispanic	303-534-7783	Women's	303-623-6683

Geographic Chambers of Commerce:

Akron	970-345-2342	Castle Rock	303-688-4597
Alamosa County	800-258-7597	Cederedge	970-856-6961
Antonito	719-376-5693	Center	719-754-2519
Arvada	303-424-0313	Central City	800-542-2999
Aspen	800-262-7736	Clear Creek	719-569-2133
Aurora	303-755-5000	Colorado Spring	719-635-1551
Avon/Beaver Creek	970-949-5189	Conifer	303-271-0178
Basalt	970-927-4031	Copper Mountain	970-968-6477
Bayfield	970-884-9782	Cortez	970-565-3414
Berthoud	970-532-4200	Costilla County	719-672-3355
Boulder	303-442-1044	Craig	970-824-5689
Breckenridge	970-453-6018	Crawford Area	303-821-4725
Brighton	303-659-0223	Creede-Mineral Cty	800-327-2102
Broomfield	303-466-1775	Crested Butte	800-545-4505
Brush Area	800-354-8659	Cripple Creek	800-526-8777
Buena Vista	800-831-8594	Custer County	719-783-9163
Burlington	719-346-8070	Del Norte	719-657-2845
Canon City	800-876-7922	Delta	970-874-8616
Carbondale	970-963-1890	Denver, Greater	303-534-8500

CHAPTER EIGHT: MONEY FOR NOTHING

Denver, Metro N.	303-450-0335	Logan County	800-544-8609
Denver, N.W. Metro	303-424-0313	Longmont	303-776-5295
Denver, S. Metro	303-795-0142	Louisville	303-666-5747
Dinosaur	970-882-4018	Loveland	970-667-6311
Divide	719-687-6011	Lyons	303-823-5215
Dolores	970-882-4018	Manitou Springs	800-642-2567
Dove Creek	970-677-2274	Meeker	970-878-5510
Durango	800-525-8855	Monte Vista	719-852-2731
Eads	719-438-5590	Montrose County	800-873-0244
Eagle Valley	970-328-5220	Monument	719-481-3282
Elizabeth	303-646-4287	Nederland	800-221-0044
Englewood	303-789-4433	Newcastle	970-984-2311
Estes Park	800-443-7837	North Park	970-723-4600
Evans Area	970-330-4204	Norwood	970-327-4707
Evergreen Area	303-674-3412	Olathe	970-323-5708
Florence	303-784-3544	Ordway	719-267-3179
Florissant-Lk George	719-748-8000	Ouray County	303-325-4746
Fort Collins	970-482-3746	Pagosa Springs	970-264-2360
Fort Lupton	303-857-4474	Palisade	970-464-7458
Fort Morgan	970-867-6702	Paonia	970-527-3886
Fountain	719-390-4066	Parker	303-841-4268
Fowler	719-263-5285	Plateau Valley	970-487-3402
Franktown	303-688-5301	Platte Canyon Area	303-674-8333
Fruita	970-858-1000	Platteville	303-758-2560
Georgetown	303-569-2888	Pueblo	800-233-3446
Gilpin County	303-582-5077	Rangely	970-675-529S
Glenwood Springs	800-221-0098	Red Feathers Lake	800-462-5870
Golden	303-279-3113	Ridgway	970-626-5868
Granby	800-325-1661	Rifle	970-625-2085
Grand Junction	970-242-3214	Rocky Ford	719-254-7483
Grand Lake	800-531-1019	Salida	800-831-8594
Greeley/Weld	970-352-3566	Saquache	719-655-2620
Greenhorn Valley	719-676-3000	Silverton	800-752-4494
Gunnison Country	800-274-7580	Snowmass	800-332-3245
Haxtun	970-774-6104	South Fork	719-873-5512
Hayden	970-276-3425	Springfield	719-523-4061
Holyoke	970-854-3517	Steamboat Spgs	970-879-0880
Hotchkiss	970-872-3226	Stratton	800-777-6042
Huerfano County	719-738-1065	Summit County	970-668-5800
Idaho Springs	800-685-7785	Surface Creek Val	970-856-6961
Johnstown-Milliken	970-587-4661	Swink	719-384-7155
Julesburg	970-474-3504	Telluride	800-525-3455
Keenesburg	970-732-4246	Trinidad	719-846-9285
Keystone Resort	970-468-4123	Ute Pass	719-684-9797
Kit Carson	719-962-3249	Vail	970-476-1000
Kremmling	970-724-3472	Vallecito Lake	970-884-9782
La Junta	719-384-7411	Victor	719-689-0558
La Veta	719-742-3676	West Jefferson Co.	303-233-5555
Lafayette	303-666-9555	West Yuma	970-848-2704
Lake City	800-569-1874	Windsor	970-686-7189
Lamar	719-336-4379	Winter Park	970-726-4118
Las Animas	719-456-0453	Woodland Park	719-687-9885
Leadville	800-933-3901	Wray	970-332-4431
Limon	719-775-2346		

Colorado Small Business Incubators: Small business incubators are designed to assist business start-ups during the most critical formative years (embryo stage). These incubators provide workshops to teach business skills and to improve knowledge of business operations and management. Other benefits to utilizing an incubator include formal and informal networks of business assistance, consulting services, multi-tenant office space, shared office services (to reduce overhead), and improved access to financial resources. Call the following incubator sites for more information: Denver Enterprise Center, (303) 296-9400, Jefferson County Business and Innovation Center, (303)238-0913, Boulder Technology Incubator, (303) 678-8000, Western Colorado Business Development Corporation, (970) 243-5242, Pueblo Business and Technology Center, (719) 546-113, Fremont County Economic Development Corporation and Business Development Center, (719) 275-8601, Colorado Bio-Venture Center (Lakewood), (303) 237-3998.

US West Home Office Consulting Center: Virtually all local phone service in Colorado is handled by US West. Recently they created the Home Office Consulting Center which offers free advice and service from consultants who are specially trained to provide creative, cost-efficient ideas for work-at-home professionals and entrepreneurs. I can tell you from experience they really know their stuff. With so many new services available (custom ringing, priority calling, caller ID, voice messaging, call forwarding, fax mail, conference calls, on and on), it really pays—although you won't have to—to have one of these professionals work out the best system for your home-office. Call 1-800-872-4658.

Rocky Mountain Home-Based Business Asociation: This non-profit association offers networking opportunities, educational seminars, a quarterly newsletter, and special events designed specially for those with home-based businesses. Call (303) 367-1918 for more information.

U.S. Department of Commerce	
International Trade	303-844-6623
Census Bureau	303-969-7750
Internal Revenue Service	303-825-7041 or 800-829-1049
U.S. Department of Labor	303-844-4405
Occupational Health and Safety Administration	303-844-3061 or 800-321-6742
Immigration and Naturalization Service	303-371-3041
U.S. Customs Service - Import/Export	303-361-0712
U.S. Environmental Protection Agency	800-227-8917
U.S. Postal Service-Requirements and Permits	303-297-6120
U.S. Small Business Administration	All numbers are area code 303
SCORE/Denver	844-3983
Office of Economic Development	844-3984
Finance Division	844-3461
International Trade	844-5239
Minority Enterprise Development	844-6444
Veterans Programs	844-5240
Woman Business Ownership	844-3984
Surety Bond Program	844-5231

CHAPTER NINE
THINGS TO DO IN DENVER
WHEN YOU'RE DEAD

STATE-WIDE RECREATION, ENTERTAINMENT AND CULTURE

Communing With Nature, Winter Activities, Water Sports, Bicycling, Sky-High Adventure, Weekend Getaways, Tours, Professional Sports, Downtown Denver, Leisure, Fun & Unusual Things To Do, The Arts & Culture

So you're in Colorado and bored. Try one of the following: Arts, Amusement Parks, Archaeological Tours, Ballet, Ballooning, Bed & Breakfast, Bicycle Touring, Boating, Brew-Pubs, Camera Safari, Camping, Concerts, Cross-Country Skiing, Dog Sledding, Downhill Skiing, Festivals and Events, Flying, Four-Wheel-Drive Trips, Gambling, Glider Rides, Gold Panning, Golf, Hang Gliding, Hiking/Backpacking, Historic Tours, Horseback Riding, Hot Springs, Ice Climbing, Ice Skating, Kayaking, Llama Trekking, Mine Tours, Mountain Biking, Mountaineering, Museums, Narrow-Gauge Train Rides, Nature Walks, Opera, Paragliding, Plays, Planetariums, Professional Baseball, Basketball, Football, or Hockey, River Rafting, Rock Climbing, Running, Sailing, Scenic Drives, Scuba Diving, Skydiving, Sleigh Rides, Snowshoe Walks, Snowboarding, Snowmobiling, Swimming, Tennis, Trail Walks, Water Skiing, Weekend Getaways, Windsurfing, Winery Tours, Zoos.

COLORADO: A Newcomer's Manual

As you can tell from the above list, there are unlimited options when it comes to things to do in Colorado. You might also guess it would be impossible to adequately cover all these options in this one book. The intent of this chapter is to provide an overview of the possibilities and direct you to sources of more complete information. In fact, there are dozens of books available on Colorado's cultural and recreational activities. If you are interested in a particular activity, I recommend the books listed throughout this chapter.

When you think of New York City, you imagine skyscrapers, crowded streets and rude taxi drivers. When you think of Florida, you imagine vast stretches of beach, palm trees and water sports. When you think of Colorado, you imagine thousands of square miles of wilderness and all the activities that go with them. Colorado has 2 national parks, 6 national monuments, 12 national forests, 43 state parks, 2 national recreation areas, 24 ski areas/resorts, and dozens of large lakes and reservoirs. These areas offer a multitude of things to do during all four seasons.

COMMUNING WITH NATURE

Camera Safaris/Nature & Trail Walks; Camping; Hiking/Backpacking; Horseback Riding; Llama Trekking; Mountaineering; Rock Climbing

> *Recommended Reading:* Colorado Publishers produce excellent books on these subjects, please see these listings in Appendix A: All Points Publishing / Fulcrum Publishing / Johnson Books / Outdoor Books & Maps / Pruett Publishing / Roberts Rinehart Publishing / University Press of Colorado / Westcliffe Publishing

Please observe the following rules while visiting or camping in any National Park, National Monument, or National Forest. See map on page 214 and check with each location for additional rules and regulations:

Dogs, cats and other pets are not allowed on trails or away from roadways and must be on a leash at all times.
Do not feed or touch wild animals (do not keep food in tents).
Prohibited: Hunting and harassment of wildlife / picking wildflowers and plants / hitchhiking / loaded firearms / open alcoholic beverages in vehicles.
Fishing requires a valid Colorado state fishing license.
Camping is restricted to designated areas.
A permit is required for all overnights in the backcountry.
Fires may be built only in picnic areas and campsites with grates.
Vehicles must remain on roads or in parking areas.
Trail bikes, snowmobiles, and all other vehicles are restricted to roads.
Remove all your own trash from picnic areas and campsites.

Mesa Verde National Park: MVNP is located in southwestern Colorado. Established in 1906, the park contains ancient cliff dwellings dating back to 1200 A.D. The most notable of the cliff dwellings are Cliff Palace in Cliff Canyon, which contains more than 200 rooms and 23 kivas (ceremonial chambers); Spruce Tree House in Spruce Tree Canyon, with 114 rooms and 8 kivas; and Balcony House in Soda Canyon, a small cliff dwelling of at least 30 rooms. The Park covers 81.4 square miles and includes two museums and a 494-unit campground. For additional information call 970-529-4461.

CHAPTER NINE: THINGS TO DO

Rocky Mountain National Park: RMNP is located 62 miles (as the crow flies) Northwest of Denver. Covering 414 square miles, the park includes 113 named peaks above 10,000 feet including Longs Peak at 14,255 feet. The Park has 57 miles of paved road (including Trail Ridge Road), 14 miles of gravel road, and 355 miles of hiking trails. RMNP has 5 campgrounds with a total of 500 sites. For additional information call 970-586-1206.

NATIONAL MONUMENTS

Black Canyon of the Gunnison NM	Montrose, CO	970-249-7036
Colorado NM	Fruita, CO	970-858-3617
Dinosaur NM	Dinosaur, CO	970-374-2216
Florissant Fossil Beds NM	Florissant, CO	719-748-3253
Great Sand Dunes NM	Mosca, CO	719-378-2312
Hovenweep NM	Mesa Verde NP	970-529-4461

NATIONAL FORESTS

Rocky Mountain Region National Forest Service		303-275-5350
Arapahoe National Forest	Ft. Collins, CO	970-498-1100
Grand Mesa National Forest	Delta, CO	970-874-7691
Gunnison National Forest	Delta, CO	970-874-7691
Pawnee National Grassland	Greeley, CO	970-353-5004
Pike National Forest	Pueblo, CO	719-545-8737
Rio Grande National Forest	Monte Vista, CO	719-852-5941
Roosevelt National Forest	Ft. Collins, CO	970-498-1100
Routt National Forest	Steamboat Sprgs	970-879-1722
San Isabel National Forest	Pueblo, CO	719-545-8737
San Juan National Forest	Durango, CO	970-247-4847
Uncompaghre National Forest	Delta, CO	970-874-7691
White River National Forest	Glenwood Sprgs	970-945-2521

NATIONAL RECREATION AREAS

Arapahoe Ntl Rec Area	Ft. Collins, CO	970-498-1100
Curecanti Ntl Rec Area	Gunnison, CO	970-641-2337

WILDERNESS AREAS

WILDERNESS	APPROX. ACRES	MANAGEMENT
Black Cyn / Gunnison	11,180	Black Cyn of the Gunnison N. M
Buffalo Peaks	43,410	Pike, San Isabel N. F.
Byers Peak	8,095	Arapaho N. F.
Cache La Poudre	9,308	Roosevelt N. F.
Collegiate Peaks	118,900	Gunnison, San Isabel, White R. N. F.
Comanche	66,901	Roosevelt N. F.
Eagles Nest	133,915	Arapaho, White River N. F.
Flat Tops	235,230	Routt White River N. F.
Fossil Ridge	33,060	Gunnison N. F.
Great Sand Dunes	33,450	Great Sand Dunes National Mon.
Greenhorn Mtn	22,040	San Isabel N. F.
Holy Cross	123,410	San Isabel, White River N. F.
Hunter-Fryingpan	82,780	White River N. F.

WILDERNESS	APPROX. ACRES	MANAGEMENT
Indian Peaks	70,894	Arapahoe, Roosevelt N.F., Rocky Mtn. N.P.
La Ganta	129,626	Gunnison, Rio Grande N. F.
Lizard Head	41,496	San Juan, Uncompahgre N. F.
Lost Creek	120,151	Pike N. F.
Maroon Bells-Snowmass	183,871	Gunnison, White River N. F.
Mesa Verde	8,100	Mesa Verde National Park
Mt. Evans	74,401	Arapaho, Pike N. F.
Mt. Massive	28,047	San Isabel N. F.
Mt. Sneffels	16,527	Uncompahgre N. F.
Mt. Zirkel	160,648	Routt N. F.
Neota	9,924	Roosevelt, Routt N. F.
Never Summer	21,090	Arapaho, Routt N. F.
Platte River	743	Roosevelt N. F.
Powderhorn	60,100	Bureau of Land Management
Ptarmigan Peak	13,175	Arapaho N. F.
Raggeds	65,430	Gunnison, White River N. F.
Rawah	73,886	Roosevelt, Routt N. F.
Sangre de Cristo	226,455	Rio Grande, San Isabel N. F.
Service Creek	47,140	Routt N. F.
South San Juan	158,790	Rio Grande, San Juan N. F.
Uncompahgre	102,790	Uncompahgre N. F.
Vasquez Peak	12,300	Arapaho N. F.
Weminuche	492,418	Rio Grande, San Juan N. F.
West Elk	176,412	Gunnison N. F.

COLORADO STATE PARKS

FEES: A valid parks pass is required on every vehicle entering a state park. A daily pass is $3; an annual pass—good for the entire calendar year at all state parks—is $30. Camping permits are $6-$12 per night, depending on the facilities available. Day-use areas are generally open for 5 a.m. to 10 p.m. and campgrounds (when open) are open 24 hours a day.

For additional information call 303-866-3437. For camping reservations call 303-470-1144 or 1-800-678-CAMP. Before using any state parks you should request a copy of the State Park Regulations. The written regulations are literally the size of a fold-up road map. See map on page 215 for the location of the parks listed below:

Arkansas	Salida, CO	719-539-7289
Barbour Ponds	Longmont, CO	970-669-1739
Barr Lake	Brighton, CO	303-659-6005
Bonny Lake	Idalia, CO	970-354-7306
Boyd Lake	Loveland, CO	970-669-1739
Castlewood Canyon	Franktown, CO	303-688-5242
Chatfield	Littleton, CO	303-791-7275
Cherry Creek	Aurora, CO	303-690-1166
Colorado State Forest	Walden, CO	970-723-8366
Crawford	Crawford, CO	970-921-5721
Eldorado Canyon	Eldorado Springs, CO	303-494-3943
Eleven Mile	Lake George, CO	719-748-3401
Golden Gate Canyon	Golden, CO	303-592-1502

CHAPTER NINE: THINGS TO DO

Harvey Gap (no pets)	Silt, CO	970-625-1607
Highline	Loma, CO	970-858-7208
Island Acres	Palisade, CO	970-464-0548
Jackson Lake	Orchard, CO	970-645-2551
Lake Pueblo	Pueblo, CO	719-561-9320
Lathrop	Walsenburg, CO	719-738-2376
Lory	BelivueCO	970-493-1623
Mancos	Mancos, CO	970-883-2208
Mueller	Divide, CO	719-687-2366
Navajo	Arboles, CO	970-883-2208
North Sterling	Sterling, CO	970-522-3657
Paonia	Paonia, CO	970-921-5721
Pearl Lake	Clark, CO	970-879-3922
Ridgway	Ridgway, CO	970-626-5822
Rifle Falls	Rifle, CO	970-625-1607
Rifle Gap	Rifle, CO	970-625-1607
Roxborough (no pets)	Littleton, CO	303-973-3959
San Luis	Mosca, CO	719-378-2020
Spinney Mountain	Lake George, CO	719-748-3401
Stagecoach	Oak Creek, CO	970-736-2436
Steamboat Lake	Clark, CO	970-879-3922
Sweitzer Lake	Delta, CO	970-874-4258
Sylvan Lake	Eagle, CO	970-625-1607
Trinidad Lake	Trinidad, CO	719-846-6951
Vega	Collbran, CO	970-487-3407

ADDITIONAL ACTIVITIES AND RESOURCES

Horseback Riding: Colorado Outfitters Association, 303-368-4731
Llama Trekking: Colorado Llama Outfitters/Guides Assoc, 303-526-0092.
Mountaineering: International Alpine School, 303-494-4904
Rock Climbing: Boulder Mountaineer Climbing School, 303-442-8355
                Boulder Rock School (Boulder Rock Club), 303-447-2804
American Camping Association (Kid's summer camp), 303-778-8774
Bureau of Land Management, 303-239-3600
Colorado Association of Campgrounds, Cabins & Lodges, 303-499-9343
Colorado Division of Wildlife, 303-297-1192
Colorado Geological Survey, 303-866-2611
Colorado State Parks, 303-470-1144 or 1-800-678-2267
National Park Service, 1-800-365-2267
The Colorado Trail (465-mile biking & hiking trail), 303-526-0809
US Forest Service, 303-275-5350 or 1-800-280-2267

WINTER SPORTS

Cross-Country Skiing; Dog Sledding; Downhill Skiing; Ice Climbing; Ice Skating; Snowboarding; Snowmobiling; Snowshoeing; Sleigh Rides

> *Recommended Reading:* Colorado Publishers produce excellent books on these subjects, please see these listings in Appendix A: Fulcrum Publishing / Westcliffe Publishers

Colorado is world-famous for its winter sports. Many summer sports have their counterparts in winter (hiking/snowshoeing, rock climbing/ice climbing, in-line skating/ice skating) which allows you, with the proper change of clothing, to enjoy your favorite type of activity year-round.

Cross-County Skiing: It's not unusual to see the city parks full of C-C skiers after the first good snowfall of the season. Many are just warming-up for serious treks into the backcountry. Cross-country skiing is becoming increasingly popular with many novices heading straight for the woods. This can be very dangerous. Every year skiers die in avalanches usually caused by their own activity and perfect avalanche conditions. Don't get in over your head (literally). Don't let your enthusiasm override your experience.

Colorado Cross-Country Ski Association, 970-887-2152
Colorado Avalanche Information Centers: Aspen, 970-920-1664; Colorado Spgs, 719-520-0020; Denver, 303-236-9435; Durango, 970-247-8187; Ft. Collins, 970-482-0457; Summit County, 970-668-0600; Vail, 970-827-5687

Downhill Ski Areas and Resorts: You won't have any problem finding complete information about the 24 ski areas in Colorado. Every fall dozens of magazines and directories become available for the new ski season. One of the best sources is from Colorado Ski Country USA, 303-837-0793. Many resorts offer special rates, ski schools, and multi-day passes. It can get as confusing as buying discount airline seats so please check with each resort for details. The prices below are for the full-rate 1995-96 season.

Ski Area	Reservations	Snow Report	Adult	/Child
Arapahoe Basin	800-222-0188	970-468-4111	$42	$19
Arrowhead	800-525-2257	970-476-4888	$30	$20
Aspen Highlands	800-525-6200	970-925-1221	$49	$27
Aspen Mountain	800-525-6200	970-925-1221	$49	$27
Beaver Creek	800-622-3131	970-476-4888	$46	$33
Breckenridge	800-800-2732	970-453-6118	$42	$19
Copper Mountain	800-458-8386	970-968-2100	$39	$18
Crested Butte	800-544-8448	970-349-2323	$42	$21
Cuchara Valley	800-227-4436	719-742-3163	$26	$16
Eldora	303-440-8700	303-440-8700	$32	$15
Keystone	800-222-0188	970-468-4111	$42	$19
Loveland	800-736-3754	n/a	$32	$13
Monarch	800-332-3668	800-332-3668	$29	$17
Powderhorn	800-241-6997	970-268-5700	$27	$18
Purgatory	800-525-0892	n/a	$37	$19
Silvercreek	800-754-7458	800-754-7458	$30	$16

CHAPTER NINE: THINGS TO DO

Ski Area	Reservations	Snow Report	Adult	Child
Ski Cooper	800-748-2057	719-486-2277	$23	$15
Ski Sunlight	800-445-7931	n/a	$28	$17
Snowmass	800-525-6200	970-925-1221	$49	$27
Steamboat Springs	800-922-2722	970-879-7300	$42	$25
Telluride	800-525-3455	970-728-3614	$43	$24
Tiehack	800-525-6200	970-925-1221	$49	$27
Vail	800-535-2257	970-476-4888	$46	$33
Wolf Creek	970-264-5629	n/a	$31	$19

ADDITIONAL ACTIVITIES AND RESOURCES

Ice Climbing: High Peaks Mountain Guides, 303-258-7436
Snowboarding: National Snowboard, Inc., 303-397-7676
Snowmobiling: Colorado Snowmobile Association, 800-235-4480
Snowshoeing: Mountain Sports, 303-443-6770
Colorado Highway Patrol, 303-639-1234
Colorado Mountain Club (Denver), 303-922-8315
Colorado Mountain Club (Boulder), 303-449-1135
Cross-Country Ski Reports, 303-573-SNOW
National Weather Service, 303-398-3964
Road Conditions (within 2 hours of Denver), 303-639-1111
Road Conditions (state-wide), 303-639-1234

WATER SPORTS

Boating; Kayaking; River Rafting; Sailing; Scuba Diving; Swimming; Water Skiing; Windsurfing

> *Recommended Reading:* Colorado Publishers produce excellent books on these subjects, please see these listings in Appendix A: All Points Publishing / Outdoor Books & Maps

My last abode when I left Florida was a classic 38' wooden yacht. While driving to Colorado I thought I would never see another boat, windsurfer, or jet ski again. How wrong I was. Colorado has over 150 major lakes and reservoirs that provide the water enthusiast with ample opportunities. When you add in some of the best rafting rivers in the country, no one should be left unsatisfied. However, before you rush out to hookup the boat trailer or buy a surplus 2-person survival raft to hit the rapids, be advised that since most boating areas are "controlled" lakes and reservoirs they are subject to many rules, regulations and restrictions. Unless you are a very experienced kayaker or rafter, don't hit the rapids on your own. This can be hazardous to your health. There are numerous outfitters who can provide a fine white-water experience.

Believe it or not, scuba diving is actually quite a popular sport in Colorado. There are many lakes and reservoirs in the state that provide interesting dive experiences. You must be certified to dive but there are several area centers that provide the training.

ADDITIONAL ACTIVITIES AND RESOURCES

Boating: Colorado Division of Wildlife, 303-297-1192
Colorado State Parks, 303-470-1144 or 1-800-678-2267
National Park Service, 1-800-365-2267, US Forest Service, 800-280-2267

Rafting: Colorado River Outfitters Association, 970-369-4632
Scuba Diving: Check your local Yellow Pages for listings

BICYCLING
Mountain Biking; Bicycle Touring; Bicycle Races

> *Recommended Reading:* Colorado Publishers produce excellent books on these subjects, please see these listings in Appendix A: Concepts In Writing / Outdoor Books & Maps / Pruett Publishing / Sage Creek Press

It seems there are as many bicycles in Colorado as there are automobiles. Many two-car garages have the better car in one side and 3-6 bicycles in the other. There are literally thousands of miles of designated bike paths in the state. If you were allowed to camp along the way (which you're not), you could spend an entire week touring the greater Denver metro area without ever leaving the bike paths. Home to some of the most beautiful scenery in the country, Colorado also hosts several of the most grueling cycling events in the world.

Probably the best known annual, multi-day bicycle tour is the week-long *"Ride the Rockies"* sponsored by the Denver Post. This fully supported ride (the sponsors provide campsites and transport all gear) is very strenuous and most participants (limited to 2,000) spend most of the summer training for this one ride. For more information call the Denver Post at 303-820-1338.

The downside to this sport's growing popularity is the inevitable conflict between cyclists and automobiles or hikers vying for the same limited spaces. Many of the state's best hiking trails have recently become two-foot-deep ruts due to overuse by mountain bikes. Collisions and other altercations are becoming almost commonplace. Please follow the "Golden Rule," use common sense, and respect the environment while cycling.

COLORADO BICYCLE ORGANIZATIONS

Aspen Cycling Club	Aspen, CO	970-925-7334
Bicycle Colorado	Littleton, CO	303-798-1429
Bicycle Racing Assoc. of Colorado	Boulder, CO	303-440-5366
Boulder Bicycle Commuters	Boulder, CO	303-499-7466
Boulder Off-Road Alliance	Boulder CO	303-447-9378
Boulder Old Wheelers	Boulder, CO	303-447-0619
Boulder Seniors on Bikes	Boulder, CO	303-443-7623
Boulder Velo Club	Longmont, CO	303-772-2264
Breckenridge Fat Tire Society	Breckenridge, CO	970-453-5548
Canon City Cycling Club	Canon City, CO	719-275-1963
Clear Creek Bicycle Club	Idaho Springs, CO	303-569-2729
Colorado Heart Cycle Assoc.	Denver, CO	303-267-1112
Colorado Mountain Club	Golden, CO	303-279-3080
Colorado Off-Road Point Series	Gunnison, CO	970-641-0285
Colorado Plateau Bike Trail Assoc.	Grand Junction, CO	970-241-9561
Colorado Springs Cycling Club	Colorado Springs, CO	719-594-6354
Denver Bicycle Touring Club	Denver, CO	303-756-7240
Douglas County Cycling Club	Franktown, CO	303-688-0587
Durango Wheel Club	Durango, CO	970-247-4066
Pedal Pueblo	Pueblo, CO	719-543-3454

Rocky Mountain Cycling Club	Denver, CO	303-290-8406
Team Babes on Bikes (B.O.B.)	Ft. Collins, CO	970-490-2969
Team Evergreen	Evergreen, CO	303-674-6048
Team Mad Dog Media	Colorado Springs, CO	719-380-9592
Winter Park FATS	Winter Park, CO	970-726-4118

SKY-HIGH ADVENTURE

Ballooning; Flying; Glider Rides; Hang Gliding; Para Gliding; Skydiving

Recommended Reading: Colorado Publishers produce excellent books on these subjects, please see these listings in Appendix A: All Points Publishing / Fulcrum Publishing

If at times you find yourself in awe at Colorado's natural beauty, you ought to see it from the air (and not from 30,000 feet in route to DIA).

A Balloon Affair	Denver	303-691-3322
A Balloon Safari Company	Denver	303-289-5455
A Real Escape Company	Arvada	303-421-4600
AAA Aviation Adventures Aloft	Fort Collins	970-226-5833
Above It All Balloon Company	Rifle	970-625-4154
Aero Cruise Bln Adventures Ltd	Broomfield	303-469-1243
Aero Cruise Bln Adventures Ltd	Avon	970-845-9907
Aero Sports Ballonists	Steamboat Springs	970-879-7433
Aeronautical Adventures	Edwards	970-926-4456
AIR Boulder Inc	Boulder	303-442-5253
Balloon America	Vail	602-299-7744
Balloons Out West	Colorado Springs	719-578-0935
Balloons Over Steamboat	Steamboat Springs	970-879-3298
BIG Horn Balloon	Montrose	970-249-9744
BIG Horn Balloon	Crested Butte	970-349-6335
Camelot Balloons	Vail	970-476-4743
Co Hang Gliding & Paragliding	Golden	303-278-9566
Colorado High Balloon Co.	Pueblo	719-544-9043
Fair Winds	Boulder	303-939-9323
Fantasy Balloons	Denver	303-478-3531
Free Spirit Bln Ride & Bungee	Colorado Springs	719-390-3332
Golden Wings Hang Gliding	Golden	303-278-7181
Grand Junction Balloon	Grand Junction	970-243-8553
Life Cycle Balloon Rides Ltd	Denver	303-759-3907
Looney Balloons Inc	Littleton	303-979-9476
Morning Glory Ballooning	Fort Collins	970-223-4191
Mountain Balloon Adventures	Vail	970-476-2353
Mountain Breeze Ballooning	Masonville	970-482-0118
Parasoft Inc Paragliding School	Boulder	303-494-2820
Pegasus Balloon Tours	Steamboat Springs	970-879-9191
Rocky Mountain Skydive	Boulder	303-430-1752
SAN Juan Balloon Adventures	Ouray	970-325-4257
SAN Juan Balloon Adventures	Telluride	970-728-3895
SAN Juan Balloon Adventures	Ridgway	970-626-5495
Sky Dive Colorado	Boulder	303-777-0225
Sky Fighters, Inc	Denver	303-790-7375
The Cloud Base (gliding)	Boulder	303-530-2208
Unicorn Balloon Company	Aspen	970-925-5752

WEEKEND GETAWAYS

Bed And Breakfast Accommodations; Cabins, Cottages & Lodges; Scenic Drives; RV Parks; Dude and Guest Ranches

> *Recommended Reading:* Colorado Publishers produce excellent books on these subjects, please see these listings in Appendix A: Fulcrum Publishing / Roberts Rhinehart Publishers / Rocky Mountain Vacation Publishing

While I lived in Florida, almost all available activities were within 10-15 miles of home. To drive an hour to do something was stretching it. In Colorado, almost every portion of the state offers something to do or see that is worth the drive. However, getting up at 4 a.m., driving 2-4 hours to do something and then driving back the same day is not my idea of fun. Neither is sleeping on the hard ground without running water. Fortunately, there are options. In fact, one of the most popular forms of entertainment in Colorado is the weekend getaway. The best book for planning a getaway is *The Colorado Guide* by Fulcrum Publishing. This book lists almost every town and city in Colorado and describes activities, lodging and dining. The other publishers listed above also produce great books for different aspects of weekend getaways.

Bed & Breakfast Accommodations: There are over 350 Bed & Breakfast establishments in Colorado spread out among 119 towns, cities, and villages.

Cabins, Cottages, or Lodges: If a cabin, cottage, or lodge is more your style you can choose from over 230.

RV Parks & Campgrounds: Colorado has 400% more RV Parks and campgrounds in the mountains than any other state in the country. If you own or rent an RV (which is as close to camping as I will ever get), you can choose from over 200 RV parks and campgrounds.

Dude & Guest Ranches: They say reservations at dude and guest ranches sharply increased with the release of the movie *City Slickers*. If true, that was good news for the 40 or so operating in Colorado.

ADDITIONAL RESOURCES

Association of Historic Hotels of the Rocky Mountain West, 303-546-9040
Bed & Breakfast Innkeepers of Colorado Association, 800-832-6657
Bed & Breakfast Rocky Mountains, 303-860-8145
Colorado Association of Campgrounds, Cabins, and Lodges, 303-499-9343
Colorado Dude & Guest Ranch Association, 970-887-3128 / 970-724-3653
Colorado Hotel and Lodging Association, 303-297-8335
Colorado Reservation Service, 800-777-6880
Distinctive Inns of Colorado, 800-777-6880

CHAPTER NINE: THINGS TO DO

TOURS

Mine Tours; Winery Tours; Archaeological Tours; Historical Tours; Four-Wheel-Drive Tours

> *Recommended Reading:* Colorado Publishers produce excellent books on these subjects, please see these listings in Appendix A: Fulcrum Publishing / Johnson Books Preutt Publishing

The word "tour" usually conjures up visions of being hoarded around with a bunch of strangers on a pre-planned, packaged, and boring walk or drive through an area that you can look at but not touch. This kind of tour is available in Colorado but that is not what this section is about. Since Colorado has such a rich history (both pre- and modern), sites with historical value or interest literally cover the state. If your interest lies in dinosaur fossils, Indian petroglyphs, or still active gold mines, you're in luck.

If on the other hand, you are a bit of a wine lover, the 9 or so Colorado wineries always welcome guests for tastings. There is even an annual bicycle tour which can be quite grueling (it's only 30 miles on flat terrain, but it stops at every winery and vineyard along the way).

Ever wonder what the backcountry of Colorado is really like? Many mountain locations offer four-wheel-drive tours that get you back to where even hikers or horses fear to tread.

Colorado Mining Districts: Old mining districts are great places for prospecting, gold panning, ghost towns, and mine tours. The following cities were once active gold and/or silver mining areas: Alma; Aspen; Bonanza; Breckenridge; Boulder County; Central City; Climax; Creede; Crested Butte; Cripple Creek; Empire-Georgetown-Silver Plume; Fairplay; Garfield; Gilman; Idaho Springs; Lake City; La Plata; Leadville; Montezuma; Ouray; Rico; Silver Cliff; Silverthorn; St. Elmo; Summitville; Telluride; Tincup-Pitkin.

WARNING: There are over 23,000 open mine shafts and tunnels in Colorado. Most are unmarked, nearly invisible until it's too late, and some are several hundred feet deep. Use extreme caution while in mining backcountry.

Mine Tours:

Bachelor-Syracuse Mine	Ouray, CO	970-325-0220
Compromise Mine	Aspen, CO	970-925-3699
Country Boy Mine	Breckenridge, CO	970-453-4405
Edgar Experimental Mine	Idaho Springs, CO	303-567-2911
Lebanon Mine	Georgetown, CO	303-569-2403
Lost Gold Mine	Central City, CO	303-642-7533
Mollie Kathleen Mine	Cripple Creek, CO	719-689-2466
Old One Hundred Mine	Silverton	800-872-3009
Smuggler Mine	Aspen	970-925-2049

Colorado Wineries and Vineyards: (call for hours and directions)

Carlson Vineyards	Palisade, CO	970-464-5554
Colorado Cellars	Palisade, CO	970-464-7921
Grand River Vineyards	Palisade, CO	970-464-5867
Minturn Cellars	Minturn, CO	970-827-4065
Pikes Peak Vineyards	Colorado Springs, CO	719-576-0075
Plum Creek Cellars	Palisade, CO	970-464-7586
Rocky Hill Winery	Montrose, CO	970-249-3765
Terror Creek Cellars	Paonia, CO	970-527-3484
Vail Valley Vinters, Ltd	Palisade, CO	970-464-0559

ADDITIONAL RESOURCES

Dinosaur National Monument, Dinosaur, CO., 970-374-2216
Mesa Verde National Park (cliff dwellings), 970-529-4461
Historical Society of Colorado, 303-866-3682
Historical Society of Colorado, Archaeology, 303-866-3395
4 Wheeling America, Denver, CO., 303-778-9144
Blazing Trail Jeep Tours, Snowmass, CO., 970-923-4544
Colorado Association of Four-Wheel Drive Clubs, Inc., 303-343-0646
Colorado West Jeep Rent & Tours Ouray, CO   970-325-4014

PROFESSIONAL SPORTS

> *Recommended Reading:* Colorado Publishers produce excellent books on these subjects, please see these listings in Appendix A: Roberts Rinehart Publishers / Westcliffe Publishing

I think it must be a state law to be a sports fanatic if you live here. At least in Denver it seems that Professional Sports is the unofficial religion. Key players instantly qualify for sainthood and the best are elevated to demi-god status. When a home team does well, such news takes precedent over any national or international event. The good side is, when a home team is playing the city is virtually vacant, except for the hundreds of sports bars. It's a perfect time to go shopping or anything else non-sports related. That being said, Denver is one of only ten cities in the U.S. with four professional sports teams. Over 4.5 million fans attended home games during the 1994 baseball, basketball, and football seasons. The Rockies play at the new Coors Field which seats 50,000. The Broncos play at Mile High stadium which seats 75,000 and both the Nuggets and Avalanche use McNichols Sports Arena with 19,000 seats.

Baseball: The Colorado Rockies, Coors Field, 303-762-5437
Basketball: The Denver Nuggets, McNichols Sports Arena, 303-893-3865
Football: The Denver Broncos, Mile-High Stadium, 303-433-7466
Hockey: The Colorado Avalanche, McNichols Sports Arena, 303-893-6700

DOWNTOWN DENVER
Elitch Gardens; Brew-Pubs; Other Activities

When I first arrived in Denver about 10 years ago, the state was in an economic bust, the downtown business district had a high vacancy rate and LODO (lower downtown)

CHAPTER NINE: THINGS TO DO

was a collection of abandoned and boarded-up warehouses and was not a safe place after dark. How times change.

Today, 7,000 companies employ over 100,000 people downtown. Many commute to work via mass transportation such as RTD's new light-rail service which transports an average of 14,000 riders a day with 8 stops in the downtown area. RTD also operates 20 daily routes from downtown to Denver International Airport. With so many visitor attractions, downtown Denver offers in excess of 4,100 hotel rooms. In 1990, Denver completed its new Colorado Convention Center which has almost 300,000 square feet of exhibit space and hosted nearly 900,000 people for various conventions and meetings during 1994.

Once nearly forsaken by full-time residents, many of the new loft projects downtown are commanding some of the highest prices in the state. Today the area has roughly 9,000 residents who are literally surrounded by many of the state's largest-drawing attractions and a vibrant night-life.

The most popular area is LODO. Literally transformed from skid-row to the hottest spot in the state in a matter of a few years, LODO offers a dazzling array of activities and attractions. LODO is home to 40 some art galleries and most of Denver's 20 brewpubs which offer a selection of fine, hand-crafted brews and full menus. But if you don't care to dine at a brewpub, over 80 new restaurants have opened in downtown with 30 or so in LODO. In addition, with the recent opening of Coors Field, sports bars are popping up by the dozens. Any of the "Visitor's Guides" available everywhere contain complete information on what to see and do in LODO.

Elitch Gardens, the first amusement park in the country to relocate to a downtown area, is now located in the Platte River Valley in close proximity to Coors Field. Open only during the summer, Elitch's has 21 rides including a huge wooden roller coaster which consumed 500,000 board feet of lumber, 14 tons of nails, 32 tons of nuts, washers, and bolts, and 3,450 gallons of paint (just for the first coat). With 6 entertainment stages, 6 restaurants and 84,000 feet of gardens, you can plan on spending an entire day there. For more information call 303-595-4386 or 800-ELITCHS.

LEISURE, FUN & THE UNUSUAL

Concerts; Festivals; Limited-Stakes Gambling; Hot Springs; Narrow-Gauge & Scenic Train Rides, Golf, Tennis

Recommended Reading: Colorado Publishers produce excellent books on these subjects, please see these listings in Appendix A: Fulcrum Publishing / Pokerbook Press / Westcliffe Publishers

Concerts and Festivals: If you have read this chapter so far, you should be fairly impressed by all the recreation and entertainment Colorado offers. I won't even attempt to list all the festivals and concerts that take place in this state every year. They literally number in the hundreds. In addition to the hundreds of annual events, there are probably an equal number of one-time, unique gatherings occurring across the state at any given time. Many annual events, such as the Renaissance Festival in Larkspur or the People's Fair in downtown Denver draw hundreds of thousands. On the other hand, during the summer, it's not uncommon to see a few hundred people sprawled out in a small city park listening to free concerts by a variety of artists. But don't worry about missing anything. There is always a special section in most newspapers highlighting upcoming events for every season.

Limited-Stakes Gambling: A few years ago, several historic mining towns decided their economic salvation could be found in gambling. They went through the legal necessities and hence, Black Hawk, Central City, and Cripple Creek have become wall-to-wall casinos. Colorado casinos are limited to slots, blackjack, and several varieties of poker with the maximum bet being $5. However, most allow you to play several hands of blackjack at once and there is currently an effort underway to raise the limit to $25. Driving and parking can be a hassle (especially if you plan to have a cocktail or two), so many casinos and private companies offer shuttle service from many areas including several ski resorts. For more information contact the Black Hawk Gaming Owners Association, 303-420-8583; the Central City Public Information Office, 303-582-1889; or the Cripple Creek Chamber of Commerce, 800-526-8777.

Hot Springs: Long before the advent of hot tubs, the Ute Indians discovered the almost magical powers of the huge hot springs and vapor caves of Glenwood Springs. Today the enormous hot-spring-fed pools are still the major attraction in Glenwood (800-221-0098) but certainly not the only one. Almost all the other activities mentioned thus far in this chapter are available in the area. Other towns with natural hot springs include Alamosa, Buena Vista, Durango, Gunnison, Hot Sulphur Springs, Idaho Springs, Nathrop, Ouray, Pagosa Springs, Ridgway, Salida, and Steamboat Springs. Each Town's Chamber of Commerce or Visitor's Center will have additional information.

Narrow-Gauge & Scenic Train Rides: The original narrow-gauge railways were built to supply the mines and export their products. Today many of these railways and trains have been restored and offer some of the most spectacular scenery in Colorado. Most run summer only so call before making plans: Buckskin Joe Park and Railway, Canon City, CO., 719-275-5485
Cripple Creek/Victor Narrow-Gauge Railroad, 719-689-2640
Cumbres & Toltec Scenic Railroad, Antonito, CO., 719-376-5483
Durango-Silverton NG Railroad, 970-247-2733
Georgetown Loop Railroad, Metro: 670-1686, or 303-569-2403
Manitou and Pikes Peak Cog Railroad, 719-685-5401

Golf & Tennis: Colorado Golf Association, 303-779-4653; Colorado Golf Resort Association, 303-770-0100; Colorado Golf Country USA, 303-688-8262; Colorado Tennis Association, 303-695-4116

THE ARTS & CULTURE

Theater; Opera; Dance; Museums/Planetariums/Zoos

The capital of Florida is Tallahassee which is not much more than a small cow-town that happens to house the state government. On the other hand, Denver, the capital of Colorado, is also the state's largest city with most of the better locations for the arts &

culture. The best are highlighted below followed by a state-wide list sorted by city or town.

The Denver Performing Arts Complex: Located in downtown Denver, the "Plex" is the largest performing arts center under one roof in the world. It contains 9 theaters with a total of 9,212 seats. This complex hosts over 1,200 performances a year including many Broadway productions. 303-893-3272.

Denver Art Museum: Newly renovated in 1993, the DAM houses the largest Native American collection in the world. 303-640-2793.

Denver Botanical Gardens: Located in Denver's Capital Hill neighborhood, the DBG is famous for its award-winning Tropical Conservatory with an extensive collection of orchids, numerous water gardens, the Rock Alpine Garden, and a Japanese Garden complete with teahouse. 303-331-4000.

Denver Zoo: Home to the world-famous baby polar bears "Klondike and Snow," the zoo is also well-known for its large, naturalistic habitats including the new Tropical Discovery. This exhibit is a complete indoor rain-forest with an amazing diversity of tropical plants and animals. 303-331-4110

Denver Museum of Natural History/ Gates Planetarium/ IMAX Theater: All located in City Park under one roof, this complex has been known to draw immense crowds during the summer months or during the premieres of special exhibits. The Museum of Natural History is the fifth-largest in the country and can literally take all day to walk through. Gates Planetarium offers regular laser-light concerts and special events while the IMAX Theater, with its 4 story high screen, is an experience not to be missed. 303-370-6300.

COLORADO MUSEUMS, GALLERIES, AND PERFORMING ARTS

Washington County Museum	Akron	303-345-6446
Alma Firehouse Museum	Alma	719-836-2803
Arvada Center for the Arts & Hum	Arvada	303-431-3939
Arvada Flour Mill Museum	Arvada	303-431-1261
Aspen Art Museum	Aspen	303-925-8050
Aspen Historical Society	Aspen	303-925-3701
Intrntl Endangered Wildlife	Aspen	303-920-3258
Aurora History Museum	Aurora	303-340-2220
Confederate Air Force Co Wing	Aurora	303-693-3031
Melvin Schoolhouse Museum Lbry	Aurora	303-693-1500
Plains Conservation Center	Aurora	303-693-3621
Lace House	Black Hawk	303-582-5382
Collage Childrens Museum	Boulder	303-440-9894
Fiske Planetarium Univ Colo	Boulder	303-492-5001
Leanin' Tree Museum of Western Art	Boulder	303-530-1442
University Of Co Art Galleries	Boulder	303-492-8300
University Of Co Univ Hrtg Ctr	Boulder	303-492-6329
University Of Colorado Museum	Boulder	303-492-6892
Summit Historical Society	Breckenridge	303-453-9022
Adams County Museum Complex	Brighton	303-659-7103
Buena Vista Heritage	Buena Vista	719-395-8458
Burlington Museum Old	Burlington	719-346-7382
Co Bighorn Mus Amtr Rdo	Byers	303-822-9868

Canon City Municipal Museum	Canon City	719-269-9018
Prison Museum & Park	Canon City	719-269-3015
Marble Historical Society	Carbondale	303-963-0358
Central City Opera	Central City	303-292-6700
Gilpin History Museum	Central City	303-582-5283
Hahns Peak School House	Clark	303-879-6781
Carriage House Museum	Colorado Springs	719-634-7711
Cheyenne Mtn Zoological Pk	Colorado Springs	719-633-9925
Colorado Springs Pioneers Mus	Colorado Springs	719-578-6650
Gllry Contemp Art Univ Co Co	Colorado Springs	719-593-3567
McAllister House Museum	Colorado Springs	719-635-7925
Museum Amercn Numismatic Assn	Colorado Springs	719-632-2646
PRO Rodeo Hall Fame & Mus	Colorado Springs	719-528-4761
Turin Shroud Exhibit	Colorado Springs	719-599-9249
Western Museum Of Min & Indust	Colorado Springs	719-488-0880
WLD Figure Skating Mus & Hall	Colorado Springs	719-635-5200
Museum Of Northwest Colorado	Craig	303-824-6360
Sundance Research Inst & Mus	Craig	303-824-6123
Cripple Creek District Mus Inc	Cripple Creek	719-689-2634
OLD Homestead	Cripple Creek	719-689-3090
RIO Grande County Museum	Del Norte	719-657-2847
Delta County Historical Scty	Delta	303-874-8721
Fort Uncompahgre Lvng Hist Mus	Delta	303-874-8349
Black Amercn W Mus & Hrtg Ctr	Denver	303-292-2566
Byers Evans House	Denver	303-620-4933
Central City Opera House Assn	Denver	303-292-6500
Children's Museum of Denver	Denver	303-433-7444
Colorado Ballet	Denver	303-837-8888
Colorado History Museum	Denver	303-866-3682
Colorado State Museum	Denver	303-866-3681
Colorado Symphony	Denver	303-640-7539
Denver Art Museum	Denver	303-575-2793
Denver Botanical Gardens	Denver	303-331-4000
Denver Firefighter's Museum	Denver	303-892-1436
Denver History Museum	Denver	303-620-4795
Denver Mus Miniature Dolls & Toys	Denver	303-322-1053
Denver Museum Of Natural History	Denver	303-370-6387
Denver Zoo	Denver	303-331-4110
Forney Transportation Museum	Denver	303-433-5896
Four Mile Historic Park Inc	Denver	303-399-1859
Gates Planetarium	Denver	303-370-6351
Grant Humphreys Mansion	Denver	303-894-2506
Hall Of Life Health Educ Ctr	Denver	303-329-5433
History Museum State Museum Gr	Denver	303-894-2505
Kids Port	Denver	303-333-6507
Mizel Museum Of Judaica	Denver	303-333-4156
Molly Brown House Museum	Denver	303-832-4092
Museo De Las Americas	Denver	303-571-4401
Museum Of Western Art	Denver	303-296-1880
State Historical Society Of Co	Denver	303-866-3682
Theatre on Broadway	Denver	303-777-3292
Triamon Museum and Art Gallery	Denver	303-623-0739
Turner Museum	Denver	303-832-0924
Summit Historical Museum	Dillon	303-468-6079

CHAPTER NINE: THINGS TO DO

La Plata County Hist Scty	Durango	303-259-2402
The Museum of Outdoor Arts	Englewood	303-741-3609
Enos Mills Cbn Mus & Nature	Estes Park	303-586-4706
Estes Park Area Historical Mus	Estes Park	303-586-6256
Macgregor Ranch Museum & Ofc	Estes Park	303-586-3749
Hiwan Homestead Museum	Evergreen	303-674-6262
Southpark City Museum	Fairplay	719-836-2387
Fleming Museum	Fleming	303-265-2591
Price Pioneer Museum	Florence	719-784-3157
Florissant Fossil Beds Natl	Florissant	719-748-3253
Curfman Gllry & Duhesa Lng	Fort Collins	303-491-6626
Discovery Center Science Mus	Fort Collins	303-493-2182
Fort Collins Museum	Fort Collins	303-221-6738
Gustafson Gallery	Fort Collins	303-491-1983
ONE West Art Center	Fort Collins	303-482-2787
Fort Garland Museum	Fort Garland	719-379-3512
OLD Fort Garland	Fort Garland	719-379-3512
Fort Morgan Museum	Fort Morgan	303-867-6331
Frisco Historical Society	Frisco	303-668-3428
Georgetown Historical Society	Georgetown	303-674-2625
Georgetown Loop Railroad Inc	Georgetown	303-569-2403
Hamill House	Georgetown	303-569-2840
Frontier Historical Museum	Glenwood Springs	303-945-4448
Astor House Hotel Museum	Golden	303-278-3557
Buffalo Bill's Museum and Grave	Golden	303-526-0747
Colorado Railroad Museum	Golden	800-365-6263
Colorado Schl Mines Geolgy Mus	Golden	303-273-3815
Golden DAR Pioneer Museum	Golden	303-278-7151
Rocky Mountain Quilt Museum	Golden	303-277-0377
Cr Orch Lvng Histroy Frm Cntry	Grand Junction	303-434-9814
Dinosaur Valley Museum	Grand Junction	303-243-3466
Doozoo	Grand Junction	303-241-5225
Museum Of Western Colorado	Grand Junction	303-242-0971
Grand Lake Area Hist Scty	Grand Lake	303-627-3351
Greenley Municipal Museum	Greeley	303-350-9220
Museums Centennial Village	Greeley	303-350-9224
Museums Meeker	Greeley	303-350-9221
Gunnison Cnty Pnr & Hist Scty	Gunnison	303-641-4530
Hayden Heritage Center	Hayden	303-276-4380
Phillips County Museum	Holyoke	303-854-2129
Grand County Museum	Hot Sulphur Springs	303-725-3939
Lincoln County Museum	Hugo	719-743-2209
Clear Creek Hist Min & Mil Mus	Idaho Springs	303-567-2421
Underhill Museum	Idaho Springs	303-567-4100
Underhill Museum	Idaho Springs	303-567-4709
Southern Uteindian Cltrl Ctr	Ignacio	303-563-4531
Fort Sedgwick Depot Museum	Julesburg	303-474-2264
KIT Carson Historical Society	Kit Carson	719-962-3306
Bents Old Fort Natl Hist Site	La Junta	719-384-2596
Lafayette Miners Museum	Lafayette	303-665-7030
Jefferson County Planetarium	Lakewood	303-237-4786
Lakewoods Hist Belmar Vlg	Lakewood	303-987-7850
BIG Timbers Museum	Lamar	719-336-2472
KIT Carson Museum	Las Animas	303-456-2005

Healy House Dexter Cabin	Leadville	719-486-0487
Heritage Museum & Gallery	Leadville	719-486-1878
House With The Eye Museum	Leadville	719-486-1227
Matchless Mine Museum	Leadville	719-486-0371
Tabor Opera House Museum	Leadville	719-486-1147
Littleton Historical Museum	Littleton	303-795-3950
Dougherty Antique Collection	Longmont	303-776-2520
Longmont Museum	Longmont	303-651-8374
Loveland Museum & Gallery	Loveland	303-962-2410
Lyons Redstone Museum	Lyons	303-823-6692
Miramont Castle Museum	Manitou Springs	719-685-1011
White River Museum	Meeker	303-878-9982
Montrose Childrens Museum	Montrose	303-240-4833
Montrose County Hist Scty Mus	Montrose	303-249-2085
Great Sand Dunes National Mnmt	Mosca	719-378-2312
Rimrock Hist Mus W Montrose	Naturita	303-864-7837
Ouray County Museum	Ouray	303-325-4576
Fred Harman Art Museum	Pagosa Springs	303-731-5785
MUS Upper San Juan Hist Scty	Pagosa Springs	303-264-4424
Lucretia Vaile Museum	Palmer Lake	719-481-3622
Fort Vasquez Museum	Platteville	303-785-2832
El Pueblo Museum	Pueblo	719-583-0453
Eppys Art Studio	Pueblo	719-542-7785
Pueblo County Hist Mus & Lbry	Pueblo	719-543-6772
Rosemount Victorian House Museum	Pueblo	719-545-5291
Rangely Museum	Rangely	303-675-2612
Rifle Creek Museum	Rifle	303-625-4862
Rocky Ford Historical Museum	Rocky Ford	719-254-6737
Robbers Roost Old West Museum	Rye	719-489-3559
Saguache County Museum	Saguache	719-655-2557
Salida Museum	Salida	719-539-2311
Silver Cliff Museum	Silver Cliff	719-783-2394
George Rowe Museum	Silver Plume	303-569-2562
SAN Juan County Hist Scty Mus	Silverton	303-387-5838
Tread Of Pioneers Museum	Steamboat Springs	303-879-2214
Tread Of Pioneers Museum	Steamboat Springs	303-879-2214
Overland Trail Museum	Sterling	303-522-3895
Telluride County Hist Mus	Telluride	303-728-3344
Tiny Town (kid-sized village)	Tiny Town	303-697-6829
A R Mitchell Western Museum	Trinidad	719-846-4224
Baca House	Trinidad	719-846-7217
Louden Henritze Archaeology	Trinidad	719-846-5508
Trinidad Childrens Museum	Trinidad	719-846-8220
Colorado Ski Heritage Center	Vail	303-476-1876
Butterfly Pavilion and Insect Center	Westminster	303-469-5441
Cozens Ranch	Winter Park	303-726-5488
Pikes Peak Museum	Woodland Park	719-687-3041
Wray Museum	Wray	303-332-5063

ADDITIONAL RESOURCES

Colorado Consortium of Community Arts Council, 303-623-1845
Colorado Council on the Arts, 303-894-2617
Colorado Historical Society,
Colorado/Wyoming Association of Museums, 970-434-9814

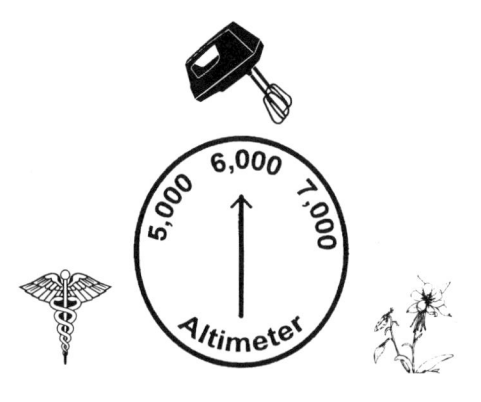

CHAPTER TEN
EIGHT MILES HIGH

HIGH-ALTITUDE LIVING
Health Precautions
Cooking
Gardening

> The information in this chapter was compiled from various sources including, but not limited to, government reports and publications (Federal, State, and Local); materials provided by business and civic organizations; and books produced by independent Colorado publishers including:
>
> *Crème de Colorado Cookbook,* C&C Publications
> *Colorado Cache Cookbook,* C&C Publications
> *Cooking with Colorado's Greatest Chefs,* Westcliffe Publishers, Inc.
> *The Xeriscape Flower Gardener,* Johnson Books
>
> For a complete description of the above books and related titles, please see the Publisher's listing in Appendix A.

In the event you skipped the topography section of chapter one, we need to review some basic facts about Colorado. Colorado may be many things, but "sea-level" is not one of them. Colorado's highest point is Mt. Elbert at 14,433 feet. The lowest is in the valley created by the Arkansas River at 3,350 feet, with 6,800 feet being the average elevation for the state.

High-altitude living can present unique challenges for the inexperienced low-lander. The air is literally thinner, the atmospheric pressure lower, the sun is a mile or two closer, and the seasonal transitions can be unpredictable. The uninitiated can experience medical maladies, culinary catastrophes, and botanical botcheries. All these, however, can be avoided with a little understanding of how the world works at nose-bleed altitudes.

HEALTH PRECAUTIONS

Newcomers to Colorado may experience a variety of medical problems ranging from shortness of breath to a bloody nose to full-blown altitude sickness. To better understand the causes behind these symptoms we need to start with a little basic physics.

Our atmosphere, containing 21 percent oxygen by volume, has a normal atmospheric pressure of 760 torrs (14.7 pounds per square inch) at sea-level. The barometric pressure decreases with an increase in altitude (12.28 lb/sq in. at 5,000 feet; 10.2 lb/sq in. at 10,000). Human life can be sustained by the barometric pressure up to altitudes of approximately 15,000 feet. Keeping in mind the average altitude in Colorado is 6,600 feet, you should consider FAA regulations require airliner cabins to be pressurized to the equivalent of 6,000 feet and military pilots are required to use pressurized oxygen while flying at or above 10,000 feet. Many of Colorado's mountain towns approach this limit.

Oxygen is used by the human body to cleanse toxins and although muscles can function temporarily without oxygen, a build-up of toxins quickly limits metabolic functions. Oxygen deficiency most directly affects brain and eye tissues, and a decrease in barometric pressure can cause minute blood vessels to swell or rupture. Outlined below are the most common aliments experienced by newcomers and tips on avoidance.

ALTITUDE SICKNESS AND RELATED SYMPTOMS

NOSE-BLEEDS

I was born and raised on the gulf-coast of Florida. Having spent my entire life at sea-level, I was perplexed by unexplained nose-bleeds every time I would visit my sister in Denver prior to actually moving here. Within hours of leaving the airport, I would begin the ritual of creating crimson Rorschach inkblots on an endless procession of tissues, paper-towels and finally, my newly purchased handkerchiefs. After consulting several experts (bartenders, cab drivers and the like), I determined the nose-bleeds were caused by both a decrease in atmospheric pressure, causing the nasal blood-vessels to swell, and the remarkably low humidity levels of high-altitude, thus causing the nasal/sinus membranes to dry out allowing the blood-vessels to rupture. The bottom-line is there is not much you can do to prevent this occurrence, although, in most cases the symptoms last only 72 hours or so. However, as we are constantly reminded by the over-the-counter drug companies, "If symptoms persist for more than seven days, consult a physician."

SHORTNESS OF BREATH

During physical exertion at high-altitudes, even the most physically fit athletes experience a degree of breathlessness until acclimatization has occurred. Because the air is thinner up here, it contains less oxygen by volume than sea-level. Therefore, even heavy breathing can barely compensate for the lack of oxygen until your body has readjusted. Many professional sports teams arrive in Denver several days before a big game just to allow the players time to acclimatize. Likewise, most seasoned skiers spend a couple of days at mid-altitudes before hitting the 12,000 foot slopes. The best advice here is to avoid heavy exertion until you have had time to adjust to new heights.

EYE IRRITATION

Many people experience varying degrees of eye irritation after arriving in Colorado. This is caused by the same factors as nose-bleeds. As mentioned above, brain and eye tissue is most quickly effected by a lack of oxygen and the low humidity tends to dry out the sensitive tissues of the eyes. Also, if you happen to be in the Denver Metro area, this irritation can be aggravated by our infamous "brown cloud" of toxins which can rival Los Angeles. The quickest relief comes from lubricating eyedrops.

ALTITUDE SICKNESS

I have met visitors to Colorado who claim to be experiencing altitude sickness as soon as they climb a flight of stairs in Denver (5,280 feet). I also know a few mountain climbers and hikers who can't wait to reach a 14,000 foot peak so they can have a cigarette, seemingly with no ill effects. I'm not sure why some display symptoms in the foot-hills and others can climb K2 in the Himalayas without oxygen. The one thing I do know is altitude sickness is most unpleasant and should be taken very seriously.

The condition itself results from a state of acute oxygen deficiency (hypoxidosis) which can most definitely occur at altitudes above 12,000 - 13,000 feet. Symptoms of hypoxidosis include mild intoxication and stimulation of the nervous system, followed by progressive loss of attention and judgment. If left untreated, unconsciousness will occur and a prolonged lack of sufficient oxygen may cause permanent brain damage.

For newcomers, a mild case of altitude sickness can be combined with the aforementioned conditions to produce light-headedness, nausea, and overall "I wish I were dead" symptoms. It should be noted the consumption of alcohol at high-altitudes may increase the effects or likelihood of the above. Take it easy the first couple of nights at the ski-lodge and if you think you are experiencing altitude sickness, slow down, descend to lower altitudes and don't be shy about asking for help.

SUNBURN

At higher altitudes, concern also needs to be given to nuclear radiation dangers (sunburn). The earth's atmosphere acts as a filter for the sun's harmful ultra-violet rays. At higher altitudes, the air is actually thinner than at sea-level and thus can not screen-out the same amount of radiation. In fact, at 6,000 feet UV rays are approximately 50-60 percent higher than at sea-level. Simply put, sunburn can occur more quickly and severely at altitude, especially on snow-covered terrain where the sunlight is reflected. Use sunblock during outdoor activities!

HIGH-ALTITUDE COOKING

Without exception, every time my father visits Colorado, whether he is in my sister's kitchen or mine, we can count on the failure of even his most prized recipes. Immediately following, we wait for the blame to fall on our "damn ovens" or "!#&*? stoves." Having lived in Florida his entire life and having perfected his recipes through thousands of experiments, my dad refuses to accept the fact further adjustments are necessary at high-altitude. I must admit it took me six years of living here to figure out how long to properly boil an egg. Besides, my dad can scream at my oven all he wants as long as I finally get one of his home-made cheesecakes!

Adding to the basic physics covered in the previous section, we discover the source of most culinary catastrophes experienced by visitors and residents alike. Remembering the relationship between altitude and air pressure, we add the following facts. As air pressure drops, water boils at lower temperatures. At sea-level, water boils at 212°F. Each 500-foot increase in altitude causes a drop of approximately 1°F in the boiling point. At very high altitudes, water boils at a relatively low temperature and since heat, not boiling, cooks food, more time is required for food to reach the desired internal cooking temperature. In addition, water evaporates much more quickly than at sea-level. Below is a quick-reference guide for standard adjustments followed by more detailed directions:

Foods cooked by boiling take more time to reach cooking temperature.

Pressure cookers require an adjustment in pressure within the cooker, or a longer period of processing, since they, too, are affected by altitude.

Sea-level temperatures for candies and frostings must be lowered as altitude increases to prevent over-concentration of the sugar mixture from excessive evaporation of the water.

Recipes must be adjusted for flour mixtures that contain considerable amounts of sugar and shortening, and are leavened with carbon dioxide gas from baking powder or soda and acid. When air is used for leavening, as in angel cakes, or steam is used, as in popovers, few adjustments are necessary.

Since deep-frying vaporizes the moisture in foods, and liquids vaporize at lower temperatures in higher altitudes, temperatures used in deep-frying should be reduced in proportion to the rise in altitude.

When **baking**, use the following adjustments: Reduce each teaspoon of **baking powder** by 1/4; Decrease each cup of **sugar** by 2-3 tablespoons; Increase by 3-4 tablespoons each cup of **liquid**; For **fats**, no adjustments are necessary unless substituting, then 1 cup of shortening equals 3/4 of butter or oil; **Oven temperature** should be increased by 25°F. Reduce by 25°F when using glass containers; Slightly increase all **cooking times**; and for best results at higher altitudes, use smaller pans and grease and flour or parchment paper, especially for cakes.

RICE, SOUPS AND VEGETABLES

Rice, soups and vegetables all require approximately 1/4 cup more water for each cup used and 10 - 15 minutes of additional cooking time. Vegetables such as green cabbage, Irish potatoes, parsnips, rutabagas, squash, sweetpotatoes and turnips require

CHAPTER TEN: EIGHT MILES HIGH

4-11 percent more time at 5,000 feet; 20-25 percent more time at 7,200 feet; and 55-66 percent more time at 10,000 feet. Cauliflower, onions, beets and mature carrots may require at least twice the cooking time at 5,000 feet as at sea-level.

High altitudes make little or no difference in temperatures for **baking** vegetables such as squash, potatoes, and sweetpotatoes.

Quick cooking conserves flavor and food value in vegetables. Small vegetables may be cooked whole, but larger ones should be cut up for faster cooking. Add vegetables to rapidly boiling water. Bring temperature back to boiling point rapidly and maintain it at this point throughout the cooking period. Better flavor and color will result from pressure saucepan cooking instead of long boiling. Cook only until tender to save both minerals and vitamin C. Because minerals and water-soluble vitamins C and B dissolve, the cooking water should be used.

Frozen Vegetables

Frozen vegetables, commercial or home packed, cook faster than similar fresh products. Usually it is sufficient to add only a minute or two to the time designated for sea-level cooking. Dense vegetables, such as cauliflower, will require additional cooking time. Keep your own records as to the time required at your altitude. No hard and fast rules can be applied. Peas, snap beans, and mixed vegetables may be cooked without thawing. Solid pack vegetables, such as greens, should be partially thawed before cooking.

Meat

Meat cooked by simmering or braising requires additional time at higher altitudes. In general, one-fourth more time may be required at 5,000 feet than at sea level. Use the sea-level time table for meats cooked in the oven, because oven temperatures are not affected by altitude change.

Eggs

In boiling eggs at varying altitudes, you must do your own testing. This means timing the eggs and recording the desired results. Try to use the same covered saucepan for cooking eggs and note whether you get the best results from eggs which are at refrigerator or room temperature. The "three-minute" egg may take up to six minutes or longer, according to altitude and cooking conditions. In Denver, I have found it takes exactly eleven minutes after the water comes to a boil to make perfect hard-boiled eggs. However, the best thing I recommend is a little egg-shaped plastic gizmo you put in with the eggs. It changes color as the eggs go from raw to hard-boiled and has never failed me at any altitude. However, my two-year old recently destroyed mine and I have not been able to find a replacement.

Pressure Saucepans

These conveniences may reduce some of the problems of vegetable cookery at high altitude. The temperature of the boiling water in the saucepan is raised because of the pressure built up within the sealed container. The boiling water and steam will cook foods faster than open kettle boiling.

At most altitudes, the cooking time of vegetables in the pressure saucepan is no more than 1 to 2 minutes over sea-level timing.

Canning

Non-acid fruits and vegetables should be processed in a pressure cooker, with an increase of one pound pressure for each 2,000 feet elevation. It is also desirable to increase processing time—by one minute for each 1,000 feet above sea level, if indicated time is 20 minutes or less, and by two minutes per 1,000 feet when sea level requirement is more than 20 minutes.

High-acid fruits and vegetables may be safely canned in a boiling water bath.

FROSTINGS AND CANDIES

Just as water boils at a temperature below 212° F. at the higher altitudes, all other liquids also boil at lower temperatures. Boiling causes loss of moisture through evaporation. The lower the boiling point, the sooner evaporation begins. At high altitudes, when sugar mixtures are cooked at the temperatures suggested in sea-level recipes, the faster loss of water causes the mixture to become too concentrated. Depending on the type of sugar mixture being prepared, the results may be "sugary" (where sugar recrystallizes out), or "hard."

To adjust sugar recipes for altitude, reduce the finish temperature. If you use a candy thermometer, test first the temperature at which water boils. While there will be minor changes from day to day, due to weather conditions, the range is usually slight. At 5,000 feet altitude, water boils at approximately 202° F., ten degrees less than at sea level. Thus, correct the finish temperature for the candy or frosting by subtracting the 10°. Example: If a sea-level recipe for creamy fudge gives a finish temperature for syrup at 238° F., at 5,000 feet the thermometer reading would be 228° F.

The tests in cold water are reliable when a thermometer is not available. At altitudes above 3,500 feet, increase the oven temperature 25°F over the temperature required at sea level. For example, cakes baked at sea level at 350°F should be baked at 375°F at all altitudes over 3,500 feet. The faster baking "sets" the cell framework within the flour mixture and helps to prevent falling.

In high altitudes, flour may become excessively dry unless it is stored in airtight containers. More liquid than the recipe calls for may be necessary to bring a batter or dough to the correct consistency.

Cakes

Some sea-level cakes are delicate and defy adjustment to varying altitudes. In which case, choose a new favorite from altitude tested recipes. Some other recipes are so well balanced that little if any adjustment may be necessary up to 5,000 feet. This is especially true of some of the commercial cake mixes. Keep a written record of any adjustments you make.

Without fat: Air, incorporated in the beaten eggs, is the leavening agent in cakes without fat. The eggs should be beaten less at high altitudes, so less leavening power is given to the batter. In angel food cakes beat the whites just until they form soft peaks; in sponge cakes beat the egg or eggs (yolks) only until they are slightly thickened.

CHAPTER TEN: EIGHT MILES HIGH

With fat: The emulsified shortening available on the market today gives good results in altitude baking. Because the emulsifier enables the shortening to tolerate a larger amount of liquid, it is preferable for the "speed-mix" cakes with high sugar ratio.

Flour: All purpose flour is preferable in most recipes. Sift before measuring and make the following adjustments: 3,500 to 5,000 feet add 1 tablespoon; 5,000 to 6,500 add 2 tablespoons; 6,500 to 8,000 feet add 3 tablespoons; and 8,000 feet and over add 4 tablespoons.

Eggs: An additional egg may be added to prevent the cake from being too dry and too tender.

Leavening: All types of baking powders and baking soda are treated alike in reductions for increased altitudes. When both baking powder and soda are used in a recipe, make the suggested adjustments in both ingredients. Accurate measurement of leavening is of increasing importance-as the altitude increases. The leavening adjustments begin with 2,000 feet elevation. The adjustments are: 2,000 to 3,500 feet decrease by 1/4 to 1/3 teaspoon; 3,500 to 5,000 feet decrease by 1/3 to 1/2 teaspoon; 5,000 to 6,500 feet decrease by 1/2 to 2/3 teaspoon; 6,500 to 8,000 feet decrease by 2/3 to 3/4 teaspoon; and 8,000 feet and over decrease by 3/4 teaspoon.

Commercial cake mixes: Buy only mixes which give directions for adjusting to altitudes, and follow directions given. In most instances, this adjustment comes in the addition of a measured amount of flour to the batter, and in a higher oven temperature. If the resulting cake seems excessively tender, an extra egg added to the batter will strengthen the cell structure and make the cake more easily handled. Bake in pans of the size recommended on the package.

Be sure to store commercial and home-made mixes in airtight containers to avoid excessive loss of moisture.

Cookies: No adjustments are usually needed unless cookies are rich, full of chocolate, nuts, snickers bars or the like. In this case, reduce the sugar and the baking powder as for a baked good. Baking a sample cookie may prevent ruining an entire batch.

Doughnuts: The sea-level recipe is usually too rich for use at higher elevations. The dough will absorb too much fat and crack during the frying. As in the case of some cakes, it is suggested that, instead of trying to adapt an old favorite recipe to the altitude, you adopt a new favorite that has been developed and tested to conditions.

YEAST BREADS

In short, use less flour per cup of liquid when mixing. Yeast breads rise faster at higher altitude and first rise should not be quite double in size. Final rise should be about 20-30 minutes. Increase oven temperature by 25° and bake for 10-15 less time.

Good basic recipes for yeast breads can be relied on at different altitudes. The fermentation of sugar in the bread is faster and bread may overproof unless it is watched. The general preference seems to be to reduce the proofing time rather than the amount of yeast. Do not add more flour than is necessary to make a dough than can be handled.

One adjustment that applies to all leavened foods is to bake the product "faster" at higher temperatures. At altitudes over 3,500 feet increase the baking temperature 25° over the sea level temperature.

Biscuits

Any standard recipe can be relied on to give good results at varying altitudes. An additional tablespoon of milk to each cup of flour improves the quality of the product.

Muffins

Slightly less sugar can be used than in a standard sea-level recipe. Try reducing sugar by one teaspoon if finished product does not meet your standards.

Quick Breads

Where the amount of sugar is low, little adjustment is needed for increased altitude. Slightly more liquid may be desirable if breads seem to dry excessively in baking. Decrease the temperature in proportion to the rise in altitude. It is difficult to give the definite number of degrees because of the variety of foods fried, but a general recommendation is to decrease the temperature two to three degrees for each 1,000 feet elevation. For example, a recipe for doughnuts gives a temperature of 370° F. When frying at 5,000 feet elevation, use a temperature in the range of 350° F. to 360° F.

The cook books mentioned at the beginning of this chapter are highly recommended. Not only do they contain recipes which are the cream of the crop, all recipes have also been adjusted for the average altitude in Colorado. See Appendix A for complete descriptions and information.

HIGH-ALTITUDE GARDENING

Colorado offers unique challenges and conditions for any type of horticulture (gardening, landscaping, farming). This is especially true for newcomers to the state who may have come from lower altitudes with more predictable weather patterns and seasonal transitions. When first arriving here, many folks jump right into gardening and landscaping without considering the subtle, yet major differences in Colorado's growing conditions. Recently, there was a story on the news about the onslaught of irate customers most greenhouses and nurseries were dealing with. It seems the vast majority of these customers were newcomers who purchased and then planted their gardens in late March or April. And why not? We were experiencing warm days and mild evenings with plenty of rain to boot. Besides, it was officially Spring and they had always planted this time of year. What they didn't expect was a couple of hard freezes in May. These folks were showing up with trunk-fulls of dead plants demanding refunds.

Due to Colorado's altitude, low humidity, intense sunlight, soil conditions and totally unpredictable weather, one would be well advised to do a little research before breaking out the shovels and potting soil. This section, as with most in this book, is intended to provide only the basics, to act as a guide. The end of this chapter contains a list of additional resources where complete information can be obtained. Let's look at some basics for the Rocky Mountain region:

Humidity: In Florida, like many coastal areas, it is not uncommon to have both temperature and humidity in the 90's. There is a vast difference between that and temperatures in the 90's with humidity in the teens. Combined with intense sunlight and prolonged heat waves, the evaporation rate of water is tremendous. It is not uncommon for evaporation rates in parts of Colorado to exceed 50 inches of water per year while receiving only 10-20 inches from precipitation. The end result is increased need for supplemental irrigation. In Denver, the average noon humidity during January is 43% while in July it averages 36%.

Sunlight: As noted previously, the effects of sunlight are intensified at higher altitudes. This holds true everywhere. However, because of Colorado's latitude and geography, we also get about 3 additional hours of sunlight per day compared to cloudier regions and on the average have 300 days of sunshine per year. All this combined means many plants which require full sun elsewhere may grow very well in partial shade here.

Growing Seasons: Sheridan, WY. has a frost-free growing season of 123 days (May 21 - Oct 21); Salt Lake City, UT.'s is 202 days (Apr 12 - Nov 1); Denver's is 159 days (May 6 - Oct 12). There are parts of the country where by mid-May you would be almost ready to harvest your first crop of vegetables. If you came from one of those areas it is hard to adjust to having to wait until May 6th or later to even safely plant. Please take note: 159 days is the season for Denver, not Colorado! Because of the great diversity in altitudes and weather conditions, parts of Colorado have longer seasons and many places have much shorter ones. Check with your local experts before planting. If you simply can't wait until mid-May I highly recommend using "walls-of-water." This product is a tee-pee shaped, double-walled, multi-chambered vinyl contraption which you fill with water and place around new plantings. The water traps the heat of sunlight during the day and slowly releases it at night when it gets cold. The manufacturer claims it can jump-start your growing season by six weeks and I have personally had good luck with them. The devices are available everywhere come Spring.

Temperature Extremes: Having grown-up in Florida, I was accustomed to very mild temperature fluctuations. The temperature and humidity usually ranged from unbearably hot and sticky to almost unbearably hot and sticky. Allowing for the slight change in seasons, the vegetation in Florida knew what to expect. Not so in Colorado! Temperature fluctuations can be drastic and sudden, regardless of season. During Spring, we can have stretches of hot weather lasting days or weeks immediately followed by a week of snow and hard freezes. In Winter, the temperature can suddenly rise (in a matter of minutes) from below freezing to almost tee-shirt weather due to "Chinook" winds, only to drop again by day's end. This kind of fluctuation is very stressful on many types of plants (not to mention most people). On average, the daily January temperatures in Denver range from 15 - 42 degrees, while in July they range from 57-88 degrees. These are averages, not examples of the very common extremes experienced.

Micro-Climates: Not only do different weather conditions occur throughout various parts of Colorado, due to everything discussed so far, you can also experience very different growing conditions within the boundaries of your own yard. You can literally have desert-like conditions along a south wall and "Aspen meadow" conditions on the north. The differences between the south and north side of the same house can be equivalent to several thousand feet of mountain elevation change or several thousand miles of latitude change on the plains.

Xeriscape: Xeriscape! Xeriscape! Xeriscape! Forty to Sixty percent of clear, cool, drinking water supplied to cities throughout the region is used for landscape irrigation! A Xeriscape approach to landscaping can result in a 50 percent reduction of needed irrigation. Additional benefits are lower initial cost per square foot and greatly reduced maintenance needs. If done properly, most Xeriscaped yards not only save a tremendous amount of water, they also give the yard's owners a lot more time to enjoy other aspects of Colorado's outdoors. *The Xeriscape Flower Gardener*, by Jim Knopf is an excellent resource for learning about all the benefits of this environmentally friendly art.

ADDITIONAL RESOURCES

High-Altitude Recipes

Crème de Colorado Cookbook, C&C Publications
Colorado Cache Cookbook, C&C Publications
Cooking with Colorado's Greatest Chefs, Westcliffe Publishers, Inc.
See Publisher's listing in Appendix A for details

High-Altitude Gardening

The Xeriscape Flower Gardener, A Waterwise Guide for the Rocky Mountain Region, Johnson Books. See Appendix A.
Successful Gardening for Colorado and the *Rocky Mountain Plant Guide*, both available from most nurseries and greenhouses.
Colorado Nurserymen's Association, 303-758-6672
Associated Landscape Contractors of Colorado, Inc., 303-757-5611
Garden Centers of Colorado Members, 303-427-8132
Colorado Chapter, American Society of Landscape Architects, 303-830-0094

Public Xeriscape Demonstration Areas:
City of Arvada Public Works Center, 303-420-0984
Colorado Springs Mesa Treatment Plant, 719-520-0300
Career Enrichment Park, Westminster, CO, 303-428-2600
Denver Water Department, 303-628-6329
Denver Botanical Gardens, 303-331-4000
Denver Botanical Gardens Chatfield Arboretum, 303-973-3705
Douglas County Executive Building, 303-688-3096
Longmont Public Library, 303-651-8360
Oxley Homestead, Golden, CO, 303-526-0284
Fort Collins Xeriscape Demonstration Garden, 970-221-6681

Denver Botanical Gardens: DBG offers numerous classes, instruction, and advice about high-altitude gardening and xeriscape. In addition, they have a complete library with over a dozen books on xeriscaping and and their staff includes botanists, horticulturists, landscapers, and professional gardeners. Call 303-331-4000.

CHAPTER ELEVEN
SO FAR AWAY

GETTING FROM THERE TO HERE
Moving Tips
Moving With Children
Temporary Housing
Relocation Services

Recommended Sources for Additional Information (See Appendix A):
Moving With Children, Gylantic Publishing Company

I have moved more times than I can remember. What I do remember is swearing to myself (after every move) I would never do it again. I recently told my wife, if we ever find the property we are looking for, build our dream house and move, we will sell our current home fully furnished with all accessories, and whatever doesn't fit in the cars, will stay.

We've all been there. The endless lists, the sleepless nights (going over the lists), the packing, the loading, the cleaning, the trip, the unloading and unpacking, the utilities, new bank accounts, on and on. Unplanned and unprepared, a major move can put the best of us down for the count. Hopefully, this chapter will assist you in making the most of your next move.

MOVING TIPS

Moving across town or across the country can be made easier if you break it down into three phases: The Preparation Phase, The Work Phase, and The Settling-in Phase. Use the tips below to make a checklist for each phase.

THE PREPARATION PHASE

One Month Prior To Moving: Make all reservations and arrangements for truck rentals or moving companies (see moving company tips below). Start acquiring necessary moving supplies such as boxes, tape, labels, etc. If you plan to drive to your new home, plan the travel route. Start a special file to save all moving receipts: many moving costs may be tax deductible. Develop your plan for packing (see Work Phase below). Make sure important records (legal, insurance, medical) are in a safe and accessible place. Notify the Post Office of your new address.

Two Weeks Prior To Moving: Notify all utilities (phone, gas, electric, water) of your move and sign up for necessary services at your new location. Completely service your car if it will be used or driven. Start recruiting help for the move (this is the test of true friendship). Confirm all reservations made previously. Confirm payment requirements from any moving companies. Make arrangements to close or transfer all bank accounts.

THE WORK PHASE

Packing: Have all packing supplies in one place (boxes, bubble wrap, marking pens, tape measure, furniture pads, rope, tools and knife, tape and scissors). Label boxes with the contents and the room where they belong in your new home. Number each box and keep a list of the contents. Make sure fragile items are clearly marked. Designate certain boxes or suitcases for personal items you'll need during the move. Keep a medical kit handy.

Cleaning: Cleaning is 90% planning and 10% effort so make a plan! Start with all necessary cleaning supplies so your momentum isn't broken. Do a preliminary job on the bathroom and kitchen, but expect them to be used up until the last time you close the door to your old home. It's easy to be immersed in your work so keep the "Child Safety" rules in mind around cleaning supplies.

THE SETTLING-IN PHASE

Physical: Make sure your new home (especially the bathroom and kitchen) are perfectly clean (you'll never go back and do it right once they are full of stuff). Check-off every numbered box from your list as it comes into the house. The first box in should be your tool kit of unpacking supplies (knife, tape measure, large trash bags, necessary tools for re-assembly). The second thing in should be a radio or tape player. Get all boxes and used packing out of the house as soon as they are emptied.

Emotional: The following suggestion applies to all phases of moving: Without fail, schedule in some time to relax and enjoy yourself (a movie, a bike ride, pizza and wine on the balcony). Allow yourself to grieve the loss of moving (friends, family, favorite places). Look forward to meeting new friends, your new job, and finding new favorite places. Accept the fact moving is a major thing. Take it easy, you don't have to adjust to everything at once.

MOVING WITH CHILDREN

If you're a parent you already know children do not think, feel, or react as adults. What may seem like a logical, well-planned, check-listed sequence of events to you may be very traumatic for children. While tending to the million details of a move, it's easy to overlook how it might effect your children. *Moving With Children* is an outstanding book by Gylantic Publishing. It covers every aspect of the moving process in general and offers the following information.

Preparation Phase Stress Factors For Children: The unpredictability of the moving schedule. The presence of strangers in the house. The disruption of familiar family routines and activities. Reduced time and attention and possible periods of separation from parents. Unaccustomed travel to visit a new neighborhood or community prior to the move. The process of having to break the news and answer questions about the move to friends, classmates, and neighbors.

Work Phase Stress Factors For Children: The disruption of a comfortable family structure. The physical demands of packing and cleaning. The necessity of giving away or leaving behind familiar belongings. Physically leaving friends and neighbors. The excitement, disruption and physical labor of moving day. The possible rigors of traveling to a new house.

Settling-In Phase Stress Factors For Children: The possible delay, loss of or damage to possessions during the move. The physical demands of unpacking, storing and decorating. The work of making home comfortable. The re-establishment of familiar family routines and schedules. The absence of a familiar support group. The process of becoming acquainted with a new community and meeting new neighbors.

If ignored or improperly handled, the tremendous amount of stress placed on children during a move can result in a wide-range of emotional and physical symptoms. If you are planning a family move and don't have a Ph.D. in child psychology I recommend the book mentioned above.

Moving Company Tips: The Better Business Bureau reports a 38% increase in complaints about moving companies since 1990. Money Magazine offers the following tips on how to protect yourself from scams and incompetence:

Get a binding estimate before the move and make sure the amount is written into the contract. It costs about $3,285 to move the contents of a three-bedroom house to a different state.

Before hiring, inquire about the company with the local BBB and state or local consumer affairs department. The Interstate Commerce Commission allows interstate movers to give you only 60 cents per pound for lost or damaged goods. To cover potential damage, check your existing homeowners or renters policy and buy extra coverage if necessary.

Ask about expected gratuities before hiring and write them into the contract. If your mover demands more money anyway and you're stuck, consider paying but write your protest on the bill as evidence. Write into the contract the company will be held responsible for damage to items you packed.

Storage Tips: If you plan to have your possessions in storage for more than a few days, find out how the moving company plans to do this. It is common for companies simply to park the semi-trailer in their lot and leave it until you are ready. In Colorado this can be the wrong thing to do. Due to our intense sunshine, during the summer temperatures inside the trailer can exceed 130 degrees for extended periods. That combined with our low humidity can play hell with furniture finishes, glue joints, framed art, music collections and the like. During the winter, temperatures inside a trailer can fluctuate 50 - 80 degrees between day and night. Excessive expanding and contracting can also damage furniture. Find another method of storage if possible or get written guarantees about damage from the companies who will, of course, deny any of the above is true.

TEMPORARY HOUSING/RELOCATION SERVICES

If you find yourself here before your belongings or will have an extended wait while your new home is finished, you will need temporary housing. There are numerous companies in Colorado that specialize in matching people with apartments, condo's, or rental homes. Most of their clients are making a permanent move but these companies also work with newcomers who need temporary housing for one month, six-months or longer. Most have computerized databases and can quickly locate just what you need. The best part is, usually there is little or no cost to you because costs are paid by the landlord or management company. If you are not already working through a relocation service, contact one of the companies below:

Apartment Hunters	Aurora	303-755-4636
A Apartment Store	Colorado Springs	719-550-1100
Apartment Connection	Colorado Springs	719-574-1974
Apartment Hunters	Colorado Springs	719-593-0055
Apartment Hunters	Colorado Springs	719-596-7368
Apartment Rental Information	Colorado Springs	719-597-7800
Colorado Springs Relocating Service	Colorado Springs	719-576-6620
Colorado Springs Relocating Service	Colorado Springs	719-574-7070
A Anne Dressers Apartment Str	Denver	303-758-8888
Anne Dressers Apartment Store	Denver	303-758-4811
Apartment Finders International	Denver	303-759-9904
Apartment Finders International	Denver	303-452-2211
National Apartment Finders	Fort Collins	970-221-2152

Relocation Concepts	Aurora	303-695-0971	(Individual)
Relocation Resources	Denver	303-297-0500	(Corporate)

Colorado Relocations Services at 303-971-0971 specializes in short and long-term, fully-furnished temporary housing (in fact, this is all they do). They can locate anything from a one-bedroom apartment to a five-bedroom house.

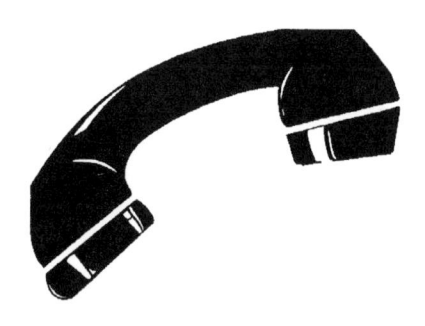

CHAPTER TWELVE
NEW KID IN TOWN

RESOURCES / PHONE LISTS

INDEX OF PHONE LISTS ELSEWHERE IN THIS BOOK

LIST OF:	Pages
State Government Departments/Agencies	37-56
School Districts	62-67
Institutions of Higher Education	70-72
Corporate and Private Libraries	73-74
County Clerks	90-91
Drivers' License Offices	98-99
Small Business Development Centers	151
Access Colorado Library & Information Network	152
Service Corps of Retired Executives Offices	152
Job Service Centers	153
Governor's Job Training Offices	153
Local Economic Development Offices	153-154
Chambers of Commerce	154-155
National Monuments	159
National Forest	159
Colorado State Parks	160-161
Ski Areas / Resorts	162-163
Colorado Bicycle Organizations	164
Ballooning, flying, glider companies	165
Mine Tours	167
Colorado Wineries and Vineyards	168
Museums, Galleries, and Performing Arts	171-174
Apartment Locators and Relocation Services	188

PREFIXES IN THE 970 AREA CODE

At Colorado's current rate of growth, the state will run out of telephone prefixes by the end of 1995. To remedy this situation a new area code, 970, has been added. No prefixes in the 719 area code were changed. However, a great number of phone numbers that were previously in the 303 area code are now in the new 970 area code. Until January 1, 1996, all 970 prefixes can be reached by either 970 or 303. When calling a number that may have been printed more than a year ago, check the list below to see if it's in the new area code.

970

		282	351	396	483	544	630	726	858	901
		283	352	401	484	547	632	728	859	920
		284	353	408	485	554	635	729	862	921
203	243	285	354	409	487	560	638	731	864	923
204	244	301	356	410	490	562	641	734	865	925
209	245	302	357	416	491	563	645	735	867	926
210	246	304	358	418	493	564	653	736	870	927
216	247	309	359	432	495	565	655	737	872	928
217	248	318	362	434	498	566	656	749	873	929
218	249	323	365	435	520	568	662	768	874	931
219	250	325	374	437	521	574	663	774	875	942
221	253	326	376	448	522	580	664	785	876	943
222	256	327	379	453	523	583	667	824	878	944
223	257	328	380	454	524	586	668	827	879	945
224	259	330	381	463	527	587	669	834	881	946
225	260	332	382	464	529	588	675	835	882	948
226	262	334	383	468	531	593	677	842	883	949
227	264	335	385	471	532	596	679	845	884	962
228	265	339	386	474	533	597	686	846	885	963
229	268	345	387	476	535	619	708	847	886	967
240	269	346	389	479	537	625	723	848	887	968
241	272	349	390	481	539	626	724	854	895	984
242	276	350	395	482	542	627	725	856	897	

Prefix list current as of July 14, 1995.

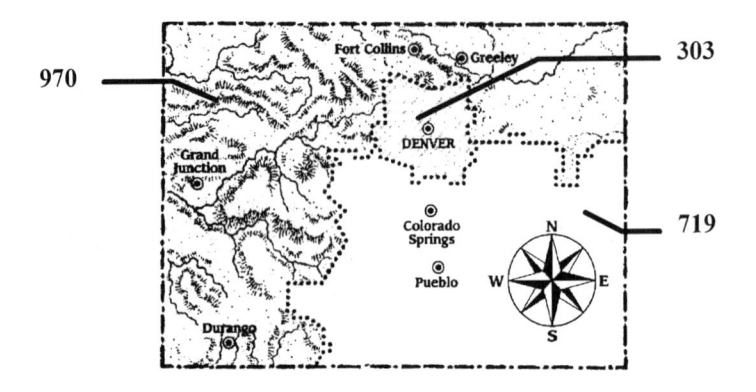

CHAPTER TWELVE: NEW KID IN TOWN

CONVENTION & VISITOR'S BUREAUS

In addition to Chambers of Commerce, which are list in Chapter Eight, Convention & Visitors Bureaus are a great source of information when evaluating a new place to live.

Boulder Conv. & Visitors Bureau	800-444-0447
Central City Public Information	800-542-2999
Chaffee County Visitors Bureau	800-831-8594
Clear Creek County Tourism Board	800-882-5278
Colorado Springs Conv. & Visitors Bureau	800-368-4748
Denver Metro Conv. & Visitors Bureau	800-645-3446
Fort Collins Area Conv. & Visitors Bureau	800-274-3678
Georgetown Visitor Information Center	303-569-2888
Grand Junction Conv. & Visitors Bureau	800-962-2547
Greeley Conv. & Visitors Bureau	800-449-3866
Idaho Springs Visitor Information Center	800-882-5278
Mancos Visitors Center	970-533-7434
Park County Tourism Office	719-836-4279
Poudre Cayon Visitor Information	800-462-5870
San Luis Valley Information Center	800-835-7254
San Luis Valley Visitor Center	719-672-3355
Telluride Visitor Services	800-525-3455

REFFERAL SERVICES

The Denver Post and TouchTOWN Information Freeway offer a free service that is very helpful to newcomers to the greater Denver metro area. The service is a 24 hour per day information retreval system you can access from any phone. To use this service you simply dial 778-7800, touch * and the extention number of your choice. TouchTOWN has hundreds of selections from which to choose. A partial list follows:

	Professional Services		**Sports**
*490	Health-Care Providers	*333	Sports, Scores and Reports
*501	Mental-Health Care	*213	Picks and Point Spreads
*894	Dental Offices	*214	The Golf Report
*911	Legal Offices	*448	Soccer Scene
*841	Financial Services	*446	Sports Trivia Challenge
	Arts and Entertainment		**The World of Music**
*479	Book Reviews	*434	Classical Music Releases
*489	New Movies	*495	Best Pop
*693	Museums/Galleries	*496	Best Rock
*300	Family Fun	*497	Best Jazz
*301	Vacation Hotline	*498	Best R & B
	Dow Jones Financial		**Loans**
*645	Financial Headlines	*488	Mortgage Loans
*646	Stock Market Updates	*844	Auto/RV Loans
*649	Dow Jones	*843	Consumer Loans
*656	Bond Updates	*842	Home Equity Loans

METRO AREA PROFESSIONAL CHILD-CARE ASSN. REFERRALS:

By County (all 303):
Adams	451-1061	Denver	733-2345
Arapahoe	766-0563	Jefferson	969-8772
Boulder	469-5596		

CIVIC CLUBS AND ORGANIZATIONS

Colorado is home to chapters of virtually all national civic clubs and organizations. The list below is not complete. Several organizations have many chapters in the same city. In those cases, only one is shown to act as a point of contact.

American Legion	Arvada	303-424-0324
American Legion	Aurora	303-680-6424
American Legion	Boulder	303-442-9551
American Legion	Brighton	303-659-5792
American Legion	Broomfield	303-466-1278
American Legion	Buena Vista	719-395-8024
American Legion	Canon City	719-275-9919
American Legion	Carbondale	970-963-2381
American Legion	Colorado Springs	719-599-8624
American Legion	Cortez	970-565-8151
American Legion	Denver	303-238-2401
American Legion	Durango	970-247-1590
American Legion	Estes Park	970-586-6118
American Legion	Florence	719-784-6125
American Legion	Golden	303-279-6200
American Legion	Grand Junction	970-243-0882
American Legion	Haxtun	970-774-9240
American Legion	Holyoke	970-854-3486
American Legion	Ignacio	970-563-9502
American Legion	Laporte	970-484-0418
American Legion	Longmont	303-776-2034
American Legion	Louisville	303-666-6314
American Legion	Manitou Springs	719-685-4724
American Legion	Pagosa Springs	970-264-4884
American Legion	Paonia	970-527-6252
American Legion	Pueblo	719-561-8319
American Legion	Sterling	970-522-5688
American Legion	Stratton	719-348-5202
American Legion	Walsh	719-324-9909
American Legion	Windsor	970-686-9966
Bnai Brith Lodge	Denver	303-393-7358
Boys & Girls Club	Alamosa	719-589-0151
Boys & Girls Club Pikes Peak	Colorado Springs	719-473-3490
Boys & Girls Clubs Metro	Denver	303-893-8150
Boys And Girls Club	Greeley	970-353-5190
Colorado Mountain Club	Boulder	303-449-1135
Colorado Mountain Club	Colorado Springs	719-635-5330
Colorado Mountain Club	Golden	303-279-5643
Colorado POW/MIA Coalition	Denver	303-499-2554
Disabled American Veterans	Colorado Springs	719-392-9923
Disabled American Veterans	Denver	303-922-3428
Disabled American Veterans	Fort Collins	970-484-1795
Disabled American Veterans	Grand Junction	970-242-1627
Disabled American Veterans	Pueblo	719-543-8343
Disabled American Veterans	Wheat Ridge	303-424-0545
Elks Home	Florence	719-784-3892
Elks Home	Fort Morgan	970-867-6711
Elks Home	Trinidad	719-846-2980

CHAPTER TWELVE: NEW KID IN TOWN

Elks Home & Lodge Rooms	Leadville	719-486-0236
Elks Lodge	Akron	970-345-2294
Elks Lodge	Alamosa	719-589-2362
Elks Lodge	Arvada	303-424-2278
Elks Lodge	Aspen	970-925-3516
Elks Lodge	Aurora	303-360-7204
Elks Lodge	Boulder	303-442-5003
Elks Lodge	Brighton	303-659-2802
Elks Lodge	Broomfield	303-469-1708
Elks Lodge	Canon City	719-275-1880
Elks Lodge	Central City	303-582-5181
Elks Lodge	Colorado Springs	719-633-5077
Elks Lodge	Cortez	970-565-3557
Elks Lodge	Craig	970-824-3557
Elks Lodge	Creede	719-658-2661
Elks Lodge	Cripple Creek	719-689-2625
Elks Lodge	Deer Trail	303-769-4480
Elks Lodge	Delta	970-874-3624
Elks Lodge	Denver	303-455-3557
Elks Lodge	Durango	970-247-2296
Elks Lodge	Evergreen	303-674-5591
Elks Lodge	Fort Collins	970-493-3777
Elks Lodge	Glenwood Springs	970-945-2286
Elks Lodge	Golden	303-279-2740
Elks Lodge	Grand Junction	970-243-0675
Elks Lodge	Greeley	970-330-3557
Elks Lodge	Gunnison	970-641-1527
Elks Lodge	Hotchkiss	970-872-3355
Elks Lodge	Idaho Springs	303-567-9996
Elks Lodge	La Junta	719-384-9161
Elks Lodge	Littleton	303-794-1811
Elks Lodge	Longmont	303-776-1055
Elks Lodge	Louisville	303-666-8600
Elks Lodge	Monte Vista	719-852-2456
Elks Lodge	Montrose	970-249-4852
Elks Lodge	Ouray	970-325-4510
Elks Lodge	Pueblo	719-544-6452
Elks Lodge	Rangely	970-675-8533
Elks Lodge	Rifle	970-625-2195
Elks Lodge	Salida	719-539-6976
Elks Lodge	Silverthorne	970-468-2561
Elks Lodge	Sterling	970-522-0515
Elks Lodge	Victor	719-689-2974
Elks Lodge	Walsenburg	719-738-1210
Elks Lodge	Westminster	303-429-2227
Elks Lodge	Wray	970-332-4907
Fraternal Order of Eagles	Aspen	970-925-9912
Fraternal Order of Eagles	Brighton	303-659-4973
Fraternal Order of Eagles	Broomfield	303-466-4928
Fraternal Order of Eagles	Fort Collins	970-498-9535
Fraternal Order of Eagles	Glenwood Springs	970-945-5506
Fraternal Order of Eagles	La Salle	970-284-6880
Fraternal Order of Eagles	Trinidad	719-846-3821
Fraternal Order of Eagles	Walsenburg	719-738-1900

Irish Fellowship Club Of Colorado	Aurora	303-752-7037
Jaycees	Arvada	303-431-5849
Jaycees	Denver	303-744-0591
Jaycees	Grand Junction	970-241-8706
Jaycees	Sterling	970-521-9546
Jaycees Colorado State Office	Wheat Ridge	303-420-4018
Kiwanis Club Of Denver	Englewood	303-779-8715
Kiwanis Rocky Mtn District Ofc	Arvada	303-422-7852
Knights of Columbus	Arvada	303-423-4603
Knights of Columbus	Aurora	303-366-6314
Knights of Columbus	Brighton	303-659-0661
Knights of Columbus	Burlington	719-346-7600
Knights of Columbus	Canon City	719-275-1412
Knights of Columbus	Cheyenne Wells	719-767-5353
Knights of Columbus	Colorado Springs	719-637-8052
Knights of Columbus	Commerce City	303-287-0945
Knights of Columbus	Denver	303-455-6888
Knights of Columbus	Englewood	303-789-0132
Knights of Columbus	Fort Collins	970-484-1881
Knights of Columbus	Grand Junction	970-242-9746
Knights of Columbus	Greeley	970-352-9774
Knights of Columbus	La Junta	719-384-2120
Knights of Columbus	Lakewood	303-238-8740
Knights of Columbus	Lamar	719-336-3591
Knights of Columbus	Trinidad	719-846-0450
League Woman Voters Araphoe Cnty	Denver	303-863-0437
Lions Club	Aurora	303-366-4323
Lions Club Foundation	Arvada	303-420-4766
Lions Club Of Denver	Denver	303-388-2025
Lions Den	Holyoke	970-854-3111
Masonic AF & FM	Akron	970-345-6522
Masonic AF & FM	Alamosa	719-589-2361
Masonic AF & FM	Arvada	303-424-9941
Masonic AF & FM	Aurora	303-366-0402
Masonic AF & FM	Boulder	303-449-2711
Masonic AF & FM	Brighton	303-659-3484
Masonic AF & FM	Brush	970-842-2503
Masonic AF & FM	Burlington	719-346-8872
Masonic AF & FM	Canon City	719-275-3818
Masonic AF & FM	Carbondale	970-963-8869
Masonic AF & FM	Castle Rock	303-688-4131
Masonic AF & FM	Cedaredge	970-856-3062
Masonic AF & FM	Center	719-754-3472
Masonic AF & FM	Central City	303-582-5525
Masonic AF & FM	Colorado Springs	719-471-9587
Masonic AF & FM	Craig	970-824-5882
Masonic AF & FM	Del Norte	719-657-3635
Masonic AF & FM	Denver	303-393-7825
Masonic AF & FM	Dolores	970-882-7945
Masonic AF & FM	Durango	970-259-5416
Masonic AF & FM	Englewood	303-789-9805
Masonic AF & FM	Estes Park	970-586-8097
Masonic AF & FM	Fort Morgan	970-867-7534
Masonic AF & FM	Georgetown	303-569-2811

Masonic AF & FM	Glenwood Springs	970-945-5013
Masonic AF & FM	Golden	303-279-9902
Masonic AF & FM	Grand Junction	970-242-0120
Masonic AF & FM	Greeley	970-353-1776
Masonic AF & FM	Hayden	970-276-3433
Masonic AF & FM	Holyoke	970-854-3518
Masonic AF & FM	Hotchkiss	970-872-3384
Masonic AF & FM	Idaho Springs	303-567-2811
Masonic AF & FM	Johnstown	970-587-4516
Masonic AF & FM	La Junta	719-384-2271
Masonic AF & FM	Lafayette	303-665-6876
Masonic AF & FM	Lamar	719-336-5331
Masonic AF & FM	Leadville	719-486-1775
Masonic AF & FM	Littleton	303-794-1771
Masonic AF & FM	Longmont	303-776-3515
Masonic AF & FM	Mancos	970-533-7721
Masonic AF & FM	Manitou Springs	719-685-5304
Masonic AF & FM	Monte Vista	719-852-3913
Masonic AF & FM	Montrose	970-249-3943
Masonic AF & FM	Monument	719-488-3785
Masonic AF & FM	Pagosa Springs	970-264-5864
Masonic AF & FM	Pueblo	719-542-9738
Masonic AF & FM	Rocky Ford	719-254-3861
Masonic AF & FM	Salida	719-539-2708
Masonic AF & FM	South Fork	719-873-5327
Masonic AF & FM	Springfield	719-523-6531
Masonic AF & FM	Steamboat Springs	970-879-0062
Masonic AF & FM	Sterling	970-522-2366
Masonic AF & FM	Trinidad	719-846-2861
Masonic AF & FM	Westminster	303-429-9895
Masonic AF & FM	Woodland Park	719-687-2732
Masonic AF & FM	Wray	970-332-4939
Moose Lodge	Aurora	303-366-2061
Moose Lodge	Canon City	719-275-1790
Moose Lodge	Colorado Springs	719-632-2914
Moose Lodge	Denver	303-457-3391
Moose Lodge	Grand Junction	970-242-4754
Moose Lodge	Longmont	303-776-4911
Moose Lodge	Loveland	970-667-2525
Moose Lodge	Nucla	970-864-7610
Moose Lodge	Pueblo	719-542-9618
ODD Fellows	Alamosa	719-589-6670
ODD Fellows	Arvada	303-427-0412
ODD Fellows	Boulder	303-442-5669
ODD Fellows	Canon City	719-275-1606
ODD Fellows	Colorado Springs	719-633-4838
ODD Fellows	Delta	970-874-4588
ODD Fellows	Denver	303-233-0372
ODD Fellows	Durango	970-247-8420
ODD Fellows	Fort Lupton	303-857-2970
ODD Fellows	Glenwood Springs	970-945-5632
ODD Fellows	Golden	303-279-1272
ODD Fellows	Grand Junction	970-245-9576
ODD Fellows	Greeley	970-353-0061

COLORADO: A Newcomer's Manual

ODD Fellows	Longmont	303-776-4588
ODD Fellows	Loveland	970-667-4584
ODD Fellows	Pueblo	719-542-0804
ODD Fellows	Sterling	970-522-3028
Paralyzed Veterans of America	Denver	303-322-4402
Paralyzed Veterans Of America	Sterling	970-522-2837
Rotary Club	Boulder	303-444-2407
Rotary Club	Denver	303-893-1919
Rotary District	Denver	303-477-0654
Rotary Meeting Information	Colorado Springs	719-473-4514
Shrine Club	Colorado Springs	719-632-3881
Shrine Club	Englewood	303-789-0272
Shrine Office	Denver	303-455-3470
Veterans Club	Akron	970-345-6584
Veterans Club	Holyoke	970-854-9444
Veterans Club	Johnstown	970-587-4500
Veterans Club	Loveland	970-667-4722
Veterans Club	Wray	970-332-4760
Veterans of Foreign Wars	Alamosa	719-589-9329
Veterans of Foreign Wars	Arvada	303-424-3824
Veterans of Foreign Wars	Ault	970-834-1212
Veterans of Foreign Wars	Brighton	303-659-9902
Veterans of Foreign Wars	Broomfield	303-460-9557
Veterans of Foreign Wars	Canon City	719-275-9886
Veterans of Foreign Wars	Colorado Springs	719-632-9874
Veterans of Foreign Wars	Commerce City	303-286-8658
Veterans of Foreign Wars	Craig	970-824-7145
Veterans of Foreign Wars	Denver	303-825-4341
Veterans of Foreign Wars	Durango	970-247-0384
Veterans of Foreign Wars	Englewood	303-781-0090
Veterans of Foreign Wars	Evans	970-339-3025
Veterans of Foreign Wars	Fort Collins	970-493-9909
Veterans of Foreign Wars	Fort Lupton	303-857-9984
Veterans of Foreign Wars	Golden	303-279-2119
Veterans of Foreign Wars	Grand Junction	970-242-9940
Veterans of Foreign Wars	Gunnison	970-641-0948
Veterans of Foreign Wars	Hotchkiss	970-872-3502
Veterans of Foreign Wars	Hugo	719-743-9994
Veterans of Foreign Wars	Lafayette	303-665-9993
Veterans of Foreign Wars	Lamar	719-336-9934
Veterans of Foreign Wars	Las Animas	719-456-2822
Veterans of Foreign Wars	Longmont	303-776-8590
Veterans of Foreign Wars	Mancos	970-533-7202
Veterans of Foreign Wars	Ordway	719-267-4735
Veterans of Foreign Wars	Pagosa Springs	970-731-2424
Veterans of Foreign Wars	Penrose	719-372-3719
Veterans of Foreign Wars	Platteville	970-785-9989
Veterans of Foreign Wars	Pueblo	719-547-2770
Veterans of Foreign Wars	Steamboat Springs	970-879-9959
Veterans of Foreign Wars Auxiliary	Brush	970-842-4337
Vietnam Veterans of America	Pueblo	719-583-2155
Vietnam Veterans of America	Westminster	303-650-2648
Womans Club Of Denver	Denver	303-839-1655
Womens Club Of Colorado Springs	Colorado Springs	719-633-3279

DAILY / WEEKLY NEWSPAPERS

When my wife & I are looking for property in different areas of Colorado, we always pick up a copy of the local paper. This helps us get a feel for the area. Many newspapers will mail you a recent copy of their publication.

Akron News Reporter	Akron	970-345-2296
Valley Courier	Alamosa	719-589-2553
Arvada Sentinel Newspaper	Arvada	303-425-8755
Jefferson Arvada Sentinel	Arvada	303-239-9890
Olde Towner Newspaper	Arvada	303-423-5306
Wheat Ridge Jefferson Sentinel	Arvada	303-425-0214
Aspen Daily News	Aspen	970-920-2118
Times Daily	Aspen	970-925-3414
Aurora Adcovate	Aurora	303-343-9020
Aurora Sentinel Aurora Pblshng	Aurora	303-750-7555
Gateway Gazette	Aurora	303-340-8142
Korean Denver News	Aurora	303-364-4500
Korean Post	Aurora	303-366-6006
Korean Times	Aurora	303-367-5900
Vail Trail	Avon	970-949-4004
Vail Valley Times	Avon	970-949-4402
Fairplay Flume	Bailey	303-838-2108
Park County Republican	Bailey	303-838-4423
Pine River Times Inc	Bayfield	970-884-2331
Berthoud Recorder Newspaper	Berthoud	970-532-3715
Boulder Weekly	Boulder	303-939-0055
Colorado Daily Newspaper	Boulder	303-442-3914
Daily Camera	Boulder	303-444-3444
Handicapped Coloradan	Boulder	303-938-8288
Breckenridge Journal	Breckenridge	970-453-2331
Brighton Standard	Brighton	303-659-2522
Brush News Tribune	Brush	970-842-5516
Chaffee County Times	Buena Vista	719-395-8621
Burlington Record	Burlington	719-346-5381
Daily Record/Market Place	Canon City	719-275-7565
Castle Rock News Press	Castle Rock	303-688-3128
Mountain Valley News	Cedaredge	970-856-7499
Center Post Dispatch	Center	719-754-3172
Greenhorn Valley News Inc	Colorado City	719-676-3304
Black Forest News	Colorado Springs	719-473-4370
Colorado Springs Bus Jrnl Inc	Colorado Springs	719-634-5905
Daily Transcript	Colorado Springs	719-634-1593
Gazette Telegraph	Colorado Springs	719-632-5511
Independent News Weekly	Colorado Springs	719-577-4545
Commerce City Beacon	Commerce City	303-289-4600
Commerce City Express	Commerce City	303-288-7987
Cortez Newspapers Inc	Cortez	970-565-8527
Northwest Colorado Daily Press	Craig	970-824-7031
Mineral County Miner	Creede	719-658-2603
Mt Crested Butte Mountain Sun	Crested Butte	970-349-6124
Crestone Eagle	Crestone	719-256-4956
Cripple Creek Woodland Pk News	Cripple Creek	719-689-2375
TRI County Tribune	Deer Trail	970-769-4646

DEL Norte Prospector	Del Norte	719-657-2211
El Informador Inc	Delta	970-874-8054
Montrose Daily Press Delta Bur	Delta	970-874-7500
American Chinese Times	Denver	303-758-6094
Beacon Review	Denver	303-692-8940
Bingo Journal	Denver	303-759-1764
Cherry Creek Local	Denver	303-377-0510
Colorado Chinese News	Denver	303-722-8268
Daily Journal	Denver	303-756-9995
Denver Business Journal In	Denver	303-837-3500
Denver Post	Denver	303-820-1010
Front Range Woman Inc	Denver	303-296-3447
Handicapped Coloradan	Denver	303-860-1491
Herald Dispatch	Denver	303-936-7778
Intermountain Jewish News	Denver	303-861-2234
Life On Capitol Hill	Denver	303-839-1738
Pueblo Star Jrnl & Chieftain	Denver	303-861-7202
Rocky Mountain Jiho	Denver	303-295-1848
Washington Park Profile	Denver	303-778-8021
Westword Corp	Denver	303-296-7744
Dolores Star	Dolores	970-882-4486
Dove Creek Press	Dove Creek	970-677-2214
Four Corners Weekly	Durango	970-385-6963
Eagle Valley Enterprise	Eagle	970-328-6656
Colorado Computeruser	Englewood	303-770-4707
Estes Park Trail Gazette	Estes Park	970-586-3356
Canyon Courier	Evergreen	303-674-5534
Flagler News	Flagler	719-765-4466
Coloradoan Newspaper	Fort Collins	970-493-6397
Eagle Country Scene	Fort Collins	970-490-1009
Senior Voice News Magazine	Fort Collins	970-229-9204
Fort Morgan Times	Fort Morgan	970-867-5651
El Paso County News	Fountain	719-382-5611
Fowler Tribune	Fowler	719-263-5311
Copper Cable Newspaper	Frisco	970-668-3022
Summit Daily News	Frisco	970-668-3998
Summit Sentinel	Frisco	970-668-0750
Fruita Times	Fruita	970-858-3924
Daily Sentinel	Glenwood Springs	970-945-1206
Glenwood Post	Glenwood Springs	970-945-8515
Golden Transcript	Golden	303-279-5541
Rocky Mountain Sports & Gaming	Golden	303-384-0026
Daily Tribune	Granby	970-887-3334
Daily Sentinel	Grand Junction	970-242-5050
Senior Beacon Newspaper	Grand Junction	970-243-8829
Gunnison Country Times	Gunnison	970-641-1414
Hayden Valley Press	Hayden	970-276-3202
Eastern Colo Plainsman	Hugo	719-743-2371
Johnstown Breeze	Johnstown	970-587-4525
Julesburg Advocate	Julesburg	970-474-3388
Middle Park Times	Kremmling	970-724-3350
Conejos County Citizen	La Jara	719-274-4192
Arkansas Valley Journal Inc	La Junta	719-384-8121
Lafayette News	Lafayette	303-665-6515

CHAPTER TWELVE: NEW KID IN TOWN

Lamar Daily News	Lamar	719-336-2266
Rocky Mountain News	Leadville	719-486-1451
Limon Arrow	Limon	719-775-8101
Limon Leader	Limon	719-775-2064
Columbine Community Courier	Littleton	303-933-2233
Englewood Herald Newspaper	Littleton	303-794-7877
South Jeffco Echo	Littleton	303-933-6300
Country Register The	Longmont	303-651-6830
Longmont Daily Times Call	Longmont	303-776-7440
Loveland Daily Teporter Herald	Loveland	970-351-6363
OLD Lyons Recorder	Lyons	303-823-6625
Mancos Times Tribune	Mancos	970-533-7766
Catholic Herald	Manitou Springs	719-685-5202
Journal Newspapers	Manitou Springs	719-685-9201
Meeker Herald	Meeker	970-878-4017
Daily Press	Montrose	970-249-3444
El Paso County Tribune	Monument	719-481-3423
TRI Lakes Times	Monument	719-488-9362
Mountain Ear	Nederland	303-258-7075
Otis Weekly Star	Otis	970-246-0160
Pagosa Sun	Pagosa Springs	970-264-2101
Palisade Tribune	Palisade	970-464-5614
Delta County Independent	Paonia	970-527-4537
High Country News	Paonia	970-527-4898
Valley Chronicle	Paonia	970-527-6585
Weekly News Chronicle	Parker	303-841-5497
Chieftain & Star Journal	Pueblo	719-544-3520
Pueblo Business Journal Inc	Pueblo	719-542-3616
Senior Beacon	Pueblo	719-544-3232
Womans Focus Newspaper	Pueblo	719-544-0303
Rangely Times	Rangely	970-675-5033
Costilla Cnty Free Prs Nwsppr	San Luis	719-672-3764
Silverton Standard Newspaper	Silverton	970-387-5477
South Fork Tines	South Fork	719-873-5592
Baca Weekly	Springfield	719-523-6600
Rocky Mountain News	Steamboat Springs	970-879-7225
Journal Advocate	Sterling	970-522-1990
South Platte Sentinel	Sterling	970-522-8148
Eastern Colo News	Strasburg	970-622-4417
Telluride Daily Planet	Telluride	970-728-9788
Telluride Times Journal	Telluride	970-728-4301
Chronicle News Publishing Co	Trinidad	719-846-3311
El Reportero News Inc	Wheat Ridge	303-940-7859
Manifest	Winter Park	970-726-5721
Cripple Creek Woodland Pk News	Woodland Park	719-687-3006
Yuma Pioneer	Yuma	970-848-2174

RADIO / T.V. STATIONS

Every time I have moved, It would always take me a month or so to find a good radio station. Below is listed all the AM and FM radio stations for the greater Denver metro area and Front Range. Many of the larger stations have transponders which broadcast into the ski resorts and mountain areas.

Call Letters	Frequency	Format	Phone
KLZ	560 AM	Christian Contemporary	433-5500
KHOW	630	Talk	694-6300
KNUS	710	News	477-7110
KTLK	760	Talk/Sports	893-8500
KLT	800	Christian/Country	433-8000
KOA	850	News/Talk	893-8500
KPOF	910	Christian/Classical	428-0910
KKFN	950	Sports	321-0950
KRKS	990	Christian	779-8797
KLMO	1060	Country	449-3224
KYBG	1090	Sportstalk	721-9210
KCUV	1150	Mexican/Latin Hits	861-1158
KBCO	1190	Alternative Music	444-5600
KBNO	1220	Hispanic	292-5266
KXKL	1280	Oldies Rock	832-5665
KKYD	1340	Kid Radio	989-1340
KJME	1390	Mexican Music	623-1390
KCOL	1410	All News/Talk	1-303-482-5991
KEZW	1430	Big Band/Nostalgia	696-1714
KBKS	1490	Alternative/Rap	444-1490
KDKO	1510	Urban Contemporary	295-1225
KQXI	1550	Christian Music/Talk	761-1550
KYGO	1600	Classic Country	321-0950
KGNU	88.5 FM	Public Radio/BBC	449-4885
KUVO	89.3	Latin/Jazz/Blues/News	480-9272
KCFR	90.1	Public Radio/Classical	871-9191
KWBI	91.1	Christian Ministry/Music	697-5924
KYBG	92.1	New Rock	721-9210
KZDG	92.5	Country	832-5665
KTCL	93.3	Alternative Music	571-1232
KRKS	94.7	Christian	779-8797
KHIH	95.7	Contemporary Jazz	694-6300
KGLL	96.1	Country	1-303-223-0435
KXPK	96.5	Alternative Rock	989-1340
KBCO	97.3	Alternative Music	444-5600
KYGO	98.5	Hot New Country	321-0950
KUAD	99.1	Contemporary Country	1-303-686-2791
KVOD	99.5	Classical	936-3428
KMJI	100.3	'70's Hits	741-5654
KOSI	101.1	Adult Contemporary	696-1714
KTRR	102.5	'70's/'80's Hits	1-303-223-0435
KRFX	103.5	Classic Rock	893-3699
KQKS	104.3	Top 40	721-9210
KXKL	105.1	Oldies Rock	832-5665
KALC	105.9	Adult Contemporary	534-6200
KBPI	106.7	Album Rock	893-3699

200

CHAPTER TWELVE: NEW KID IN TOWN

KWMX	107.5	Adult Hits	321-0950
KIMN	107.9	Adult Contemporary	1-303-482-5991

Aspen Channel	Aspen	303-925-9579
Channel Thirty Eight	Aurora	303-671-0938
KTV Channel 10 Jones Intercable	Broomfield	303-465-2365
FOX 21 KXRM TV	Colorado Springs	719-596-2100
K 43CG TV Channel 43	Colorado Springs	719-574-7777
KKTV TV	Colorado Springs	719-634-2844
KMGH TV Southern News Bureau	Colorado Springs	719-633-7777
KRDO TV	Colorado Springs	303-825-5552
KXRM Partnership	Colorado Springs	719-591-1121
3 News Sports	Craig	303-824-7265
KBDI Public TV 12	Denver	303-296-1212
KWGN TV Channel 2	Denver	303-740-2222
KCNC TV Channel 4	Denver	303-861-4444
KRMA TV Channel 6	Denver	303-892-6666
KMGH TV Channel 7	Denver	303-832-7777
KUSA TV Channel 9	Denver	303-871-9999
KBDI Public TV Channel 12	Denver	303-296-1212
KTVD TV Channel 20	Denver	303-792-2020
KDVR TV FOX Channel 31	Denver	303-595-3131
KRMT TV OFColorado	Denver	303-423-4141
KUBD TV 59	Denver	303-751-5959
Public Broadcasting Of Colorado	Denver	303-871-9191
WCTV	Denver	303-758-1978
KREZ TV	Durango	303-259-6666
KWGN INC	Englewood	303-740-2222
KWHD TV 53	Englewood	303-773-9953
CHANNEL 8 Estes Park	Estes Park	303-586-6045
KCNC TV Northern Bureau	Fort Collins	303-224-4444
KUSA Northern Bureau	Fort Collins	303-484-5332
NEWS 4 Mountain Bureau	Frisco	303-668-0444
KREX TV	Grand Junction	303-242-5000
KUSA West Slope Bureau	Grand Junction	303-242-1999
CHANNEL 43	Lakewood	303-237-4300
KCEC Channel 50	Lakewood	303-235-0049
Channel 3	Longmont	303-776-1424
KREY TV	Montrose	303-249-9601
KDJ 24 TV	Pueblo	719-542-4277
KKTV Channel 11	Pueblo	719-542-6247
KOAA TV Channels 5 & 30	Pueblo	719-544-5781
KRDO TV News 13	Pueblo	719-544-1312
KRDO TV News 13	Pueblo	719-543-0013
KTSC TV	Pueblo	719-528-5050
KTVS TV	Sterling	303-522-2729
TCTV Telluride Community TV	Telluride	303-728-3838
TV 8	Vail	303-479-0800
Vail Valley TV	Vail	303-476-7444

201

CREDIT UNIONS

During the past 4-5 years, virtually all Colorado owned banking institutions have been bought-out, taken over or otherwise gobbled-up by out of state Mega-Banks. By no coincidence, as this state continues to grow, we are bombarded by ads from dozens of Mega-banks offering "free" checking accounts and other enticements to bank with them. You almost need a microscope to sort out the fine print to see what "free" really means. The bottom line is all banks are *for-profit* corporations.

On the other hand, all credit unions are *non-profit* corporations. This is probably why approximately one-third (1.2 million) of all Colorado citizens choose credit unions for all their financial needs. Most Colorado credit unions offer a full-range of services including loans, savings accounts, checking (share draft) accounts, payroll deductions, direct deposit, educational/financial counseling and more.

Joining a credit union may be easier than you think. Credit unions are generally sponsored by companies, churches, fraternal organizations or other groups with similar interests. Some credit unions serve residents in certain neighborhoods or communities. In addition, most credit unions extend their membership to families of current members and select employee groups. Taking a course at certain schools could qualify you for membership. For more information on how you might qualify to take advantage of a local credit union call the Colorado Credit Union Center at 303-427-4222 or 800-477-6240. As of this writing, there are 192 credit unions in Colorado.

Akron F C U	Akron	970-345-2623
Alamosa Credit Union	Alamosa	719-589-2544
Guadalupe Parish F C U	Antonito	719-376-5413
Arvada Public Employees F C U	Arvada	303-431-5970
Colorado Central Credit Union	Arvada	303-427-5005
Denver Postal F C U	Arvada	303-422-6221
Electrical F C U	Arvada	303-428-5080
Northwest United F C U	Arvada	303-424-5037
Roaring Fork Employees F C U	Aspen	970-920-5218
Aurora F C U	Aurora	303-755-2572
Aurora Scools F C U	Aurora	303-360-0987
Buckley F C U	Aurora	303-340-9829
Fitzsimons F C U	Aurora	303-340-3343
Gateway Credit Union	Aurora	303-340-2300
Rural Electric F C U	Aurora	303-695-6354
Safeway Rocky Mountain F C U	Aurora	303-369-6400
Saint Pius Tenth F C U	Aurora	303-364-3939
Saint Therese F C U	Aurora	303-364-4819
Space Age F C U	Aurora	303-369-7666
Ashoka F C U	Boulder	303-449-5900
Boulder Community Hospital FCU	Boulder	303-449-3551
Boulder Mncpl Employees F C U	Boulder	303-441-3065
Boulder Valley F C U	Boulder	303-442-8850
IBM Rocky Mountian Employees	Boulder	303-449-9600
U Of C F C U	Boulder	303-443-4672
Brighton Cooperative F C U	Brighton	303-659-7014
District 27 F C U	Brighton	303-659-6600
Community Financial F C U	Broomfield	303-469-5366
Fremont County F C U	Canon City	719-275-3261

CHAPTER TWELVE: NEW KID IN TOWN

AIR Acdmy F C U	Castle Rock	303-688-8500
Co-Operators F C U	Center	719-754-2632
Air Academy F C U	Colorado Springs	719-593-8600
C.M.S. F C U	Colorado Springs	719-471-3931
Colorado Springs F C U	Colorado Springs	719-473-4110
ENT F C U	Colorado Springs	719-574-1100
First Charter F C U	Colorado Springs	719-473-6250
Fitters Local 58 F C U	Colorado Springs	719-634-3516
H.P. Colorado F C U	Colorado Springs	719-590-2094
Harrison District 2 F C U	Colorado Springs	719-473-0218
Interstate Gas Credit Union	Colorado Springs	719-634-3100
Mountain Bell F C U	Colorado Springs	719-473-7452
Mowry Credit Union	Colorado Springs	719-389-0703
One-Thirteen F C U	Colorado Springs	719-632-7118
Pikes Peak F C U	Colorado Springs	719-473-5962
School District 3 F C U	Colorado Springs	719-392-8439
School District 14 F C U	Commerce City	303-287-8025
United Florists F C U	Commerce City	303-288-7898
Moffat County Schools F C U	Craig	970-824-7005
St. Michael's F C U	Craig	970-824-6566
Holy Name Of Mary Credit Union	Del Norte	719-657-3926
Delta F C U	Delta	970-874-7674
Joint District 50 F C U	Delta	970-874-7674
Colorado Southern F C U	Denver	303-628-0523
Colorado State Employees F C U	Denver	303-832-4816
Columbia Healthcare Employee FCU	Denver	303-320-2244
D C Credit Union	Denver	303-321-4414
Denpak F C U	Denver	303-289-5461
Denver Bar Assn F C U	Denver	303-860-1117
Denver Cmnty Developed F C U	Denver	303-292-3910
Denver Fire Dept F C U	Denver	303-458-6129
Denver Media F C U	Denver	303-572-0501
Denver Municipal F C U	Denver	303-399-1173
Denver Police F C U	Denver	303-458-6660
Denver Pub Schl Employees F C U	Denver	303-321-4209
Denver Rio Grande Credit Union	Denver	303-634-2156
Denver Stake F C U	Denver	303-451-6543
Denver Texaco Employees F C U	Denver	303-793-4910
Denver Water Department CU	Denver	303-628-6860
Diakonia F C U	Denver	303-922-8375
District One F C U	Denver	303-288-2066
Eaton Employees F C U	Denver	303-296-4800
Emmaus Luthern F C U	Denver	303-423-7892
Farmers Union F C U	Denver	303-337-5500
FBW F C U	Denver	303-831-3861
Gates Credit Union	Denver	303-744-3535
GSA-8 F C U	Denver	303-236-7283
GW F C U	Denver	303-573-6312
I.U.E.O. #9 Credit Union	Denver	303-623-3194
Manville Employees F C U	Denver	303-978-2274
Methodist Ministers F C U	Denver	303-777-9676
Metrum Community Credit Union	Denver	303-770-4468
Midtown F C U	Denver	303-861-0844
Plumbers Local F C U	Denver	303-286-2575

Porter F C U	Denver	303-691-2345
Presentation F C U	Denver	303-936-2299
Provenant F C U	Denver	303-629-3950
Public Service Employees F C U	Denver	303-691-2345
Rio Grand Operating CU	Denver	303-477-3960
Rocky Mountain News Empl. CU	Denver	303-892-2620
S M W No 9 F C U	Denver	303-934-5428
Saint Dominics F C U	Denver	303-477-1523
Samsonite F C U	Denver	303-373-7454
School District 50 F C U	Denver	303-428-9571
Sooper F C U	Denver	303-986-7500
Tramco F C U	Denver	303-722-9497
Two Blues F C U	Denver	303-831-2061
U S Consolidated F C U	Denver	303-628-5900
University Cooperative CU	Denver	303-777-0946
VAH F C U	Denver	303-321-7345
Wedenem Credit Union	Denver	303-753-0592
White Crown F C U	Denver	303-293-0071
Zion Baptist Brotherhood CU	Denver	303-861-4958
Southwest Colorado F C U	Durango	970-247-5204
Englewood Municipal F C U	Englewood	303-762-2555
Rocky Mountian Employees CU	Englewood	303-649-4111
Security Credit Union	Englewood	303-761-2210
Pueblo Govt Agy F C U	Florence	719-784-0600
Norlarco Credit Union	Fort Collins	970-221-1261
Fort Lyon F C U	Fort Lyon	719-456-2671
Fort Morgan Schools F C U	Fort Morgan	970-867-4028
District 8 F C U	Fountain	719-382-8400
C U Of The Rockies	Golden	303-273-5200
Coors Credit Union	Golden	303-279-6414
CoorsF C U	Golden	303-279-6414
CSM F C U	Golden	303-273-3417
Jeffco F C U	Golden	303-278-4907
Colorama F C U	Grand Junction	970-243-7280
Grand Junction F C U	Grand Junction	970-243-1370
Grand Junction P.S.C. Empl. F C U	Grand Junction	970-244-2618
Junction Bell F C U	Grand Junction	970-242-3100
Mesa County F C U	Grand Junction	970-243-5705
Mesa County Teachers F C U	Grand Junction	970-243-2434
Mount Garfield F C U	Grand Junction	970-243-3242
Rio Grande F C U	Grand Junction	970-243-7330
Rose Hill F C U	Grand Junction	970-244-2010
Agland F C U	Greeley	970-352-8690
College Credit Union of Greeley	Greeley	970-351-2434
Norbel F C U	Greeley	303-356-6660
State Farm Insurance Co. F C U	Greeley	970-351-5349
Weld Schools Credit Union	Greeley	970-330-9728
Bellco First F C U	Greenwood Village	303-689-7800
Gunnison Western F C U	Gunison	970-641-2482
Haxtun Commnity F C U	Haxtun	970-774-7396
Holyoke Community F C U	Holyoke	970-854-3109
Hotchkiss Community FCU	Hotchkiss	970-872-4277
CO-NE F C U	Julesburg	970-474-2617
La Junta F C U	La Junta	719-384-7251

Mennonite FCU	La Junta	719-384-5412
Otero County Teachers F C U	La Junta	719-384-7488
Cobe Employees F C U	Lakewood	303-231-4320
Credit Union Of Denver	Lakewood	303-234-1700
Jeffco Schools F C U	Lakewood	303-989-3300
VAR F C U	Lakewood	303-233-4285
Fellowship F C U	Lamar	719-336-5511
Lamar Civic F C U	Lamar	719-336-4387
Saint Francis Credit Union	Lamar	719-336-4552
Bent County Scool Employees F C U	Las Animas	719-456-0548
Lake County Schools Credit Union	Leadville	719-486-1837
Church Of St Marys F C U	Littleton	303-730-1128
F.C.I. F C U	Littleton	303-798-8181
Norgren Employees F C U	Littleton	303-763-2555
RED Rocks F C U	Littleton	303-797-2900
Mile High Turkey F C U	Longmont	303-776-6611
Saint Vrain Valley F C U	Longmont	303-772-2115
BIG Thompson F C U	Loveland	970-669-4747
HP Rocky Mountain F C U	Loveland	970-697-2812
Longs Peak F C U	Loveland	970-667-8585
Montrose County Schools F C U	Montrose	970-249-5319
Montrose F C U	Montrose	970-249-8813
Grain Millers F C U	Northglenn	303-452-0675
School District 12 F C U	Northglenn	303-451-1146
Olathe F C U	Olathe	970-323-5404
High Country F C U	Parshall	970-569-3221
Decibel Credit Union	Pueblo	719-542-5276
Educators Credit Union	Pueblo	719-545-2434
Minnequa Works F C U	Pueblo	719-564-8793
NEPCO F C U	Pueblo	719-546-0580
Power F C U	Pueblo	719-564-0710
Pueblo City Employees F C U	Pueblo	719-545-4889
Pueblo Government Agencies F C U	Pueblo	719-542-3379
Pueblo Teachers Credit Union	Pueblo	719-561-0804
Star Journal & Chieftain Credit Union	Pueblo	719-544-3520
State Hospital F C U	Pueblo	719-542-5773
Rio Blanco Schools F C U	Rangely	970-675-2372
Burning Mountain Credit Union	Rifle	970-625-0212
Rocky Ford F C U	Rocky Ford	719-254-7441
St. Joseph Credit Union	Salida	719-539-2968
Peoples F C U	Springfield	719-523-6250
Routt Schools F C U	Steamboat Spgs	970-879-2723
Sterling Community F C U	Sterling	970-522-0111
Holy Cross F C U	Thornton	303-287-4133
Holy Trinity F C U	Trinidad	719-846-3112
Las Animas County Teachers F C U	Trinidad	719-846-2647
Saint Mary Credit Union	Walsenburg	719-738-1760
Westminster F C U	Westminster	303-427-6466
Burlington Nthrn RR Employees C	Wheat Ridge	303-425-6627
Luthern Medical Center Empl. FCU	Wheat Ridge	303-425-8534
Front Range Community F C U	Windsor	970-686-7426
K.C.D. Credit Union	Windsor	970-686-4362
Yuma County F C U	Yuma	970-848-3823

PUBLIC UTILITY COMPANIES

Many cities and towns provide their own electric and gas services. Most rural areas are serviced by regional companies. Although not complete, most companies serving Colorado are listed below.

Aspen Munic Elec System	Aspen	970-920-5148
Boulder City Municipal Building	Boulder	303-441-3260
City Of Fort Collins Lgt & Pwr	Fort Collins	970-221-6700
Colorado Springs Utilities	Colorado Springs	719-448-8000
Delta-Montrose Electric Assn	Delta	970-874-8081
Eastern Colorado Utility Company	Strasburg	303-622-4220
Estes Park Light & Power Dept	Estes Park	970-586-5331
Glenwood Springs Electric Syst	Glenwood Springs	970-945-6672
Gunnison Light & Water Dept	Gunnison	970-641-2448
Highline Electric Assn	Holyoke	970-854-2236
Holy Cross Electric	Aspen	970-925-7311
Holy Cross Electric Assn	Glenwood Springs	970-945-5491
Intermountain Rur Electr Assn	Conifer	303-838-5583
Intermountain Rur Electr Assn	Woodland Park	719-687-9277
Intermountain Rurall Elec Assn	Sedalia	303-688-3100
Las Animas Municipal Light & Power	Las Animas	719-456-1621
Longmont Electric Utility	Longmont	303-776-6050
Loveland Light & Power	Loveland	970-667-6130
Lyons Munic Light & Power	Lyons	303-823-6622
Morgan County Rural Elec Assn	Fort Morgan	970-867-5688
People's Natural Gas	Castle Rock	303-688-3032
Poudre Valley Rural Elec Assn	Fort Collins	970-226-1234
Public Service Company Of Co	Boulder	303-938-2200
Public Service Company Of Co	Brighton	303-654-8405
Public Service Company Of Co	Denver	303-571-7511
Public Service Company Of Co	Evergreen	303-674-3361
Public Service Company Of Co	Fort Collins	970-225-4010
Public Service Company Of Co	Grand Junction	970-244-2790
Public Service Company Of Co	Loveland	970-667-4154
Public Service Company Of Co	Salida	719-539-2535
SAN Isabel Electric Assn Inc	Pueblo	719-547-2160
SAN Isabel Electric Assn Inc	Trinidad	719-846-2287
SAN Isabel Electric Assn Inc	Walsenburg	719-738-1401
SAN Miguel Power Assn Inc	Telluride	970-728-3825
Sangre De Cristo Electr Assn	Buena Vista	719-395-2412
Southeast Colorado Power Assn	La Junta	719-384-2551
TRI Stat Gnrtn & Trans Assoc	Durango	970-247-4950
TRI Stat Gnrtn & Trans Assoc	Salida	719-539-3484
Trinidad Mncpl Pwr & Lgt Dept	Trinidad	719-846-9843
U.S. West (Business)	Denver	800-603-6000
U.S. West (Residential)	Denver	800-244-1111
United Power	Golden	303-642-7921
United Power	Brighton	303-659-0551
Westplains Energy	Pueblo	719-545-0360
White River Electric Assn Inc	Meeker	970-878-5041
Wray Light & Power Dept	Wray	970-332-4431
Yampa Valley Electric Assn Inc	Steamboat Springs	970-879-1160

VOLUNTEER CENTERS

A good way to meet new friends and get to know your new community is to volunteer some time to a worthy cause. There are several Volunteer Centers in Colorado that act as volunteer clearinghouses for available positions.

Most volunteer centers offer a service which provides information to individuals and groups who wish to volunteer and who need to know what volunteer opportunities exist in the local community. Denver's Metro Volunteers! has approximately 1,000 volunteer positions listed, representing over 600 nonprofit organizations in the community. They can also link groups such as church groups, employee groups, school groups, etc., with one-time projects in community agencies.

In addition to the Volunteer Centers listed below, many cities in the metro Denver area have volunteer coordinators within their local government structure.

Center for Information and Voluntary Action
400 E. Main Street, Aspen, CO 81611, 303-925-7887

Volunteer Conection
2299 Pearl Street, Suite N, Boulder CO 80302, 303-444-4904

Volunteer Center, Pikes Peak United Way
830 N. Tejon, Suite 150
Colorado Springs, CO   719-632-1543

Metro Volunteers!
225 E. 16th Avenue, Suite 200, Denver, CO 80203, 303-832-6060

Volunteer Resource Center, United Way of Weld County
P.O. Box 1944, Greeley, CO 80632, 970-353-4300

In addition, many national and state-wide causes are listed below:

Amnesty International Colorado	Denver	303-894-9494
Celebrate The Earth	Denver	303-832-4819
Clean Water Action	Denver	303-839-9866
Colorado Environ Coalition	Denver	303-837-8701
Colorado Open Lands	Denver	303-894-9870
ECO Options	Boulder	303-443-4525
Environmental Defense Fund	Boulder	303-440-4901
Global Response	Boulder	303-444-0306
Greenpeace Action	Boulder	303-440-3381
Sierra Club	Aspen	970-963-3023
N Amercn Wildlife Safeguard	Colorado Springs	719-576-1564
National Audubon Society	Boulder	303-499-0219
National Audubon Society	Denver	303-696-0877
Nature Conservancy	Telluride	970-728-5291
Nature Conservancy	Boulder	303-444-1060
Nature Conservancy	Colorado Springs	719-632-0534
Plant It 2000	Littleton	719-481-8390
Rivers Colorado Alliance	Durango	970-259-3209
Sierra Club	Fort Collins	970-493-0314
Sierra Club Rocky Mtn Chptr	Denver	303-861-8819
Sierra Club Southwest Office	Boulder	303-449-5595
Volunteers For Outdoor Colorado	Denver	303-830-7792

APPENDIX A
RECOMMENDED READING FROM COLORADO PUBLISHERS

The following Colorado publishers contributed materials for this book. Many have numerous titles about different aspects of Colorado and therefore have their own catalogs. Please check with your favorite bookstore for the titles or you can order directly from the publisher. Please note the prices indicated below **do not** include shipping & handling which varies with each order. Please contact the publisher for details before ordering. All books listed are paperback unless otherwise noted.

All Points Publishing
PO Box 4832, Boulder, CO 80306, 303-447-1971
Get Out Of Town:
A Comprehensive Guide to Outdoor Activities in the Boulder Area, 304 pgs, $14.95

Bradford Publishing (Free Catalog Available)
1743 Wazee Street, Denver, CO 80202, 303-292-2590
Colorado Revised Statutes 1995 Vehicles and Traffic, 348 pgs, $9.50
Friendly Divorce Guidebook for Colorado, 433 pgs, $24.95
Landlord & Tenant Guide to Colorado Evictions, 170 pgs, $18.50
1994-1995 Catalog of Legal Forms (over 1000 pre-printed legal forms), free

C&C Publications, The Junior League of Denver, Inc.
6300 East Yale Avenue, Suite 110, Denver, CO 80222, 303-782-9244
Colorado Cache Cookbook, 430 pgs, $15.95
Crème de Colorado Cookbook, 381 pgs, Hardbound, $19.95

Communications Creativity (Free Catalog Available)
PO Box 909, 425 Cedar Street, Buena Vista, CO 81211, 800-331-8355
Big Ideas For Small Service Businesses: How to Successfully Advertise, Publicize, and Maximize Your Business or Professional Practice, 289 pgs, $15.95
Country Bound: Trade Your Business Suit Blues for Blue Jean Dreams, 433 pgs, $19.95
Discover The Good Life In Rural America: The City Slicker's Guide to Buying Country Real Estate Without Losing Your Shirt, 168 pgs, $12.95

Concepts In Writing
1135 South Garfield Street, Denver, CO 80210, 303-757-0269
Bike With A View: Colorado's Front Range and Central Mountains, 116 pgs, $12.95

Fulcrum Publishing (Free Catalog Available)
350 Indiana Street, Golden, CO 80401, 800-992-2908
Ancient Walls: Indian Ruins of the Southwest, 112 pgs, full color, $19.95
Colorado's Fourteeners: From Hikes To Climbs, 251 pgs, $15.95
Rocky Mountain National Park: Classic Hikes & Climbs, 255 pgs, $14.75
Rocky Mountain Skiing, 397 pgs, $18.95
Rocky Mountain Walks, 277 pgs, $15.95
Seasonal Guide To the Natural Year, 336 pgs, $15.95
The Colorado Guide, 3rd Edition, 643 pgs, $18.95 (Highly Recommended)
Many, many other related titles!

APPENDIX A

Gylantic Publishing Company
PO Box 2792, Littleton, CO 80161-2792, 303-797-6093
Moving With Children: A Parent's Guide To Moving With Children, 185 pgs, $12.95
Many other self-help/recovery titles.

Ice Castle Editions
PO Box 280166, Lakewood, CO 80228-0116, 303-988-6424
Leadville's Ice Palace, A Colossus in the Colorado Rockies, 391 pgs, $16.95

Johnson Books (Free Catalog Available)
1880 South 57th Court, Boulder, CO 80301, 800-258-5830
A Roadside Guide To Rocky Mountain National Park, 318 pgs, $12.95
Roadside History of Colorado, Revised Edition, 389 pgs, $12.95
Tales, Trails and Tommyknockers: Stories From Colorado's Past, 144 pgs, $7.95
The Archaeology of Colorado, 325 pgs, $14.95
The Four Corners Anasazi: A Guide to Archeological Sites, 225 pgs, $17.95
The Xeriscape Flower Gardener for the Rocky Mtn. Region, 182 pgs, $14.95
Magnificent Rocky: A CD-ROM Guide to Rocky Mt. National Park, $39.95
Many, many other Colorado titles!

League of Women Voters of Colorado
1410 Grant Street #B-204, Denver, CO 80203, 303-863-0437
Colorado: The State We're In, 1995 Revised Edition, 127 pgs, $5.00

Magnolia Street Press
2600 Magnolia, Denver, CO 80207, 303-322-2822
Colorado Private Elementary and Secondary Schools, 1995-96, 190 pgs, $10.95
The Guide to Metro Denver Public Schools, 1995-96 Edition, 300 pgs, $13.95

Outdoor Books & Maps
PO Box 417, Denver, CO 80201, 303-629-6111
Best of Northern Colorado Hiking Trails, 160 pgs, $12.95
Colorado Lakes & Reservoirs Fishing & Boating Guide, 5th Edition, 160 pgs, $12.95
The Best of Colorado Biking Trails, 2nd Edition, 96 pgs, $9.95
The Complete Colorado Campground Guide, 3rd Edition, 160 pgs, $12.95
Also produce trail information & maps for Colorado Ntl Forest and wilderness areas.

Pokerbook Press
PO Box 17851, Boulder, CO 80308, 303-665-9008
Poker, Hold 'Em, Book One, 74 pgs, $6.95 / *Intermediate*, 76 pgs, $6.95
Poker, 101 Ways To Win, 225 pgs, $17.95

Pruett Publishing Company (Free Catalog Available)
2928 Pearl Street, Boulder, CO 80301, 800-247-8224
A Climbing Guide to Colorado's Fourteeners, 3rd Edition, 255 pgs, $16.95
A Colorado History, 7th Edition, 448 pgs, $20.00
Colorado Cycling Guide, 377 pgs, $16.95
Making Tracks: An Introduction to Cross-Country Skiing, 108 pgs, $12.95
Mountain Bike Rides In The Colorado Front Range, 150 pgs, $13.95
Rocky Mountain Wineries: A Travel Guide to the Wayside Vineyards, 165 pgs, $16.95
Many, many other similar Colorado titles!

Roberts Rinehart Publishers (Free Catalog Available)
5455 Spine Road, Mezzannine West, Boulder, CO 80301, 800-352-1985
Absolutely Every Bed & Breakfast in Colorado, 320 pgs, $16.95
Alpine Flower Finder: Wildflowers Found Above Treeline, $5.95
In The Shadow of the Rockies: An Outsider's Look Inside a New Major League Baseball Team, 260 pgs, Hardbound, $21.95
Chronicles of Colorado, 210 pgs, $14.95
Colorado's Backyard Wildlife, 133 pgs, $10.95
Handbook of Rocky Mountain Plants, 4th Edition, 444 pgs, $19.95
Rocky Mountain National Park Natural History Handbook, 158 pgs, $12.95
Rocky Mountain Safari: A Wildlife Discovery Guide, 88 pgs, Full Color, $9.95
Many, many other Colorado/nature titles including several for children!

Rocky Mountain Vacation Publishing
5101 Pennsylvania Ave., Suite #5, Boulder, CO 80303-2799, 800-886-9343
Colorado Cabins, Cottages, & Lodges, 318 pgs, $12.95
Colorado RV Parks: A Pictorial Guide, 270 pgs, $19.95

Sage Creek Press
PO Box 1373, Silverthorne, CO 80498, 303-468-6372
The Mountain Bike Guide To Summit County, Colorado, 120 pgs, $9.95

University Press of Colorado (Free Catalog Available)
PO Box 849, Niwot, CO 80544, 800-268-6044
Colorado: A History in Photographs, Hardbound, $24.95
Colorado: A History of The Centennial State, 3rd Edition, 454 pgs, $24.95
Denver: Mining Camp to Metropolis, 544 pgs, $24.95
Exploring Colorado State Parks, 267 pgs, $17.95
Rocky Mountain Flora, $17.50
Rocky Mountain Mining Camps: The Urban Frontier, $17.50
Rocky Times in Rocky Mountain Ntl. Park: An Unnatural History, Hardbound, $24.95
The Colorado General Assembly, 340 pgs, Hardbound, $29.95
Many, many other similar Colorado titles available!

Westcliffe Publishers (Free Catalog Available)
PO Box 1261, Englewood, CO 80150-1261, 800-523-3692
Colorado Hut to Hut: A Guide to Skiing and Biking Colorado's Backcountry, 272 pgs, full color, $19.95
Cooking with Colorado's Greatest Chefs, 160 pgs, full color, $35.00
Explore Colorado From Plain to Peaks, full color, $19.95
Guide to Colorado Wildflowers, Volumes I & II, full color, $24.95 each
Places Around The Bases: A Historic Tour of the Coors Field Neighborhood, 177 pgs, $16.95
The Colorado Trail: The Official Guidebook, 270 pgs, full color, $19.95
The Complete Guide to Colorado's Wilderness Areas, 340 pgs, full color, $19.95
Many, many other Colorado titles and full color calendars!

APPENDIX B
THE NEW DENVER CENTRAL LIBRARY

Photo by Rhoda Pollack

COLORADO: A Newcomer's Manual

COLORADO COUNTIES

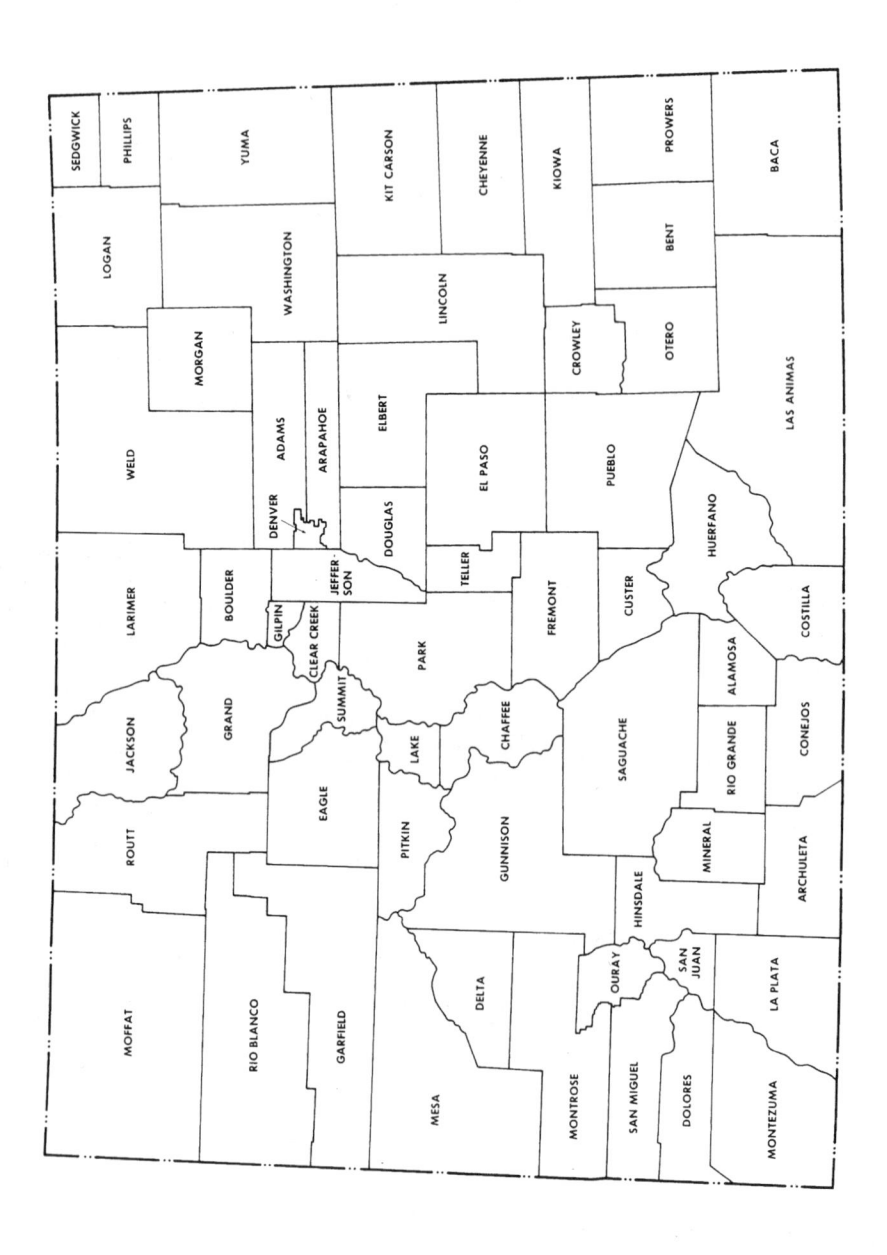

212

APPENDIX B

COLORADO SUB-STATE REGIONS

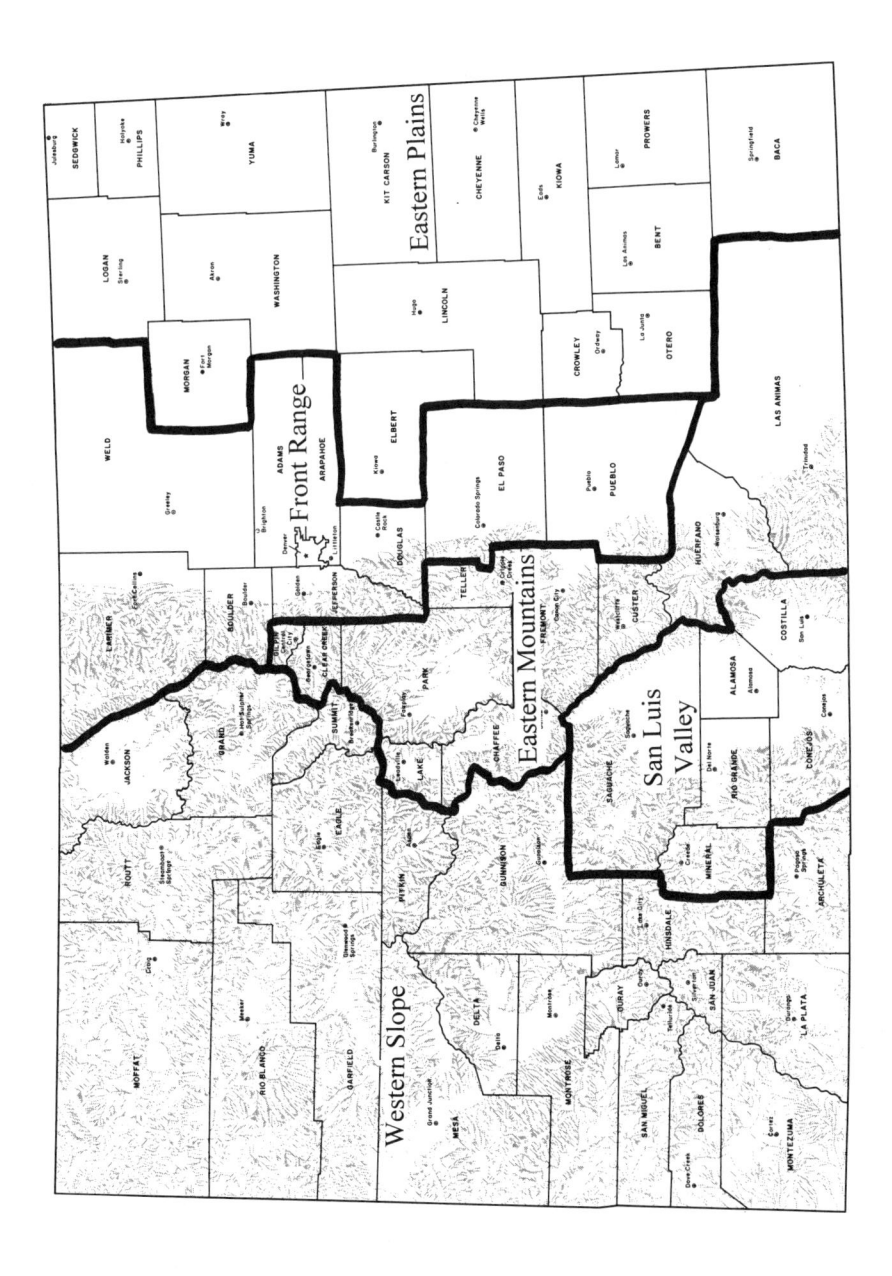

COLORADO NATIONAL FOREST

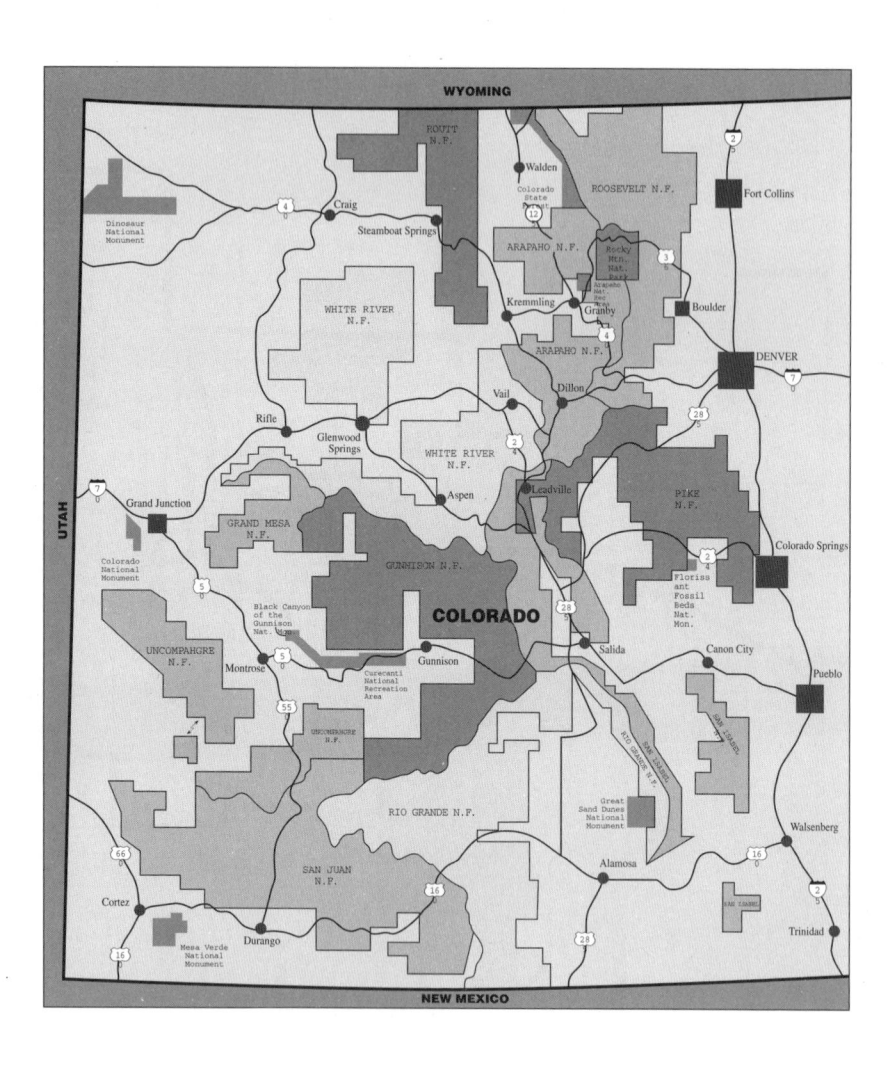

© Copyright 1995, Outdoor Books & Maps, Inc., Denver, CO

APPENDIX B

COLORADO STATE PARKS

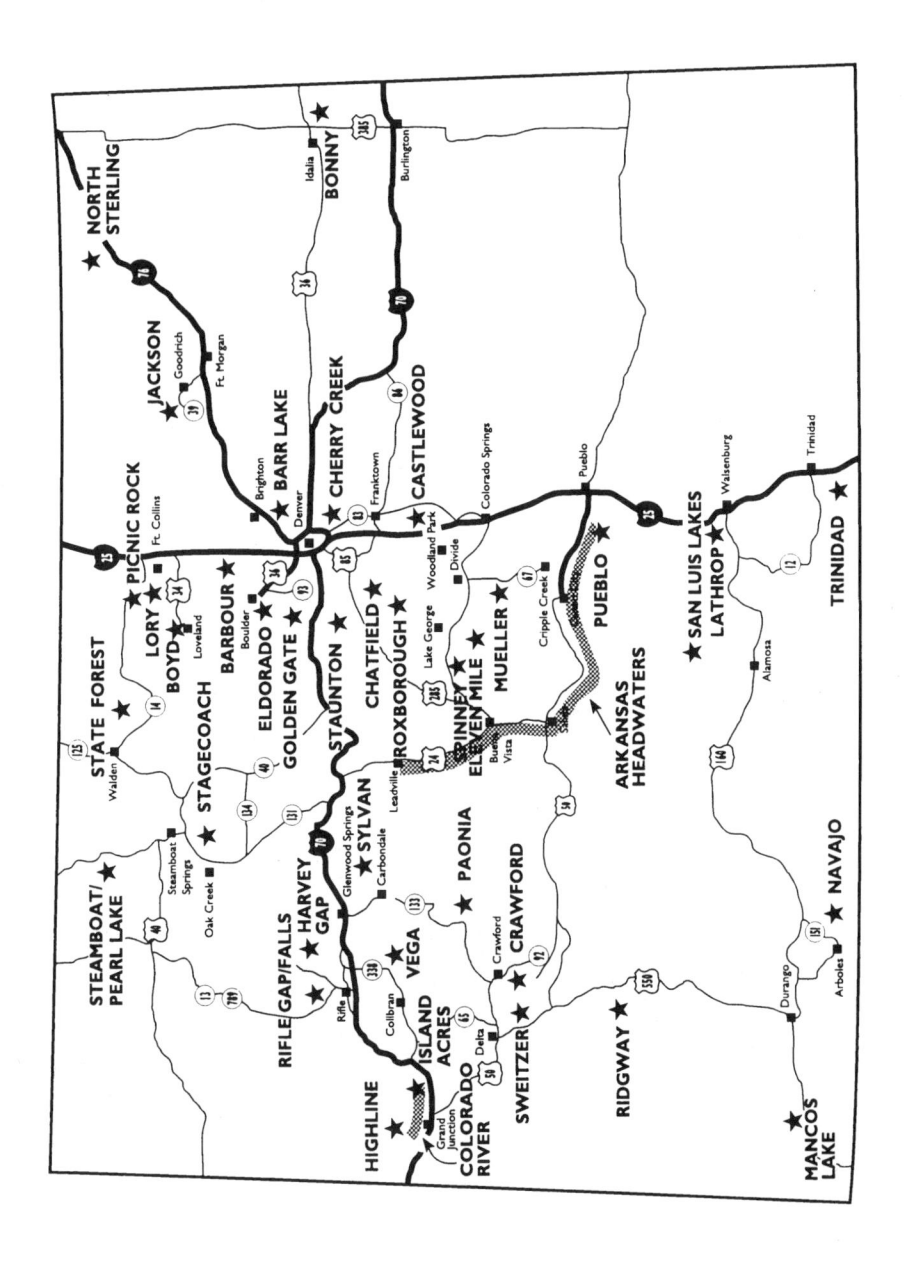

BIBLIOGRAPHY

1993 Local Government Financial Compendium, Colorado Division of Local Government, 1995

1994 Annual Report, Colorado Department of Revenue, 1994

1994-1995 Colorado Education and Library Directory, Colorado Department of Education, 1994

1994-95 Tuition and Fee Report, Colorado Commission on Higher Education, 1994

1994/95 Official Denver Visitors Guide, Denver Convention & Visitors Bureau, 1994

A Climbing Guide to Colorado's Fourteeners, Third Edition, Walter Borneman & Lyndon Lampert, Pruett Publishing, Boulder, CO, 1994

A Colorado History, Seventh Edition, Ubbelohde/Benson/Smith, Pruett Publishing, Boulder, CO, 1995

A Roadside Guide to Rocky Mountain National Park, B. Willard & S. Foster, Johnson Books, Boulder, Co, 1990

Absolutely Every Bed & Breakfast in Colorado, Third Edition, Toni Knapp, Travis Ilse Publishers, Niwot CO, 1994

Ancient Walls, Indian Ruins of the Southwest, Chuck Place, Fulcrum Publishing, Golden, CO, 1992

Best of Northern Colorado Hiking Trails, Jack O. Olofson, Outdoor Books & Maps, Denver, CO, 1995

Big Ideas for Small Service Businesses, Marilyn & Tom Ross, Communication Creativity, Buena Vista, CO, 1994

Bike With a View, Mark Dowling, Concepts in Writing, Denver, CO, 1994

Colorado: A History of the Centennial State, 3rd Ed., Abbott/Leonard/McComb, University Press of Colorado, Niwot, CO, 1994

Colorado's Fourteeners, From Hikes to Climbs, Gerry Roach, Fulcrum Publishing, Golden, CO, 1992

Colorado's Safest Communities, KUSA 9 News, 1995

Colorado at a Glance, Department of Local Affairs, 1994

Colorado Business Start-Up Kit, Colorado Business Assistance Center,

Colorado Cabins, Cottages & Lodges, Hilton and Jenny Fitt-Peaster, Rocky Mountain Vacation Publishing, Boulder, CO, 1993

Colorado Cache Cookbook, The Junior League of Denver, Inc., C & C Publications, Denver, CO, 1978

Colorado Cycling Guide, Jean and Hartley Alley, Pruett Publishing, Boulder, CO, 1990

Colorado Department of Regulatory Agencies, Department of Regulatory Agencies, 1993

Colorado Driver's License Handbook, Colorado Department of Motor Vehicles, 1995

Colorado Fact Booklet, Department of Local Affairs

Colorado Factbook, Vol. V, No. 1, Pyramid Publications, 1994

Colorado Hut to Hut, Brian Litz, Westcliffe Publishers, Englewood, CO, 1992

BIBLIOGRAPHY

Colorado Lakes & Reservoirs, Jack O. Olofson, Outdoor Books & Maps, Denver, CO, 1994

Colorado Occupational Employment Outlook 1994-1999, Colorado Department of Labor and Employment, 1994

Colorado Private Elementary and Secondary Schools, 1995-96, Margorie Hicks, Magnolia Street Press, 1995

Colorado Revised Statutes 1995, Vehicles and Traffic, Bradford Publishing, Denver, CO, 1995

Colorado RV Parks, Hilton and Jenny Fitt-Peaster, Rocky Mountian Vacation Publishing, Boulder, CO, 1995

Colorado Ski Country USA, Ski Guide 1995/96, Colorado Ski Country USA, 1995

Colorado, The State We're In, League of Women Voters of Colorado, 1995

Country Bound, Trade Your Business Suit Blues for Blue Jean Dreams, Marilyn and Tom Ross, Communication Creativity, Buena Vista, CO, 1992

Crème de Colorado Cookbook, The Junior League of Denver, Inc., C & C Publications, Denver, CO, 1987

Crime in Colorado, 1993 Annual Report, Department of Public Safety, 1994

Denver, Mining Camps to Metropolis, S. Leonard & T. Noel, University Press of CO, Niwot, CO, 1990

Discover the Good Life in Rural America, Bob Bone, Communication Creativity, Buena Vista, CO, 1994

Exploring Colorado State Parks, Martin Kleinsorge, University Press of CO, Niwot, CO, 1992

Friendly Divorce Guidebook, for Colorado, M. Hauer, J.D. and S.W. Whicher, Bradford Publishing, Denver, CO, 1994

Get Out of Town, A Comprehensive Guide to Outdoor Activities in the Boulder Area, M. Harding & F. Snalam, All Points Publishing, Boulder, CO, 1994

Governor's Advocate Corps. . A Citizen's Handbook to Colorado State Departments, Governor's Advocate Corps, 1995

Handbook of Rocky Mountain Plants, Ruth Ashton Nelson, Roberts Rhinehart Pubs, Niwot, CO, 1992

Landlord & Tenant Guide to Colorado Evictions, Victor M. Grimm, Esq., Bradford Publishing, Denver, CO, 1995

Leadville's Ice Palace, Darlene Weir, Ice Castle Productions, Lakewood, CO, 1994

Mountain Bike Rides in The Colorado Front Range, William L. Stoehr, Pruett Publishing, Boulder, CO, 1988

Moving With Children: A Parent's Guide to Moving with Children, T. Olkowski & L. Parker, Gylantic Publishing, Littleton, CO, 1993

Newcomers' Packet, Colorado Department of Education, 1995

Places Around The Bases, Diane Bakke and Jackie Davis, Westcliffe Publishers, Englewood, CO, 1995

Reports from the Colorado Economic and Demographic Information System, Colorado Division of Local Government, 1995

Roadside History of Colorado, James McTighe, Johnson Books, Boulder, CO, 1984

Rocky Mountain National Park Classic Hikes & Climbs, Gerry Roach, Fulcrum Publishing, Golden, CO, 1988

Rocky Mountain National Park Natural History Handbook, John C. Emerick, Roberts Rhinehart Pubs, Niwot, CO, 1995

Rocky Mountain Safari: A Wildlife Discovery Guide, Cathy and Gordon Illg, Roberts Rhinehart Pubs, Niwot, CO, 1994

Rocky Mountain Skiing, Claire Walter, Fulcrum Publishing, Golden, CO, 1992

Rocky Mountain Walks, Gary Ferguson, Fulcrum Publishing, Golden, CO, 1993

Rocky Mountain Wineries, L. Collison & B. Russell, Pruett Publishing, Boulder, CO, 1994

Seasonal Guide to The Natural Year, Ben Guterson, Fulcrum Publishing, Golden, CO, 1994

State Report Card 1994, Colorado Department of Education, 1994

Tales, Trails and Tommyknockers, Myriam Friggens, Johnson Books, Boulder, CO, 1979

The Archaeology of Colorado, E. Steve Cassells, Johnson Books, Boulder, CO, 1983

The Best of Colorado Biking Trails, Jack O. Olofson, Outdoor Books & Maps, Denver, CO, 1994

The Colorado General Assembly, John A. Straayer, University Press of Colorado, Niwot, CO, 1990

The Colorado Guide, 3rd Edition, B. Caughey & D. Winstanley, Fulcrum Publishing, Golden, CO, 1994

The Colorado Trail, Randy Jacobs, Westcliffe Publishers, Englewood, CO, 1994

The Complete Colorado Campgroud Guide, Jack O. Olofson, Outdoor Books & Maps, Denver, CO, 1992

The Complete Guide to Colorado's Wilderness Areas, John Fielder & Mark Pearson, Westcliffe Publishers, Englewood, CO, 1994

The Entrepreneur's Resource for Success, The Colorado Small Business Development Center

The Four Corners Anasazi, Rose Houk, San Juan National Forest Association, 1994

The Guide to Metro Denver Public Schools, 1995-96 Edition, Margorie Hicks, Magnolia Street Press, 1995

The Mountain Bike Guide to Summit County, Colorado, Laura Rossetter, Sage Creek Press, Silverthorne, CO, 1993

The Mover's Guide, Targeted Marketing Solutions, Inc, 1993

The Practical Steps to Successful Business Ownership, U.S. Small Business Administration, 1995

The Xeriscape Flower Gardener for the Rocky Mountain Region, Jim Knopf, Johnson Books, Boulder, CO, 1991

US West Guide to Home Office Success, US West, 1995

INDEX

A

Acclimatization • 176
Accreditation • 59
ACLIN • 152
Administrative Division • 32
Agriculture Statistics • 20
Alcoholic Beverage • 86, 102, 158
Amendment Two • 30
Americans With Disabilities Act • 47
Anasazi • 15, 21, 209, 218
Ancestral Rockies • 21
Apache • 22
Archaeological Tours • 157, 167
Artifacts • 21
Attorney General • 32, 44

B

Backpacking • 157, 158
Ballooning • 157, 165, 189
Bed And Breakfast Estab. • 166
Better Business Bureaus • 56
Bicycle Races • 164
Bicycle Touring • 157, 164
Bighorn Sheep • 17
Blizzards • 26
Blue River • 22, 130, 131
Board of Law Examiners • 34
Boating • 126, 157, 163, 209
Brekenridge • 25
Brown Cloud • 93, 177
Business Insurance • 138, 147

C

Cabins, Cottages • 166, 210, 216
Cakes • 178, 180, 181
Camera Safaris • 158
Camping • 126, 157, 158, 160, 161
Centennial State • 15, 23, 210, 216
Chambers of Commerce • 121, 154, 189, 191
Charter Schools • 59
Chief Justice • 34
Chinooks • 25
City Sales Tax • 86
Clean Air Act • 47
Cliff Dwellings • 16, 22, 158, 168
College Classes • 60
Colorado Consumer Protection Act • 140
Colorado Criminal Code • 33, 102
Colorado ID Card • 88, 98
Colorado Plateau • 25, 164
Colorado Revised Statues • 92, 101
Colorado State Income Tax • 86
Colorado Territory • 22, 114
Columbine • 19, 72, 127, 199
Comanche • 22, 159
Commission on Indian Affairs • 32, 44
Common Law Marriage • 105
Community College • 70, 71, 113, 116, 118, 120, 122, 124, 127, 129, 134, 151
Concerts • 157, 169
Continental Divide • 22, 24, 117, 128
Cookies • 181
Corporation • 44, 48, 76, 84, 141, 142, 147, 156
Corporations Division • 32
County Clerk • 28, 29, 90, 104, 139
County Court • 33, 99
Court Administrator • 34
Court of Appeals • 33, 34
Credit Unions • 49, 202
Crime • 80, 217
Cripple Creek • 23, 154, 167, 170, 172, 193, 197, 199
Cutthroat Trout • 17, 18

D

Department of Law • 32, 46
Department of State • 32
Dept. of Labor & Employment • 147, 152
Disadvantaged Business Certification • 47

Discipline • 44, 59
District Courts • 33
Division of Registrations • 45, 51
Dog Sledding • 157, 162
Downhill Skiing • 157, 162
Driver's Licenses • 28
Dude and Guest Ranches • 166
DUI • 97, 101, 102
DWI • 96, 102

E

Early Railways • 23
Early Voting • 28
Eastern Plains • 79
Economic Development Comm. • 40
Economic Development Offices • 153, 189
Economic Statistics • 19
Education Demographics • 18
Educator Licensing • 38
EEOC • 48
Eggs • 179, 180
Elections Division • 32
Elitch Gardens • 119, 168, 169
Emissions Test • 89
Employee Classifications • 145
Enrollment Requirements • 58
Entrance Age to School • 58
Exceptional Children's Educational Act • 58
Executive Branch • 31, 35
Eye Irritation • 177

F

Family Healthline • 42
Fastest Growing Counties • 78
Festivals • 157, 169
Financial Services Board • 49
Flying • 157, 165
Four Corners Area • 15, 21, 198, 209, 218
Four Year Colleges • 71
Fraud By Check • 102
Front Range • 24, 26, 71, 79, 113, 118, 121, 198, 200, 205, 208, 209, 217

G

General Assembly • 27, 29, 31, 32, 35, 36, 58, 68, 210, 218
General Elections • 28, 30
General Partnership • 140
Geography • 16, 24, 58, 183
Glider Rides • 157, 165
Gold • 18, 22, 23, 167
Golf • 112, 115, 117, 121, 157, 169, 170, 191
Governor's Advocate Corps • 37, 217
Grand Canyon • 23
Grand Lake • 24, 155, 173
Great Plains • 25
Greater Metro Region • 111
Grievance Boards • 52
Grievance Committee • 34
Growing Season • 183

H

Hailstorms • 26
Hang Gliding • 157, 165
Highway Statistics • 21
Hiking • 126, 157, 158, 209, 216
Historical Tours • 167
Home Study • 59
Horseback Riding • 157, 158, 161
Hot Springs • 157, 169, 170
House of Representatives • 35, 44
HUD • 48
Humidity • 25, 176, 177, 182, 183, 188

I

Ice Climbing • 157, 162, 163
Ice Skating • 157, 162
Initiatives • 29, 44
International Trade Office • 44

J

Jefferson Territory • 22
Job Service Centers • 152, 153, 189
Job Training Office • 44, 153, 189

INDEX

Joint Budget Committee • 35, 45, 48
Judicial Branch • 33, 34
Jury Duty • 35
Jury Summons • 35

K

Kayaking • 157, 163
Kiowa • 22, 94, 99, 114

L

Landlords • 103
Lark Bunting • 17
Leadville • 15, 23, 71, 99, 132, 153, 155, 167, 174, 193, 195, 199, 205, 209, 217
Leadville's Ice Palace • 15, 23, 209, 217
League of Women Voters • 27, 29, 31, 209, 217
Legislative Council • 30, 36, 74
Legislators • 35, 36, 93
License Plates • 87, 91
Licensing Division • 32
Lieutenant Governor • 31, 32
Limited Liability Company • 141, 142, 147
Limited Liability Partnership • 142
Limited Partnership • 141, 142
Liquor Stores • 102
Little Dry Creek • 22
Llama Trekking • 157, 158, 161
Local Boards of Education • 59
Local Control of Instruction • 58
Lodges • 161, 166, 210, 216
LODO • 107, 119, 169
Lottery • 43, 106

M

Magnet Schools • 59
Marriages License • 103
Media Statistics • 20
Mesa Verde • 16, 21, 75, 158, 159, 160, 168
Mesa Verde National Park • 158
Metro Highway Conditions • 43

Mexican/American War • 22
Mine Tours • 157, 167, 189
Mining • 16, 22, 23, 105, 167, 170
Minority Business Office • 151
Motion Picture & Television Comm. • 40
Motor Vehicle Office • 89
Motorcycle Endorsement • 95, 96
Mountain Biking • 157, 164
Mountain Peaks • 24, 117, 128, 130, 159, 180
Mountaineering • 157, 158, 161
Moving Company Tips: • 187
Mt. Elbert • 175
Mt. Evans • 160
Muffins • 182
Municipal Courts • 33
Museums • 157, 170, 171, 173, 174, 191

N

Nature Walks • 157
Navajo • 22, 161
Nomadic Tribes • 21

O

Occupational Education • 151
Office of Business Development • 44, 47, 150, 151
Office of Energy Conservation • 31, 44
Office of State Planning • 31, 44, 48
Open Enrollment • 59
Opera • 157, 170, 172, 174

P

Para Gliding • 165
Parole Board • 38, 40
Pikes Peak • 22, 23, 24, 71, 124, 168, 170, 174, 192, 203, 207
Planetariums • 170
Polling Places • 28, 29
Population Demographics • 16
Presidential Election • 29
Presidential Primary Election • 29

Private Colleges • 71
Private Libraries • 10
Prohibited Marriages • 104
Proof Of Insurance • 92, 96
Property Taxes • 137, 150
Prospecting • 22, 167
Public Defender • 34, 45
Public Utilities Commission • 43, 45, 50

R

Rainfall • 25
Referendum • 29
Regulatory Flexibility Act • 46
Revocation • 96, 98
River Rafting • 163
Rock Climbing • 158, 161
Rocky Mountain National Park • 24, 128, 159, 208, 209, 210, 216, 218
RV Parks • 166, 210, 217

S

S Corporation • 141
Sailing • 163
Sales Tax Licenses • 13, 143
San Juan Mountains • 24
San Luis Valley • 71, 79, 154, 191
Sangre de Cristo Mountains • 24
Sawatch Mountain Range • 24
Scenic Drives • 166
School Board • 60
School Districts • 57, 113, 189
Scuba Diving • 163, 164
Secretary of State • 29, 30, 31, 32
Senate • 35, 36, 44, 68
Shoshoni • 22
Ski Areas • 80, 131, 132, 158, 162
Skydiving • 165
Sleigh Rides • 162
Small Business • 45, 46, 47, 49, 126, 135, 136, 144, 148, 150, 151, 152
Small Business Administration • 138, 151, 152, 156, 218
Small Business Hotline • 43, 142, 143, 150
Small Business Incubators • 156

Small Claims Court • 33
Smart Growth • 108
Snow Report • 162, 163
Snowboarding • 162, 163
Snowmobiling • 162, 163
Snowshoeing • 162, 163
Soups And Vegetables • 178
Speaker of the House • 35
Special Taxes • 86
State Budget • 31, 35
State Flag • 18
State Park Regulations • 160
State Parks Pass • 160
State Primary Election • 29
State Sales Tax • 86
State Seal • 18
Stegosaurus • 17, 18
Storage Tips: • 188
Student Aid • 69
Substate Regions • 24, 79
Sunburn • 177
Sunshine • 16, 25, 183, 188
Supreme Court • 33, 34, 44, 74
Suspension • 96
Swimming • 126, 163

T

Temperature Fluctuations • 183
Tenants • 103
Tennis • 169, 170
Textbooks • 58
The Governor • 31, 34
Theater • 115, 123, 170, 171
Topography • 16, 24, 93, 175
Tornadoes • 25, 26
Traffic Violations • 33
Trail Ridge Road • 24, 159
Trail Walks • 158
Train Rides • 157, 169, 170

U

Unclaimed Property Program • 32
Uniform Consumer Credit Code • 140
Use Tax • 139
Ute • 22, 76, 155, 170
Utility Rates • 46